Yogis, Destiny and the Wheel of of Time

K.N. Rao

Vani Publications
Delhi

The Society for Vedic Research and Practices
"a nonprofit research and training organisation"

Hindu Astrology Series

Yogis, Destiny and the Wheel of Time

Published by:
K. Subhas Rao
Vani Publications
F-291 Sarawati Kunj, 25 IP Extn. Delhi - 92

Copyright with K.N. Rao

First Edition 1995
Second Enlarged Edition 1996
Third Revised Edition 2003
Fourth Revised Edition 2007

ISBN: 81-89221-10-8

Price:

Printed by
Shree System Technologies
at D.R. Printers, 4/52 Anand Parbat, Delhi

Setting and Designing
Shree System Technologies
Bharat Singh and Rajendra Singh
B-77/S-3 Dwaraka, DLF Dilshad Extn. II,
Ghaziabad-201005, Tel.: 95120-2610670, 9868616689
e-mail: srist@rediffmail.com

Dedication

My mother, K. Sarasvani Devi, my adi guru, who taught me astrology and showed me the true meaning of spiritual life.

To my father, K. Rama Rao, who instilled in all his children love for literature and healthy agnosticism.

To my mantra Guru, Swami Paramananda Saraswati, who taught me lessons through his inspiration and drew my attention to the universal religion of Yogis.

To my Jyotish Guru, Yogi Bhaskaranandji, who convinced me that astrology was not fortune-telling, but that it peeps into the divinity of life.

To Swami Moorkhanandji, who talked me out of my decision to give up astrology and argued that I should concentrate on the academic beauty of this subject.

To Mouni Baba of Ujjain, who asked me to predict less and write more.

To my brothers, sisters and their families, who witnessed some of the incidents mentioned in the book and helped me put them into proper sequence.

Acknowledgements

- I must thank my younger brothers, K.Vikram Rao and his wife, Dr.(Mrs.) K. Sudha Rao and K. Subhas Rao and his wife K.Vijaylakshmi for reading the manuscript from beginning to end and offering very constructive suggestions.
- Ms. Heide Fiechter of Switzerland, who spent a week in February 1995 on my manuscript. Also Ms. Monika Mcclain of Seattle, a Vedic astrologer of USA with experience of editing books professionally, edited the manuscript.
- Both Monica and Heide said that a book about yogis, no longer living, inspired them, but my experiences with living Yogis was the proof of my truthfulness and fire of spiritual conviction.
- To Leona Reugg for helping me revise the second edition.
- All those readers of the *Astrological Magazine,* in which some of the pieces were serialised, by writing to me and telling me that these have been the best ever articles to have appeared in the magazine. They are in the hundreds and I thank them all.
- My students of astrology, who read the articles and tested the astrological principles given here and there, showing the promise of spirituality in a horoscope.

The financial support given by **"the Society for Vedic Research and Practices"** for the reproduction of this piece of research with evidences supporting the researches is duly acknowledged and appreciated.

K. N. Rao

4

Lord Krishna

Prabhu Beejoy Krishna Goswami, my Guru's Guru

Ma Yogamaya
wife of Prabhu Beejoy Krishna Goswami

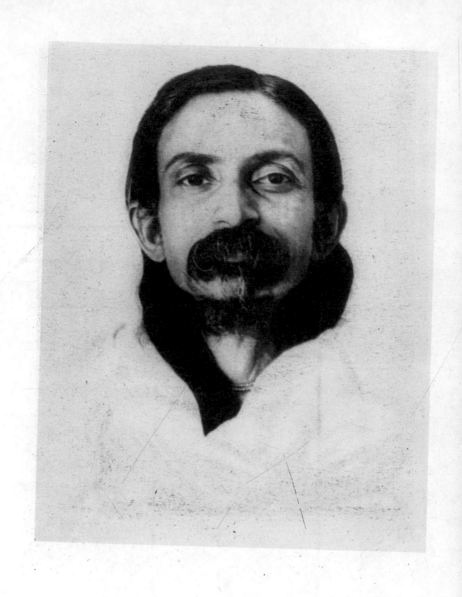

Swami Paramanand Saraswati
my *Mantra Guru*

Yogi Bhaskaranandji
my *Jyotish Guru*

Nagaridas Baba

Nagaridas Baba with K. N. Rao

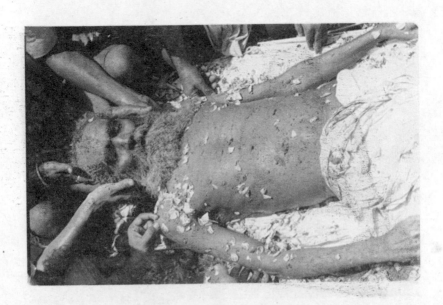

Nagaridas Baba – the last journey

Vrindavan Parikrama

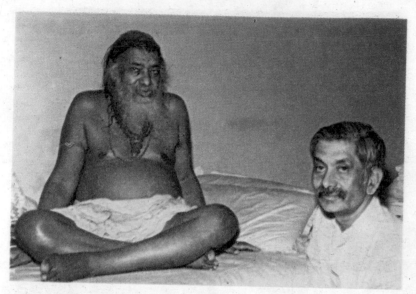

Swami Moorkhanandji (Vidyaranya) with K. N. Rao, 1981

Swami Moorkhanandji
with K.N. Rao, Dr. R.K. Caroli and Satya Prakash Yadav

Neem Karoli Baba

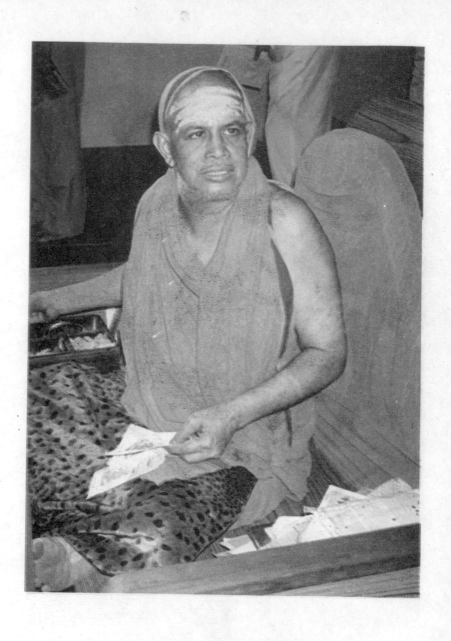

Kanchi Kamakoti Shankaracharya
Swami Jayendra Saraswati

Yogi Sri Sivananda Murthy (living)   Yogi Bankhandi

K. N. Rao, Yogi Karve (living)
and the late Mrs. Amrita Preetam the famous writer.

K. N. Rao, I.A.&A.S., Accountant General, Orissa receiving the Samant Chandra Shekhar Award, instituted by the Government of Orissa, for his contribution to astrology, in January 1986

About the Author

Rao has seen ordinary looking men and women evolve spiritually and has met great yogis, many of them still living. He writes about them, and talks about them.

But he is famous as an astrologer.

He learnt astrology from his mother and the art of writing, from his father, K. Rama Rao, who was a famous Indian journalist in English language between 1930 and 1960. Rao's mantra Guru was a Bengali from eastern India. His jyotish Guru was a Gujarati from western India. Himself, a south Indian, brought up in northern India, he is an Indian in the truest sense of the term with no parochialism, casteism, regionalism or the other types of narrowness usually associated with people all over the world. It is why he does not confine his account of spiritual experiences to one narrow region of India. His book on Devaraha Hans Baba, is a critical recording of the miracles he had witnessed for thirty six days continuously in 1994. He has the courage of conviction to write about living yogis with as much enthusiasm, as about those, who are no more with us. He narrates part of his long spiritual quest, which makes him say repeatedly in conversations that a life without spirituality is an animal life only. It is on the insistence of his friends that Rao decided to write out only a few of his own personal experiences about the undying spiritual heritage of India, here in this book. It is a first-hand account all through.

In his book, *Astrology, Destiny and the Wheel of Time,* which has by now been acclaimed as the best book to have come on Vedic astrology in English, the author has given enough hints about how lucky he had been from the childhood, when he saw from closest quarters great saints and yogis like Ma Anandmoyee, whom he served as a boy in sub-teens; how the great Neem Karoli Baba was a regular visitor to Nazarbagh, Lucknow, where he was brought up. Rao has done more original and fundamental researches in Vedic astrology in the last two decades and published them, than any other living contemporary of his. He is neither a translator of the classics of Vedic astrology nor a mere compiler, as most of the other writers, tend to be.

It is not unusual for an Indian to meet great yogis and fakirs almost all his life. India is a land of spiritual giants. K.N. Rao has been luckier than most Indians in this respect, as his great Guru Swami Paramanand Saraswati had told him, one year after his initiation, on April 24, 1962, that where ever he went he would meet great yogis. He is one of the few, who can give absolutely first hand account of what he saw, when, alone in the company of those yogis and, also describe his own spiritual experiences. Yet, as instructed by his Guru, he has restrained from narrating his own experiences and, has confined himself, mostly to others'. A great Guru forbids his disciple to discuss his own great spiritual experiences.

This book is different from any other book on spiritual phenomena in many ways—there is the splendour, grace, kindness and extraordinary powers of the yogi; there is that inscrutable harshness of the yogi, behind which remains the concealed story of his kindness, which the devotee may either not realise or, realise when it is too late. A yogi once beat a very poor man with a baton, till he bled. Few days after, he prospered. The yogi had destroyed all his misfortunes. Such inscrutable acts of yogis are well understood by Indian villagers, while the urbanite judges the yogi with his own hypocritical parameters. It is not unusual in Indian families to talk of yogis among ancestors. In the case of K.N. Rao, both from his paternal and maternal side there have been yogis who, gave up everything material and lived on *madhukari* (the rule imposed on a celibate disciple that he would get alms from one house only each day for certain number of years, and if refused in the very first house, he would have to remain hungry the whole day). One of Rao's uncles was a great yogi in Chitrakoot, in the state of Uttar Pradesh, while the other was in Kalahasti, in the state of Andhra Pradesh. The famous Jillallmudi Ma of Guntur of Andhra, who had thousands of followers, was the cousin of Rao and she had told him that after fulfilling his astrological mission he too would have to take to a life of complete renunciation.

Rao, who learnt astrology with his mother, K. Sarasvani Devi, was inspired more by his Jyotish Guru Yogi Bhaskaranandaji, to look into the spiritual depths of a horoscope first. He taught him certain secrets, which he has been asked not to reveal much, except referring to them here and there. It is what Rao has done in this book.

During his under-graduate and post-graduate days, Rao had come under an intense spell of Marx and Freud. He accepted the socialism of Acharya Narendra Dev, whom he even now regards as the greatest agnostic guru, he has met in his life. It took him away for some years

18

from the childhood experiences with yogis and, from the spiritual tradition of his mother. He spent his days questioning spiritual phenomena. But God was kind to him. Between 1959 and 1961 when he was at Allahabad, he had such rare spiritual experiences that he found it difficult to accept Freud or Marx, as anything other than geniuses, who had only a partial, distorted and fragmented view of the baser side of human life. From there, it had been for him long and agonising retracing of his traditional spiritual roots.

He spent some time in Sevagram, at Wardha with Mahatma Gandhi and, felt that the Mahatma was a truly spiritual person but, with a clearly defined political mission. It is why he does not include Mahatma Gandhi in his list of yogis or mahatmas here.

Rao's transformation began when he was transferred to Shillong in January 1962, where he met his mantra Guru, Swami Paramanand Saraswati, who not merely spiritualised his life but also rekindled his interest in astrology. The book revolves round the pivotal figure of his great Guru but, deals with so many more great Yogis, some of them living.

Rao has taught astrology to a friend's daughter and has advised her to keep in reserve her spiritual power and predict, first through astrology, systematically, then seek final clarity through her inborn psychic powers. This young woman gives amazing predictions. But when she asked Rao to become her guru, his answer was that one could become a guru only if one realised God, which had not happened to him. He did not have instructions from his Guru to initiate anyone. His clear and firm opinion is that those, who become gurus without such clear divine instructions, were fake gurus who did a lot of damage to honest spiritual tradition of India. Since 1980, Rao has been refusing to take this tempting offer of becoming a guru, who could be promoted well in the west.[1]

Rao, who was a very high ranking officer of the Government of India, retired as Director General, from the Audit Department in 1990. He has had the rare opportunity of interacting with the most westernised Indians, without any spiritual roots in the traditions of India[2] and also, interacting very intimately with most seekers.[3] It is why he has had a lot of bitter and sweet experiences and exchanges with a variety of persons. In this book he writes, as is his habit, with candidness and sometimes bitingly, about some incidents which a person, who has taken to spiritual life, has to face.

Whether it has done him good or not, is for others to decide. Yet the agnostic in him makes him reject the claims of yogis unless he witnesses them first hand. In the same vein, he insists that an astrologer should produce original research and not become a mere compiler or translator. It explains why he has so many enemies in the world of astrologers. His argument that an astrologer, who does not have a horoscope, with favourable dasha and yogas for distinction in astrology in India or abroad, should not be envious of others, who get such fame. To be envious is to disbelieve in astrology, itself. Naturally the envy of other astrologers showed their own lack of knowledge of astrology though some of them, as editors of some astrological journals, felt that they were entitled to greater honour and fame, in spite of their horoscopes, which showed more money only.

When it comes to a fake yogi, he expresses no opinion but withdraws quietly and does not meet him again, ever.

He emphasises that a true yogi gives you inner experiences, without your having to ask for it. But wait patiently and with true spirit of humility. The great yogi walks into your house, unannounced, is what he and his truly spiritual friends have experienced. Rao has seen the seamy and brighter sides of life in ashrams, because he has had to run his Guru's ashram twice, in two spells, in five years. The bliss that it was, the agony that it was, the vistas of divinity it opened out before him and the depths of human villainy that it has shown him, has made him almost apathetic to the very idea of building up big ashrams.

The most unusual topic in this book is that anytime, anywhere, anyone in India can hope to meet a great yogi, if such a spiritual quest is genuine. It is only the materialistic, the hypocritical, the agnostic, the atheistic and the close minded persons that would fail to recognize a great yogi. Rao never claims to be a yogi, though some American friends, who have seen how he lives in India, have done so.

Rao and the members of his brothers' and sisters' families have been lucky in this regard. Some of the finest yogis come into their lives, visit their homes without any previous notice or appointment. They are, *atithi* in the truest sense of the term. *Atithi* means one who comes without any previous intimation, about his arrival because the tithi (the lunar day) of his arrival is unannounced. 'A' is a negative prefix. Thus an *atithi* is not a guest, as used in English.

The purpose of this book is to tell readers that as in any field the sublime co-exists with dross. The over-publicised, the advertised yogi may be a fake or in elementary stages of spiritual development, while the great one appears suddenly and vanishes suddenly, after guiding the spiritually deserving aspirant.

The message of the book is: keep alive pure faith, have no material desires, wait and watch the great yogi, who performs miracles through the great inner transformation he brings out in you. Rao began this serious quest while playing the game of bridge to which he was addicted, when he started experiencing the supernormal. He, therefore, believes that the supernormal can be experienced anytime, anywhere by anyone because the Omnipresent God reposes in every heart, which is man's true temple, church, mosque or synagogue.

Between 1993 and 1995, Rao has visited the USA on five lecture tours. He was the Chief Guest at the Second Conference of the American Council of Vedic Astrology in 1993. He was requested to be present in the Third Conference also in 1994 on the opening day because of the crowds he would draw. His name was advertised till November 1995 also for the Fourth Conference though he had made it clear that he would not be available anymore for the American conferences.

Since June 1998 he has visited Moscow six times where he taught astrology through interpreters. It has been a great success every time, as reported by the Russian sponsors.

As a result of his academic approach, he has now thousands of students in India and hundreds in the USA and Russia. He is the Director of Astrology Course in the Bharatiya Vidya Bhawan, New Delhi. The teachers on the teaching faculty of the astrology course in the Bharatiya Vidya Bhawan have, like him, never charged any fee for teaching, which they do in an honorary capacity. What impelled Rao to do it is well explained in his own horoscope where the lagna and the 10th lords get combined in the lagna, with an exalted Jupiter in the 10th house. All this was foreseen by his Jyotish Guru, Yogi Bhaskarananda of Gujarat whom Rao describes as the last of the *Rishi astrologers* in the purest classical mould. He had told him that he would have to visit many foreign countries to give to Hindu astrology the honour, recognition and dignity, which it did not have till then. An American summed up the impact of the first ever foreign visit of Rao to the USA in 1993 as, *"Vedic astrology before Rao and after Rao"*.

What different yogis have said about astrology as a *Vedanga*, which he must not give up has been quoted in his book, *Yogis, Destiny and the Wheel of Time*. Astrology is ill-reputed as a profession because of its mercenary and exploitative nature. Rao's desire never to turn into a professional astrologer, has won him thousands of admirers and also some enemies from the community of professional astrologers who felt threatened, when around him there grew up a fine team of more than two hundred academic astrologers like him, for whom astrology is not a source of living, but a super science to delve into the

21

meaning and purpose of human life, which is what astrology, as Vedanga, should and has to be.

Both his *mantra guru,* Swami Paramananda Saraswati, and his *jyotish guru,* Yogi Bhaskarananda taught him some secrets of spiritual astrology, which are not given usually in any book of astrology. Rao has revealed some of these secrets in his book, *Yogis, Destiny and the Wheel of Time.* Among Rao's recent fundamental and most original researches are his two books *Predicting through Jaimini's Chara Dasha* and *Predicting through Karakamsha and Mandook Dasha.* It has been possible for him to produce such researches because he was told by his *jyotish guru* that what was in *parampara* (tradition) was much more than what was contained in books of astrology, which are translated literally and are without illustrations generally. His own mother, who was his first *jyotish guru,* knew many such traditional secrets, parts of which Rao has revealed in his three books, *Ups and Downs in Careers, Astrology; Destiny and the Wheel of Time* and *Planets and Children.*

It was the *mantra guru* of Rao, Swami Paramananda Saraswati, who first asked Rao not to give up astrology as it had to be an integral part of his *sadhana.* Later a great yogi, Swami Moorkhanandji, prophesied in 1982 that he would be the architect of a great astrological renaissance. Whether that is already fulfilled or not can be gauged from the impressive list of his research published.

After the first book which went fast, many appreciations have been received. Here are some. They are from different parts of India and the world.

Appreciation

23 February, 1996

Respected Sir,

I have come across few of your books in the book stall at Madras. I have purchased three of your books and one through my friend.

The books I have gone through are
1.   Astrology, Destiny and the Wheel of Time
2.   Yogis, Destiny and the Wheel of Time
3.   Astrology and Karma
4.   The Nehru Dynasty

I have found that your books are unique as they are illuminating and each sentence is pregnant with a eloquent meaning. Since I have already read the books of few writers like L.R. Chowdhury, S.S. Sareen, J.N. Bhain, M.C. Jain, P.S. Sastry, Santhanam and B.V. Raman, your books are incomparable with any of the above authors for its clarity, brevity and lucidity. I am an avid reader of astrological books, having a collection of nearly 90 books in Tamil and English including the entire collection of B.V. Raman's books. But almost all the books are either reproduction of originals or a compendium of the original books according to author's scheme. Otherwise it is not useful for a learner, where your books stand out giving clear guidance for application of various rules and enable an astrologer to come to some conclusion. Sir you have done a yeoman service to the cause of Astrology in a very high way, for learners to benefit in an immense way.

P. Soundarajan,
B-2 BHEL Quarters,
Opposite to Udayam Theatre,
Ashok Nagar,
Madras - 600083
22 May, 1996

ଓଞ୍ଚ

Dear Sri K.N. Rao,
I'm not sure why I am writing to you, especially right now of all times. In a few hours, I will be leaving with Amma for Her 10th world tour, returning to India only August 18th. I have wanted to write you for a long time, but felt very shy about it, because I am such a novice in my study of astrology. Your books have inspired me the most of all ones I've read in the past 4 years living here in Kerala with my family (wife and 2 daughters) at the ashram of Sri Mata Amritanandmayi Devi.

I've felt a kinship with you from another angle as well as my profession in Canada before coming here was management accounting.

Prasannam Herke
C% Mata Amritanandamayi Math Amritpuri PO
Kollam District
Kerala - 690525, India

ଓଞ୍ଚ

14 March, 1996
Guru Purnima

You have been a great inspiration in my life. Everyday I am thinking of some aspect of your teachings and the example you have set. You have encouraged me to become steady in my job and more dedicated to my spiritual path. Your life's example of performing your duty and simulteneously pursuing your love for astrology and spiritual path is a permanent fixture in my mind. The stories in *Yogis, Destiny and the Wheel of Time* are one of the greatest gifts that you have shared. Memories of the Yogis' lives stay with me.

I had given up the hope of studying astrology because of the confusion created over ayanamsha. You have cleared that confusion and gone further to show how divisional charts work and given us several dasha systems to experiment with along with text books of working examples from yourself and your competent students . . .

Your efforts have had a tremendous impact on America. It is hard to be fooled by articles in astrological journals now. You have made a clear difference between research that works and astrological discourse. You have placed astrology where it belongs as a spiritual practice.

Tom White, P.O. Box 286
Soquel, CA 95073

ೞ

29 May, 1996
To,
Sri K.N. Rao,

I congratulate you on your wonderful book, *Yogis, Destiny and Wheel of Time.*

As a person inclined towards spiritualism and liberation of soul in this birth itself, I was deeply fascinated by your book and hence this letter.

E Gayatri
19, Prithvi Avenue, Alwarpet,
Madras - 600018, Tamil Nadu
Tel: 499-7025

ೞ

23 April, 1996
Dear Mr. Rao,

I am enclosing the May 1996 issue of 'Yoga Journal', a very popular magazine widely distributed throughout North America. A feature article on Vedic astrology begins on page 82, in which I have incorporated many coments you made during your last trip to the San Francisco Bay Area.

I want to express my deepest gratitude for the amount of time you spent with me and other American students during your visit. Your insights into the underlying spiritual purpose of Jyotish and its connection with yoga were especially appreciated. Although the magazine just came out today, already I have been receiving phone calls from readers telling me how deeply they were affected by your remarks. Without question your comments were the highlight of the article. I very much doubt that anyone who reads the piece will fail to be profoundly inspired by your words!

Thank you also for your detailed response to the last issue of the ACVA Journal. I learned so much from your elaboration on the chart I attempted to delineate (it was my husband's birth chart actually; he is constantly involving himself in car accidents!). I also particularly appreciated the copy you gave me of *Yogis, Destiny and the Wheel of Time*. My husband and I have both read it several times. It is your best book ever!

I have always hesitated to write to you because I realize that a man of your stature is extremely busy and you are continually inundated with requests for your time. Deborah Ress, however, has advised me to be more bold in approaching you. Even now I am hesitating because I recognize that as a beginning level student of Jyotish, it is very presumptuous of me to be writing articles like that which appears in 'Yoga Journal'. Still I feel that the blessings of the lineage of sages flowed so strongly through your words, that all I needed to do was record your wisdom. May this article serve as a small token of our appreciation for your immense contribution to the science of light!

522 Joapuln Drive
Sincerely
Sonoma, CA 95476
Linda Johnsen, USA
Phone : 707/939-1787, Fax : 707/939-9448
E-mail:johnsen108@aol.com

References

1. An American regretted that he was not brown in complexion to get himself accepted as a guru in the USA. He asked Rao if he should promote him as a guru in the USA, where it can be a good multi-dollar business.
2. As the Director of International Courses in Revenue Audit, thrice, he had met them.
3. Mainly because of the ISKCON and Mahesh Yogi's great work in the USA.

Contents

Preface to the
First Edition

The supernormal has been so normal an occurrence in my life that my acceptance of the marvels of science and technology, without any sense of bewilderment, has quite often caused some surprise to some friends. People almost take the one extreme stand and, accept either the normal or the supernormal. My answer to them is: if you do not accept both, particularly having been born in India, the land of Yogis, you are wasting the advantage of your Indian birth and, are behaving like the westerner, who never had the advantage of taking a truly holistic view of life. The westerner has had to fight a cold climate to survive, and has evolved over the centuries into a being, in whom, the will to fight, to survive, is so strong that he has had no time to wait, think, pause, meditate and see the divinity in him, that vaster meaning of life, without which the view he has of the world and life must be, of necessity, a fragmented one.

Take the case of the story of the writing of this book itself. While, it was being serialised in the form of articles under the title, 'That Blissful Inspiration', in the *Astrological Magazine*, my three astrological trips to USA occurred, and in spite of writing twelve pieces, the other fifteen parts, which were not serialised, had to wait for nearly sixteen months before I could settle down to complete them.

The difficulties that crop up, get solved through divine intervention. The first great difficulty was that I had to leave the government house, which I had occupied so far, having retired from government service. To move into a rented house in Delhi, with the pension I get, would have meant spending my entire pension on rent. Then a Yogi, Mouni Baba,[1] told me to take the plunge without any hesitation. Another Yogi, a Jain,[2] saw my palm and said that I would soon have a house of my own.

I know and believe in such supernormal utterances since I do astrology, and was waiting for the right solution to emerge out. I figured out that by encashing two fixed deposits and taking out my

28

entire bank balance, I could meet half the expense of buying a house for myself in one of the new colonies of Delhi, where such a house would be within the purchasable range of my monetary resources. Then a loan from a friend, plus raising extra money through hard work, enabled me to buy a house, much sooner than I could imagine.

Then came in the other difficulty. Before leaving for USA in June 1994, I had to vacate my government accommodation and move into a rented house, along with my younger brother's family. He had suffered spinal trouble earlier in his college days. He lifted weights though he ought to have known better and, when I returned from the USA, he was lying in bed with serious spinal problem. My books and manuscripts were in disarray in the rented house. The completion of this book had to wait.

Dr. R. Sahney with his acupuncture and Dr. Vikram Dogra, an orthopaedist, both friends of Dr. K.S. Charak, FRCS, were treating my brother.

Just then walked into my house Yogi Bankhandi, who came to our earlier house before I was leaving for USA in June 1994. He saw my brother in agony and said nothing, except that he would come next day also. He came, as promised, and finding no doctor at home, as on the previous day, said, "*I will come tomorrow and cure you of this in five minutes.*"

Yogi Bankhandi is rather oldish and, has to be helped physically when he sits down, to get up. He asked my younger brother to lie down on the ground and touched his spine, pulling it from two ends with a piece of cloth. There was a clicking sound. My brother said that it was a great relief from pain. The Yogi told him to get up and walk. After fifteen days, Subhas walked as well as he did before this spinal problem. The next day, he walked up and down the stairs many times, as though, distrusting that he had been cured. My younger brothers and their family members have seen great Yogis rather often and, Subhas had no reason to *distrust this second miracle of his life in six months.*

The first miracle occurred when he had run into difficulty as a result of the betrayal of trust by a subordinate of his. This subordinate had made him authorise some foreign exchange amount to someone, who was involved in an international gang. Just then had come Yogi Hans Baba to Delhi and said, "*Maine chakkar chala diya hai. Chinta mat karo*". (I have set my weapon into motion. Don't worry.)

Then Yogi Hans Baba asked me to ask a friend of mine in a high rank in Delhi police to take energetic interest in this case, which appeared odd for two reasons: first, there was a powerful gang, which could not be proceeded against in the Indian conditions and, there was not the remotest connection between the area covered by that police officer and, the operation of this international gang. Yet, as it had to happen as seen by Yogi Hans Baba, a person involved in this gang was caught, in the very area falling in the jurisdiction of my friend, the police officer. From there, the beginning of the end of the professional trouble of Subhas became visible.

Then in November 1994, I left again for the USA and returned in December. I now decided to complete the book and worked, day and night. Part of the manuscript was also finalised. One day, I was reading out parts of it to elicit critical comments of S. Ganesh, Dr. Charak and Naresh Sharma, all well employed and also teachers of astrology with me in the Bharatiya Vidya Bhawan, New Delhi, the largest school of astrology in the world.

Compared to Yogis how small are astrologers, I was saying.

Just then there was a phone call and Yogi Bankhandi said that he was coming to my place. I told my friends that it was the same Yogi who had cured Subhas of his spinal problem, in five minutes, yes, literally, in five minutes.

They waited, and came Yogi Bankhandi, with a disciple. It was the night of February 19, 1995. Turn by turn, all touched his feet. The younger son of Subhas, Gaurav, touched his feet and seeking his blessings went back to study for his forthcoming examinations. Then came the elder son of Subhas, Gautam, whose ear trouble had been so serious that doctors had said that he would have to be treated more intensively, possibly, even operated upon surgically. In the meantime, Gautam had developed another complication, a severe headache, which was not getting cured at all. When Gautam came and touched the feet of Yogi Bankhandi, I told him that this fellow had not been well for some weeks now. The Yogiji then asked him what was wrong, and said, *"Kal sube theek ho javoge"* (You will be all right tomorrow). It must have surprised Ganesh and Naresh for whom it was a new experience. Gautam was all right from the next day onwards. Since he lives in the same complex of buildings as us, Ganesh, came the next day, to find out how Gautam was.

"Must be a powerful Yogi," said Ganesh.

"Is that not our great heritage?" I said. Since we are also astrologers, the academic astrologers, not the pop or the professional variety, we do not accept astrological claims of anyone easily, just as, no one among us would accept even the claim of supernormal powers easily, by anyone.

What do you say to what you see yourself with your own eyes?

When Yogi Bankhandi came, I was completing the manuscript of this book, with the preface yet to be written. It is only recently, in the last twenty days (of February 1995), that I learnt some use of the computer, mainly because Julia Simon of San Diego had told me in December that many of my old typewritten manuscripts would be lost forever, unless I had fed them into a computer. That suggestion made me accept the great technological facility available to writers now. I did as advised by Julia. Marie Anne Cooke presented me her old computer, to begin and get used to the computer-culture.

I told Yogi Bankhandi about the book.

"*Yes, there is a purpose behind this, a very good purpose, a divine purpose,*" he said.

That is the acceptance of the computer and, a Yogi's supernormal power, with a spontaneity, which is in the Indian blood, the acceptance of physical science and metaphysical science, without any fear of appearing ludicrous. This is a normal, and let me emphasize, the spiritual approach to life in India. I found that Yogi Bankhandi sat down there and told me, as a Yogi only can, through the inspiration he generates inside your heart, how I could start the preface. It was good, in a way, that the preface should start with the most easily verifiable proofs of the supernormal.

The other Yogi, who should attract American astrologers, both Hindu and western, is S.E. Karve with his supernormal way of finding out one's birth time, even the date, month and year of birth.

If lucky, Americans may be able to see personally Yogi Karve of Bombay and watch him tell the birth details of persons, unknown to him. Those who know it already, but are doubtful about the exactness of their birth time, will be even more surprised. Astrologers, wanting to rectify birth time without knowing the *nadi shodhan* method, commit more mistakes if they do not know the use of divisional charts of Vedic astrology. Yogi Karve visited USA sometimes in June 1995, and shows how he fixes the birth time, without the use of any of the tools of modern technology, he would have proven what I am writing here, the truth of the great synthesis that exists in the Indian life, the synthesis between the truths of physical sciences and the truths realities exist on the metaphysical plane.

Who then is a Yogi?

The easiest definition should be, he, who by concentrating on the

Cosmic Being, knows some of those truths, which are perceivable through methods not known to the physical sciences. These methods are the integral part of the Indian way of life, known as *sadhanas* or spiritual practices.

Such spiritual practices have been of vast varieties in India, and will always be so.

From the self-denying celibate meditating in the caves of the Himalayas, or Girnar in Gujarat, Mount Abu in Rajasthan, Sahyadri ranges in Maharastra and the great Deccan Plateau, to the place of worship a Hindu house-holder has in his house, even in the busiest of Indian cities, these spiritual practices, the perception of those metaphysical truths at various levels, have been maintained in an unbroken continuity.The emphasis here always has been on practice, not the theory. It has thus been the scientific method of perceiving the practical.

Such a vast variety of spiritual practices has given to the Indian mind the innate habit of not viewing any phenomena, experience, or truth, as being unbelievable. That is why, right from the ancient times, persecuted religious minorities came to India with their own beliefs, and got absorbed into the mainstream of the Indian life and the Indian way of life, without having to seek any religious conversion. The Cosmic Truth is One only, call it Krishna or by any other name. It is multi-faceted. The vast variety of Indian spiritual practices have demonstrated that. The easiest and sweetest one has always been the path of devotion. The most difficult one is the Yoga of Patanjali, which needs the highest physical and mental discipline, from the start and, strictest celibacy always. Yoga is not what it is made out to be in the west, a set of physical exercises, but the inter-linking of the Being within us all to the Cosmic Being. That link reveals metaphysical truths and gives supernormal experiences to millions in India but supernormal powers to only a few because the higher discipline which is required to evolve into that higher state is a full time attunement to the Cosmic. Those who have it, are Yogis of high status and achievements.

The tradition of the Indian house-holder respecting such Yogis always has been, the essence of the Indian way of life, because we in India have the advantage of seeing, respecting and serving such persons. In the process, some get cheated by the fraudulent, which is also not uncommon.[3] Yet the tradition of the Yogi being respected, venerated and worshipped by the house-holder, will always continue, for the reason that the Indian house-holder has the opportunity of meeting the genuine Yogi, be he a saffron-clad mahatma, the great soul as we call them, or a fakir or a Muslim saint, or even an ordinary house-holder, reaching the higher realms of spirituality through such practices at home.

I have mentioned the names of three Yogis so far. Yogi Bankhandi is a saffron-clad mahatma with no fixed place to live in. When he comes to Delhi, he rings up someone known to him and there, the pure food he wants will be prepared for him, without his ever telling that he wants it. He will demand nothing. The money we may offer to him may be, from a petty sum to a large amount, which he may spend on a railway ticket or on the bus or taxi fare. He is linked to the Cosmic in all states, walking, talking, lying, sitting or even sleeping though I have not seen him sleeping. Sitting, rather squatting, for long hours, in one posture is his normal habit. Next to my Guruji, it is his prophecies I have heard that have come out so correct. I cannot reveal them in this book, as, they relate to some of the most controversial issues before the Indian public and nation, in 1996.

The other Yogi I have referred to, Devaraha Hans Baba, is a Yogi in the Patanjali tradition, austere, rigid and distant, seated on a raised wooden platform, specially erected for him. But in recent months, he has fallen into the same trap of Maya, as many yogis fall. He wants to build an ashram of 108 rooms.

The third one, Yogi Karve is the house-holder Yogi, has wife and children, yet earns nothing. The Great Being he worships, the *"Vishwa roopa"*, looks after him. He stayed with me for four days and, in the presence of astrologer friends, told with a hundred percent accuracy, the ascendant and the planetary position in many horoscopes. In some cases, he even told us the ascendant of the husband from the horoscope of the wife. In the presence of friends, I had told him that I was struggling with the correct birth time of an American. Without waiting, he said, exact nine a.m. Yogi Karve gives the standard time of the region or, the country a person was born in. This was regarding the birth time of President Clinton of USA, about which there has been a controversy.[4] I worked on Virgo, while the *Astrological Magazine* had given Cancer. On the basis of Cancer, Dr. B.V. Raman had also made a prediction in November 1992 in the the First Vedic Astrologers' Conference at San Rafael, that Clinton would lose. On the basis of some events of Clinton's life, the early death of his father, legal education, date of marriage and getting Rhodes Scholarship, Cancer ascendant was palpably wrong.

But Yogi Karve solved my problem fastest, and left me in no doubt. Similarly, he corrected the ascendant of my nephew, K. Gaurav

Rao, from the beginning degrees of Virgo to the last degrees of Leo, (Vedic).

It is not for us, ordinary men, to judge what supernormal level they, the yogis, have reached. Venerate them, because you can see when you meet a true Yogi that he is supernormal, if there is some spiritual development in you. Or wait and watch with an open mind.

Experiencing the supernormal in the presence of the Yogi can be both external and internal. External experiences are spectacular. They get a Yogi his reputation. The inner experiences purify a devotee's heart, if such experiences are not delusions, or hallucinations, and give stability to his devotion to the Cosmic and, inner life itself.

Let me talk about Yogi Hans Baba here.

I had seen many such external miracles in March 1994, when I had to organize and spend thirty six days with him. The crowd expectations had gone up. Organizers like me got the blame, when some incurable cases got cured but, some just did not. I then wrote a critical book on Yogi Hans Baba. *Why is it then that some people were cured and some not?* That brings me to what must be described as Destiny. Destiny is easy to define as that part of the sum total of the karmas of a man's incarnations, which he has to enjoy and suffer in his present life, without fail. Astrologers, who predict successfully prove this up to a point, but upto a point only, because the astrologer is not a Yogi, 'seeing' as the Yogi does, but inferring, through vast and baffling techniques of Vedic astrology.

I have given enough proofs of it through my readings, often in writing even before I met a person whose horoscope I happened to have for scrutiny. I have also dealt with this theme in my book, *Astrology, Destiny and the Wheel of Time.*

Though the present book has some astrological discussion here and there,· particularly in the earlier chapters, this book is mainly the narration of some, some only, of my experiences with Yogis, first hand eye-witness accounts. Both the Yogi and the astrologer, the good ones only, can see through differing methods, both *karma phala* or, the results of the karma of past lives, one has to enjoy or suffer, and the *karma samskaras* or the psycho-physical, mental and spiritual tendencies arising out of the actions, thoughts, deeds and speech of an individual. In doing so, the astrologer is sometimes spectacular but mostly a failure, because of the great expertise needed along with high Yogi-like discipline in his life. Most of the astrologers are busy worldly men with their material demands, writing, editing, talking and promoting themselves like anyone else in other professional fields.

They are men with limited vision but big reputations, shallow, arrogant, pompous even, in their feigned humility.

It is the pattern of destiny that an astrologer sees in vast detail and predicts. Because some of these predictions come out correct, Vedic astrology, though badly fragmented, with many of its techniques lost, or applied without statistical replicable testing, continues and will survive as the easiest super-science available to man, providing a holistic attitude towards his own personality.

Destiny is what a common man suffers but a Yogi transcends.

In this book, instances of both types have been given.

But when will the predestined happen?

There is a time for everything, birth, infancy, youth, middle age, old age, sickness, disease, death, achievements, failures, gains, losses, and the sense of happiness or unhappiness we attach to them, according to our own individual, family, social, national, even racial, value system.

The Yogi rarely gives the time frame, in which a certain predestined event would happen. This is the area in which the astrologer works, with the dasha systems of the Hindu astrology, which is unique and unparalleled. I have had the unique advantage of both seeing and analysing astrologically, the pattern of someone's destiny, and knowing what a Yogi, whose supernormal powers I had reasons to believe in, had said about that person. The pattern of human destiny is what both a Vedic astrologer and, a Yogi can see. The Yogi is rarely interested in telling any event in detail and in a defined time-frame. But then a true Yogi's utterance is usually infallible.[5] That is what cannot be said about the astrologer. In fact, there is no great astrologer in the world at all.[6] The purpose of saying all this is to emphasize that at some stage every intelligent man must begin his quest for the quintessential meaning and purpose of life. Then begins a search, which is the beginning of the thirst, for the non-normal.

It began in the USA with drugs, and later, attractions for *sadhana*. But *sadhana* can be frustrating in these days of 'instant' culture. Something to sustain and restore belief in the Cosmic, without being cheated, can be a wish, an anguished anticipation, or even an achievement. It is here that a true Yogi's is a great spiritual presence, visibly and mostly invisibly, when you are sincere.

References

1. A Yogi about whom there is note later.
2. The best palmist I have met todate.
3. See chapter 15 Caution and Warning, later.
4. In November, 1993 I had already argued at the Third conference of America's Vedic Astrologers that Clinton's lagna had to be Kanya. On that basis, I had already included a piece on him, in my revised edition of Ups and Downs in Career. Yogi Karve's words came as a piece of good reassurance for me.
5. I say usually infallible, not infallible always.
6. No one can master astrology in a life time.

Preface to the
Second Edition

The first edition of this book was sold as fast as my other book written in the middle of 1995, *Timing Events through Vimshottari Dasha*. The appreciation received has been very encouraging from all over the world. Generally, in most of the books on spiritual themes, the torments and agonies of a spiritual aspirant followed by bliss is not elaborated and only one-sided picture is presented, which makes them lopsided and look rosy. Spiritual life is beautiful but it has many fires. It is always rewarding whether or not one makes spectacular progress in one life or not. Life without spiritual tones is animal life.

I have made some additions to this book, some very valuable spiritual lessons from ancient scriptures. This book has been re-edited by Anuradha Dutt, after introducing many punctuations, in the British style of journalism on which we Indians have been taught.

The most important additions made is the chapter, Chapter 15 on "Caution and Warning", which became necessary, as will become obvious after one has read it. Then there are scriptural instructions, which is the highest spiritual wisdom, humanity can ever have. A simple and plain understanding of world's greatest book of spiritual wisdom, India's great eternal heritage, should always be kept in the background, before accepting anyone as spiritual unlike the west where it has been reduced to a mere display of a belief, which is false.

Preface to the Third Edition

I am thankful to Ambica Gulati who proofread the third edition of the book and remarked that it was the best book I had written at a time when I had a keen desire to share some experiences and messages and that now I have got back into the shell in which I lived most of my life shunning publicity. In a way that is true, because in the last decade, India has become more globalized sharing the vulgarity of the west and its nonspiritual approach to life.

Indians have become too materialistic in the meantime, too epicurean to pay any attention to their great eternal heritage in the spiritual field. They want all those instant remedies as they want in the west and want to meet a guru who can give them instant spiritual experience. That spiritual life is a story of slow unfoldment and the result of the *karmas* of past lives is what one is not prepared to accept.

Some people asked me to write a companion volume to this book and I refused to do it es the world is not interested in spiritual matters anymore unless it fits into their epicurean materialistic frame of living.

This book in the meantime has been translated into Russian and Japanese and is being translated into Bulgarian also.

This may be the only book ever written where one has shared one's experiences with various saints, not with his own guru. In other books, the attempt has been to promote their own gurus and narrow down the spiritual canvas of India which is limitlessly vast.

...1...
That Great Guru

It is time I had recollected and put down in writing, a friend told me, something about those who called astrology sacred science, to dispel cynicism astrologers create. Avarice, malice, more boast than ability and fraudulent practices in every field of human endeavour, provokes unhappiness, but in astrology, the gullible that get cheated and become its worst victims, and, the over-ambitious consultors, who do not want an astrologer to give them a disappointing prediction, both turn hostile, first, to astrologers and, then to astrology.

Few months before he took *samadhi*, the great mahayogi, *Devaraha Baba*, had told a friend-astrologer: *"Bachcha, ye pavitra vidya hai, ise chhodana nahin"* (It is a sacred *vidya*. Do not give it up). Every great and true mahatma I have met, has called it both sacred and a *vidya*. I have heard of only one well-publicised baba that speaks against astrology. In 1984, when he was making frantic attempts to enter the then prime minister Indira Gandhi's *durbar* (court), he had it spread through his disciples that astrology and astrologers were humbug. Indira Gandhi would live for fifteen years more, as India's Prime Minister. Silent for about five years, he has now started back on his own tirade against astrology.[1] How can a mahatma, who is supposed to know Hindu scriptures speak against astrology, I ask his dumb-founded disciples. They say that they have to tolerate him because he gets them good business contacts.

I have referred in my article on Dr. Nagendra Singh, former Judge of the International Court of Justice (*The Astrological Magazine*, January 1984), how mahatmas have spoken of astrology and instructed me, not to give it up. From time to time, what they have said is :

- Astrology should be treated as a part of spiritual *sadhana,* was the advice of my late Guruji, *Swami Paramanand Saraswati*, my *mantra-Guru.*
- Astrology is the only *vidya* (branch of knowledge), which shows clearly how cosmic laws operate through planets, but at a later

39

stage, it should be given up lest it become an obstacle for *sadhana*, was the opinion of my Jyotish Guru, *Swami Bhaskaranandji*.

- His Holiness, *Shankaracharya of Kanchi Kamkoti*, Shri Jayendra Saraswati, had told me that political predictions would always be tricky and would go wrong.[2] It is in non-political areas that the percentage of successful predictions would be very high.

- *Swami Moorkhanandji* (Vidyaranya was his real name), must have told me more than a dozen times not to give up astrology. He told me that astrology had to be a mission, a service done without any monetary consideration, to keep alive its sacredness. He knew some of those secrets of astrology which, I know, that only *mahatmas* know, and are not given in any text book of astrology. He shared some of them with me, when I could be alone with him, which was rare.

- *Mouni Baba of Ujjain* told me to overcome my problems, which astrology created for me, to give consultations to least number of people and concentrate my energy on more research in a cloistered, sequestered life. This was the best practical advice I ever got.[3]

Problems of Astrologers

How do sound astrologers meet their consultors and consider their difficulties, guide and counsel them, must be a purely individual problem. A late friend of mine from Lucknow put it more clearly to me thus—eighty percent people, with their normal human tensions, seek instant and immediate remedy and have little patience; twenty percent, have high ambitions and would go to any extent to persuade an astrologer to tell them that things are favourable for them![4]

Old and respectable astrologers have their own views. An old Bengali astrologer told me that no single method of calculation of longevity could be said to be infallible. A very old astrologer, about ninety six years old or more, was rather blunt[5, 6]. He said that astrology had become a *thugee vidya* (in the hands of cheats), and he reeled off the names of many astrologers and, spoke about their lack of understanding of even elements of astrology. He, of course, impressed me with his quaint techniques of predictions, some of which given to a family known to me, were dazzling.[7] But he says that there are cheats and cheats in the field of astrology and, to become an astrologer was to become a member of a gang of cheats to which you may not belong ! Against such morbidity provoking criticism of astrology, were some of the occasional observations made by mahatmas from time to time which I would record here, giving astrological examples.

My Guruji's Observations

My Guruji's observations on astrology being the subject here, I will deal with this astrologically, referring to his own horoscope and, referring to some incidents which are, to majority of us, miracles in the truest sense of that term.

(a) Nothing that happens to an individual is outside his horoscope.

(b) Kaal Chakra dasha was the best of the dashas for great predictions.

(c) An astrologer must eat *sattvik* food and do his *japam* intensely.

(d) Astrology, honestly done, must lead to feelings of true non-attachment to life and the world.

Let me first refer to a horoscope. It is that of a lawyer of Calcutta.

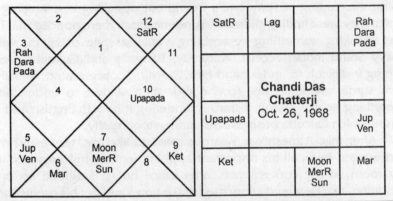

Lagna	Sun	Moon	Mars	Mercury	Jupiter	Venus	Saturn	Rahu
21°35'	10°06'	24°40'	17°15'	14°58'	15°46'	28°08'	12°17'	05°48'

41

I got this horoscope of Shri Chandidas Chatterji after 1975, perhaps in 1977, but the story I am going to narrate will start from the year 1968.[8]

I do not know much about Gulbarga district in Karnataka but, in Calcutta and later, in other cities, I did come across some practitioners of occult sciences, resembling astrology. It is not astrology in the traditional sense, casting a horoscope on the basis of time, date and place of birth. One such occult science is described as '*angushtha shastra*', being based solely on the study of an individual's thumb. *Angushtha,* means the thumb.

Though I came across many '*angushtha shastris*' later, the only one, who impressed me was Atmeshwar Swami, a plumpish, impressive personality, who was always accompanied by his uncle, Janardan Swami. I met them in Calcutta accidentally, in the business premises of Batuk Bhai, a *guru bhai* of mine, in 1968, when he was doing the reading of someone's thumb but, speaking in a language, which they were finding difficult to understand. I, then, noticed that he was speaking something resembling Varanasi style of Hindi, with heavy South Indian accent. Naturally, Bengalis and Gujaratis were finding it difficult to understand him. Slowly, I concentrated, initially, with some strain, on his accent and, then started to understand everything he was saying. I started rendering it both in English and in Hindi, which Calcutta businessmen understood easily.

After this, Atmeshwar Swami started to like me, requested me and wanted to fix all his important appointments in my presence, in my room, at my convenience, after office hours. I agreed on one condition, that he would allow me to take notes and get his predictions verified, later. He agreed cheerfully. Thus began a story of a very sweet friendship.

His method, which I described later, in a very long testimonial I gave to him, which was reproduced (without my name, of course), in *The Illustrated Weekly,*[9] in some issue in 1969, briefly was:

(a) After studying the thumb, he divided individuals into three categories: below number five thousand as insignificant men; between five thousand and ninety nine thousand as men, who would make a mark in life – the greater the number, the greater the success; and people above ninety-nine thousand, as rarest of the rare men, the epoch-makers.[10]

(b) This was based on *Ravana Samhita*, preserved in Karnataka, in some families, particularly in the Gulbarga district.

(c) This was a *guru-mukhi vidya* (passed on from gurus to disciples), and was never taught to anyone outside a close circle of family members, that too only to males.[11]

Atmeshwar Swami had given some very fine predictions, the short range ones, when fulfilled, could be got verified by us, in a matter of weeks. Let me refer to two of his pleasant predictions: the first was to Justice P.B. Mukherji, who had been superseded as the Chief Justice of Calcutta High Court, supposedly on the basis of an adverse remark on his case recorded by Pt. Jawaharlal Nehru in 1962.[12] But Atmeshwar Swami insisted that come what may, before February 1970, Justice Mukherji would become the Chief Justice. In Rajkot, I received a letter in January 1970, that Justice P.B. Mukherji had been elevated.[13]

More impressive was the prediction he gave to a person, who was described as a second-rate Congress (O) leader, in post-Congress split year of 1969.[14] To him, Atmeshwar Swami told that eight years later, he would be a Minister in the central cabinet in Delhi. It happened in 1977. I remembered it as a fantastic prediction. But to a businessman in Calcutta, he gave from commercial to sexual predictions, with so much ease and confidence, that I was both amazed and amused. I do not want to recount them here, but they clicked so well that people held Atmeshwar Swami in awesome respect.

My Guruji, who respected astrologers, and gave them money munificently, from out of the donations sent to the ashram, always respected Atmeshwar Swami, for preserving ancient knowledge. In the ashram, Atmeshwar Swami gave some wonderful predictions to many inmates and visitors, all in my presence, with me recording them. Whenever I praised Atmeshwar Swami to the skies, people asked me a question. Why did I do that, *when not a single prediction he had given me, ever came out correct!* My answer was that every astrologer had to have his percentage of failures. Mine was a case falling in this small percentage, perhaps five, of failures. Should I not praise him, seeing his over ninety percent success rate?

Towards the end of 1969, both he and I left Calcutta. But during that period, everyone except Chandibabu, whose horoscope I have given earlier, never consulted him and, even told me one day: *"I know all about my future. In 1948, one day while walking in a garden, Guruji told me all about me, my future, my wife's future and even about my children. I need not consult anyone as every word of what Guruji (in Bengali they use Thakurji for Guruji) had told me has come out correct so far."*

Surprisingly, in 1978, during the fag end of my second Calcutta posting, Atmeshwar Swami again visited Calcutta, this time, for a very brief visit as he had built up richer clientele in Bombay and Gujarat, after the article on him in *The Illustrated Weekly*, in 1969. This time, he was not even looking at the thumb. He reeled off predictions effortlessly. I asked him – why this change? He confided in me that the Dattatreya *Yantra* he was worshipping, had started giving him fullest results; his gifts had become totally supernormal.[15] It was then that he gave me the only correct prediction – I would be transferred to Delhi, from where my visits to Vrindavan would increase enormously. In Vrindavan, I would meet an extraordinary saint under a banyan tree – a classical *avadhoot*, resembling Jada Bharata of the *Srimad Bhagvatam*. It not merely came out true but, I had the extraordinary luck of meeting Nagaridas Baba, from July 1978 to July 1988, twice a month, till the Baba took *Samadhi*.

But the question that intrigued me was why Chandibabu was not telling me what Guruji had told him. Among the saints I have known, I had the benefit of seeing that my Guruji could tell anyone's future as and when he wanted with absolute precision.[16] But he did that rarely. He shared it more with me than anyone else.

I never asked Chandibabu or Guruji what these predictions were.

Sometime in 1978, few months before my transfer to Delhi, one day Chandibabu gave me his horoscope, and his wife's and asked me what I had to predict. Why was he wanting predictions from me when he knew all about his future, was my question. He melted, for the first time, and said, he was anxious and, shaken up. A prosperous lawyer like Chandibabu, who had appeared stiff-necked and snobbish to many, had controlled his emotions with dignity.

I analysed his horoscope thus:

The Charadasha sequence: Mesha ending 1913, Vrisha 1916, Mithuna 1920, Karaka 1929, Simha 1939, Kanya 1950, Tula 1960, Vrishchika 1970, Dhanu upto 1978.

It was Dhanu-Dhanu period. From the darapada the seventh house was under heaviest affliction.

In Vimshottari it was Venus-Mercury period. The dasha of the seventh lord, with retrograde Mercury in the seventh house. Was his wife safe? In Jaimini the next dasha would be of Makar, containing upapada and indicating a change in his life also.

"Not good at all for your wife," I told him.

"I knew that," he said laconically and then passed on his wife's horoscope to me.

Guru as Family Counsellor

There will always be, in India, genuinely spiritual Gurus, as sources of spiritual and mental strength to hundreds of disciples suffering family, social and professional problems. Some of them end up as good *sadhakas*, towards the end of their lives; some of them oscillate between the worldly and the spiritual with enigmatic suddenness; some of them rightly take only the spiritual messages of the Guru and lead secluded lives, in pursuit of their *sadhana*. Surprisingly for a majority of them, the Guru is a crutch on which they want to carry on their entire burden and, that of their family's. If the Guru leaves the world of mortals, they see it as the end of everything for themselves, forgetting that Guru lives through the mantra given to his disciples and, not in flesh and bone. *"Akhand Mandalakaram Vyaptam yena characharam tat padam darshitam yena tasmai shree gurave namah"* speaks of Guru as the immanent, all-pervading power not confined to his body.

Chandibabu belonged to this category. Though so prosperous, with a lucrative legal practice in the Alipore courts of Calcutta, he was haunted by the fear of life without the physical presence of Guru. In sheer desperation, he had once asked Guruji in 1948, whether he would ever have to live in the world without the physical presence of his Guru.

One day in 1948, Guruji took him for a walk and told him, *"I will be with you all for over thirty years from this year. Then within a space of six months, you, your wife and I will leave the world."*

Others only knew that Chandibabu had been told clearly about his end, but only I came to know clearly in 1978, from Chandibabu what Guruji had told him. I knew of the supernormal gifts of Guruji. I knew that haunting fears of Chandibabu had substance. They were not imaginary fears, like that of many other guru bhais. Life without Guru! That was the haunting fear of many, particularly of some women.

Chandibabu's dasha-sequence

In the case of Chandibabu, his Venus dasha had reached a very critical stage and it was *maraka* (killer) for Mesha lagna. It would be followed by the dasha of debilitated Sun.

In Jaimini, the Makar dasha would have the atmakaraka in the eighth. So his horoscope showed that period was neither good for him nor his wife.

I had worked harder on the horoscope of his wife on his own insistence and had refused to give any prediction. But I had reasons to have my own apprehensions.

His wife's Horoscope

Often when I wanted to give up astrology, it is for reasons like this. May be, my reactions were strongly subjective. There was no personal emotion involved in it. Unconsciously, I place myself in the position of the consultor and, experience the turbulence of his emotions, in the dasha running.

With my Hindu middle class background, I know the deep emotional tangles in which close knit members of a family, so emotionally interdependent, get involved. There are so many emotions, but the fear of uncertainty is chilling, and the fear of death, frightening ... I could see, even though a bachelor, that towards the end of a long and successful married life, the husband and the wife perhaps merge into each other, perhaps ... they have one emotion, the same emotion throbbing in two physical bodies. Marriage reaches a point of divinity now, perhaps.

The fear of death of his wife ... the gloom on Chandibabu's face ... then the fear of his own death as prophesied by Guruji ... and Guruji's own physical end of life's journey ... would all that come out correct? One wished it would go wrong. But wishing is mere wishing ... fluttering in a void, vainly.

In Vimshottari it was Mercury (debilitated) mahadasha and Jupiter (retrograde) sub-period, Lagna lord in the eighth and retrograde, to be followed by retrograde second lord's sub-period. I had made detailed analysis.[17]

Few days after, Chandibabu had asked me and I had repeated the same prediction.

Then, one day, he told me that his wife had breast cancer. Then another day, he told me that doctors had removed all malignant parts, successfully . . . He was cheerful.

I wished doctors would prove right. But Mercury-Saturn period?[18]

In 1978 April, I was transferred to Delhi.

In March 1980, I received the message that Mrs Chandida died of cancer, which had spread all over her body.

On 23rd June, I got a telegram about Guruji ... no more.

In September, 1980, Chandibabu also died.

It was known to Chandibabu in 1948. He did not need the prediction of the angushtha shastri, in 1968. He took me in confidence in 1977-78.

Thirty two years after 1948, all three of them left the world of mortals. *Such is the vision of a seer, for whom death is not even an emotion. It is that story of a seer, I am narrating astrologically ... the story of that blissful inspiration.*

NOTES

Devaraha Baba

The greatest Yogi, my generation and generations previous to mine, had seen in the plains of India was Devaraha Baba, who never ate or drank anything. He knew the great secrets of the Patanjali's Yoga-Sutras.[19] He was by any computation, over two hundred years old, when he left the world in 1989. He became more famous, when the former Indian Prime Minister, the late Indira Gandhi, started visiting him.

༺༻

Devaraha Hans Baba

A very ardent disciple of Devaraha Baba is the now famous Hans Baba on whom I have written a critical book, critical because though like his great guru, *he is a Yogi,* he is already surrounded by many opportunists. Whether he is the reincarnation of his great guru or, merely the disciple of a great guru whom he cannot match is the controversy that is already raging. It will go on for some years. A journalist wrote a book on him in Hindi, pronouncing his judgement that Hans Baba was the reincarnation of his guru, Devaraha Baba. Without my wanting it, I got embroiled in the controversy.[20]

I spent full 36 days with the Baba, serving him for full sixteen hours, minimum, every day.

Devaraha Hans Baba has performed many miracles before me and cured, what were medically incurable diseases. But when crowds started collecting round him, expecting to be rid of their diseases, and not to learn the great spiritual lessons he could give them, I got irritated. How can the *karmas* of so many births, whose evil consequences one has to suffer, be reduced to ashes and every human life be made blissful? That goes against the very soundly understood yet mysteriously operating laws of *karma,* I argued[21]. Organisers like me get all the blame, when someone expecting to overcome his misfortune, or ailment, feels that he has been the victim of a wrong propaganda.

༺༻

Jada Bharata

The story of Jada Bharata, of the *Srimada Bhagvatam,* is the story

48

of how great Yogic development can come to a temporary halt, through attachments, and how finally, the Yogi can get out of the entanglements, by avoiding the repetition of the mistake that had led him into rebirth.

Nagaridas Baba always reminded me of Jada Bharat, as no other Yogi, including my own Guru, Swami Paramananda Saraswati, could and ever did.

The story begins ... India which was known as Ajnabhvarsha, was renamed as Bharatvarsha, after the great spiritual and efficient king, known as Bharat.[22] The king had equally worthy sons, to whom he handed over his kingdom, as his age advanced, and prepared himself, for a life of renunciation. He started living in a hermitage, deep inside a forest where except the wild animals, the green foliage of the trees and rivulets flowing by, there was nothing to distract his attention, from the practices of his Yogic sadhana.

But Fate had willed otherwise.

One day a lion was chasing a pregnant deer which, to save her life, took a big frantic leap over a rivulet. The child in her womb fell into the river. The deer died, and the baby deer needed careful nurturing, being motherless now. The *sanyasi*, Bharat, took pity on the baby deer. He started looking after it, with affection. An attachment, leading to the creation of a new bondage, became a hurdle to further progress, in the life of the sanyasi Bharat.

Nagari Das Baba described a guru's desire to build ashrams and have disciples as something of a self-immolation, a worldy ambitious Yogi gets trapped into. He had his own disciples, but none ever near him, or serving him. Once initiated, his disciples had to do their own *sadhana*. There was no master and serf relationship in the *guru-shishya* tradition of his.[23] He used to describe a Guru wanting to build an ashram, as a building contractor.

The Guru inspires from within. His physical presence is not a necessary pre-condition to progress in *sadhana*.

The queen of a princely state had offered to Nagari Das Baba her huge palatial temple,[24] where he could live, have his ashram, with disciples. He rejected the offer and, ran away from Vrindavan for nearly ten years, to be totally out of the sight of the queen.

Nagari Das Baba's tongue was acerbic. Often, he said that a true disciple does his spiritual practice sincerely. A bad disciple keeps running round the guru instead of doing *sadhana*.

"It is *raakshasas* (demons) that worship the Guru," he said, often.

Such biting comments of Nagari Das Baba earned him many

enemies, in Vrindavan. He was poisoned thrice, twice, during the period I used to meet him (1978-88). He suffered, but without taking medicine, overcame all the effects of lethal poisoning, through his Yogic powers.

In 1988, when he took *samadhi*, the most sublime, spiritual presence in my life came to an end.

ॐ

To come back to the story of King Bharat, he died with the agony of a parent of the child-deer, in his heart. In his next birth, he had to be born as a deer, because if the thoughts in the mind of a persons at the time of death are concerning the material, not the spiritual, leading to salvation, one must get trapped into the cycle of births and rebirths. The kind God keeps alive the memory of any great *sadhana*, done by anyone in a previous birth, whatever may the next birth be, human or animal.

The Deer Bharat
Remembering the mistake of his previous birth, he ate only dry leaves, and moved around sacred places, biding time, awaiting his death.

Jada Bharat
Jada means dull, stupid. In his next birth, he was born in the family of a highly religious Brahmin. But, Bharat observed none of the normal rituals of a Brahmin. In that high transcendental state, he needed no help of rituals, whose purpose is to create that state, through which transcendental state is attained, which he had already attained, as King Bharat, earlier. He moved in the world like a mad man.[25]

To cut a long, brilliant story short, Jada Bharat remained in that state, outwardly stupid, wooden, dull but inwardly, in high transcendental bliss. He taught brilliant spiritual lessons to an arrogant king of Sindh, Raja Rahugana.[26]

In this birth Jada Bharata attained the ultimate, spiritually.

ॐ

Nagari Das Baba was the most accessible Yogi I had met, like Tapasi Baba of Dwaraka. The greatest Yogis I have met lived in the pilgrimages associated with Radha-Krishna.

He never accepted any money from anyone, never touched it. If anyone insisted on giving anything, he told him to get fodder for cows, peacocks and other birds and, feed them around the bunyan tree, near where he sat and, where peacocks and birds flocked. Cows would come every day, lick his body and would not leave him, inspite of his protesting, till they were satisfied. Elsewhere in the book, there is more about Nagari Das Baba.

ॐ

Moorkhanandji

I have referred to Swami Moorkhanandji many times in my articles in the *Astrological Magazine*. I have not met another Yogi, who knew the secrets of *mantras* so correctly, along with their *prayog* (the method of doing them with their do's and don'ts), as he knew. I was very annoyed with persons who took the fullest advantage of his extraordinary knowledge of Sanskrit, direct and personal experience of the potency of the *mantras* he chose to experiment with, wrote books which earned them national and international fame, but never mentioned that it was plagiarism, pure and simple.

In 1984, in my astrological articles on the late Dr. Nagendra Singh, former Judge in the International Court of Justice, I mentioned about him. Someone in Allahabad, who read them, told Moorkhanandji about them. Later when he met me in Delhi, he said, "So you have mentioned my name". I said that I had, and would do it many times more. The Indian habit of not mentioning the names of persons from whom such extraordinary spiritual knowledge was learnt, is the most vulgar theft in any sense of the term. It also showed lack of gratitude, I said.[27]

'*Moorkha*' in Sanskrit means, a fool. How and why did he come to be known by this name, did arouse my curiosity. I asked him about it. His actual name was Vidyaranya, or, a storehouse of knowledge or, literally, a forest of knowledge. That was the name his guru had given him. But he chose for himself the name, *Moorkha*, because he said that according to the *shastras* (spiritual-religious literature) he who has made many resolutions in life and, did not carry them out, was a '*moorkha*'.

And we all, like the fools we were, referred to him as Moorkhanandji, while he was the Wise Teacher and we, a pack of *moorkhas*.

I came to know about him from an industrialist, the late Sitaram Jaipuria who, when in crisis, consulted me astrologically, and when not in crisis, used some ever willing astrologers of Delhi, to work for him, as liaison men for shady deals. Since Sitaram knew that I did not charge any fee, for my consultations, he was surprised once, when I told that I would charge my fee. What, he had asked me. I told him that till he took me to Moorkhanandji, he would have no astrological consultations from me.

After that, between 1979 and 1985, I met Moorkhanandji, at least four or five times in one year, in Ghaziabad, near Delhi, where he stayed in the house of Sitaram Jaipuria. I have mentioned about an incident of those days in my book, *Astrology, Destiny and the Wheel of Time.*

Sometime after 1980, when my Guru had taken *samadhi* (this term means when a Yogi decides that it is time to get out of his body, meaning decision to die), I had, after 1975 decided, once again to give up astrology. During that period of my vacillations, Moorkhanandji not merely encouraged me to continue with my astrology, but even told me some secrets.

I should not give up astrology because *"Yeh vidya lupta nahi hui hai. Ast hai. Iska phir udaya hoga apke madhyam se"* (This knowledge of jyotisha or astrology is not lost but is hidden, as at sunset. There will be a revival of it and you will be the medium through whom it would happen).

Since I believe in the words of such *Mahatmas*, I knew that sometime, even in the India of my times, some chances would come and, I would be fulfilling some astrological mission of mine, about which I had hints from others, also. But none had said it in so clear a language. Today (1995), the biggest astrology classes of the world are being run in the Bharatiya Vidya Bhavan, New Delhi, of which I am the architect, with a team of new writers of excellent books on astrology, all of which are path-breaking. *These books have been acclaimed as the best ever to have come from India. In USA, where they are rather clear headed in the compliments they pay to astrologers, a common phrase now used is, "Vedic astrology in USA before Rao and after Rao". Mr Robert Hand, a giant in western astrology with whom I had a ten hour meeting at the house of Charles Drutman and Darlene, my sweet-tempered hosts at Boston, he liked my openness, as he said. It was in December, 1994. In the meantime I learn that Mr. Hand has written to some that, "Rao is the best man to come from India..." (I have heard that this sentence is being made use of to advertise my* audio cassettes in which my class room lectures on Vedic astrology, have been tape recorded with all the technological efficiency of USA.)

That is what and how a Yogi, Moorkhanandji, foresees it. And I know is, that when this mission of mine is over, I will either die suddenly or give up astrology, suddenly.

Moorkhanandji knew the secrets of *mantras*. Once a friend of mine in trouble, with the mightiest power of India of those days, Indira Gandhi, the Prime Minister, was told by Moorkhanandji, to do a *prayog* (experiment). My friend did it. The person, through whom Indira Gandhi had chosen to wreak vengeance on my friend, ran into many difficulties.

He told me, when I was alone with him, some of the most stunning secrets of spiritual progress. He asked me, when we were alone, whether I was experiencing something, which I thought was rather awesome.[28] He then told me what it meant and what would be some other symptoms, later. It was said in 1982. I experienced it for the next four years. He never touched money, had no disciples, no ashram and had not eaten rice, wheat or any cereals for over forty years. He lived only on fruits or vegetables, which he ate only at night. I have described in my book *Astrology, Destiny and the Wheel of Time*, how in the same nursing home, within a space of six months, (from December 1984 to May 1985) my two great astrological gurus, my mother and Swami Moorkhanandji, breathed their last. For my astrology, it has been an irreparable loss, the death of a great Yogi, who knew the uses of some secret Chakras of Vedic astrology, which, only Yogis know.

Mouni Baba

An ideal Guru should be like Mouni Baba of Ujjain, whom I first met in 1979, at the residence of Dr. Nagendra Singh. After my prediction about his re-election to the International Court of Justice, Dr. Singh had neither the decency to thank me for it, nor the courtesy to tell me, anything about the visits of Mouni Baba to Delhi. After a gap of more than eight years, I met him again in the house of Shri Arjun Singh, the famous Indian politician. My meetings have been more frequent since then.

On his advice, I gave up eating rice, wheat and cereals. It is ten years, now. In terms of calories, what I consume, is less than one tenth of what the world's poorest man eats. People in India and USA have seen me working for sixteen hours a day, without sleep and without rest. The instructions Mouni Baba gives to some chosen few, who he thinks take to spiritual practices properly, are precise, scientific and illuminating. But, he is not easily accessible. He maintains a vow of silence (*mouna*) and communicates, whatever he wants to say, by writing on a slate, with a chalk, in exquisite Hindi and, in beautiful hand writing. He told me that giving too many predictions to many persons should be avoided. The reasons he gave were so beautiful. But professional astrologers will not like them at all.

Shankaracharya of Kanchi

A great living saint, and a true world teacher, with deepest classical learning, lucid exposition and a winning smile is the present Shankaracharya of Kanchi, Jayendra Saraswati. I am a witness to his supernormal powers, which I should not reveal, yet. I have referred to him in my book, *Astrology, Destiny and the Wheel of Time*, also.

References

1. He has given up all attempts to enter any durbar of important politicians, as he has now realized that he has nothing to offer, ever as a fraud.
2. Astrologer can never get the correct horoscope of important figures.
3. Spiritual energy gets wasted in predicting if the astrologer is also a *Shaka*.
4. No astrologer can ever satisfy them.
5. He died in 1995, after the first edition of this book was published.
6. If he saw Mesha (sheep) and Simha (lion) coming into operation in a dasha, he would say the sheep has entered the mouth of the lion!
7. He has read some couplets in Bengali of the girl astrologer, Khana, who was a genius. She put in couplet forms some of the finest secrets of astrology.
8. Remember this important chronology of events, from 1948 to 1978.
9. It was the most dignified weekly of India once. It had the misfortune of getting such sensation mongering editors as Khushwant Singh, and, very unworthy editors, later. It collapsed, as was inevitable.
10. A very noble dacoit, Man Singh of Morena and Bhind in Madhya Pradesh had such a high number. Man Singh was adored by many villagers.
11. Females would take the secrets to the families into which they would get married.
12. The first Prime Minister of India (1947 to 19640.
13. I was then posted in Rajkot.
14. That was the first clear signal Indira Gandhi, the Indian Prime Minister, had given of her future intentions of wrecking democratic institutions of India.
15. He told a Hindu colleague of mine that a love affair had with a Muslim girl had caused lot of agony, even without looking at his thumb, as he used to do, in his earlier visit.
16. In retrospect, I can say now that he was matchless in this regard. I have

not met anyone who could see everything in a flash, as my Guruji could.

17. This is the composite technique in which I combine both Parashara and Jaimini dashas, successfully, as explained in my book, *Predicting through Jaimini's Chara Dasha.*
18. Death was looming. Doctors could not have been right.
19. Technically, only persons following the Yogic path, are to be described as Yogis.
20. I got involved in this controversy. Once bitten twice shy, I have avoided the Baba since then because of the enthusiasm of an ignorant journalist, who wrote a book on Baba calling him the reincarnation of his great, in fact very great, guru.
21. Americans should read the story of Jada Bharat before trying to pose as spokespersons of the spiritual tradition of India.
22. Should not be mistaken for the son of Shakuntala of the famous play of the great Kalidas.
23. Gurus, who make their disciples work like slaves for the fulfilment of their worldly ambitions are among the worst exploiters.
24. In Vrindavan there are many palaces in which there are magnificent temples.
25. Many great Mahatmas pretend to be dull and stupid.
26. A good caricature of the modern writer of books on spiritual themes, while the writer himself is a greedy devil.
27. I have now discovered that many foreigners, particularly of the West, are the most ungrateful people, with some notable exceptions.
28. How did he know that romantic, yet awesome, experience of mine?

...2...
A Profile of Guru's Life

When people ask me whether I believe in the supernormal powers of Yogis, my invariable answer is — one hundred percent. But to the other question, whether I believe hundred percent in the supernormal powers of all saints, my invariable answer is 'no'. There is that difference between Yogis and Yogis, the genuine, on the one hand and the pseudo saints and the lukewarmly genuine ones, on the other.

So first, cursorily the distinction I have spoken of between saints with supernormal powers.

(a) *Mantra-drashta*[1] : What mantra will suit whom can be "seen", only by such a saint as has the power to see it. How can one know whether a particular saint has such a power? It is a difficult question, which I can answer in my own way, by showing a contrast. When I was initiated by my Guruji, I was told that he would give only such *mantra* as would appear before him, at the time of initiation. He gave me a Krishna *mantra*, without his or anyone else ever knowing that Lord Krishna and Vrindavan had been dearest to me. To accept it as the appearance of a *mantra* before him was difficult for me, as it neither proved nor disproved anything as far as the claim made by my *guru-bhais* about the appearance of *mantras* before my Guruji was concerned. Later, I had many interesting experiences. The first was, when my own immediate elder sister Sharad, a Sanskrit scholar, wanted to be spiritually initiated by my Guruji, though she had picked up a Krishna *mantra* from somewhere, for her own *japam*. She was in a very pleasant daze, when Guruji gave her the same *mantra*.

(b) At least three times, during my stay in the Ashram, I met some persons who more than a decade ago had been initiated by Guruji, had gone away, consumed non-vegetarian food in spite of strict prohibition, after initiation, forgotten their *mantras* and came, seeking the "blessings" of Guruji, after they had run into some serious difficulties, with the request to be given the *mantra*, they had forgotten. They were afraid of making this request directly to Guruji and, were told that only if "Rao dada pleaded with Guruji something perhaps could be done."[2] On one such occasion, when I requested Guruji to help me, he said that the fellow, who was not serious about the *mantra* given, need not be helped. But then I had asked him politely, why did he at all initiate so many so fast without "seeing", whether they were worthy of being initiated at all! In a way, I pointed it out as the fault of Guruji himself and not of the disciple, going astray.[3] All of them were not merely re-initiated but, were given the same *mantra*, as was given previously. They were ecstatically surprised, stupefied and told me that they had no doubt about Guruji being *mantra-drashta*, "seer" of *mantras*. Many had been first initiated in their dreams by Guruji, and later, when they came to him for formal initiation, they got the same *mantra*, exactly.

This is the only living proof I have of a *mantra-drashta*. When I discussed it with a *guru-bhai*, he told me that he had known it all along, as he had been given a Kali *Mantra*, while his wife, a Krishna *mantra*. On the wife protesting to Guruji, why they had been initiated separately and given separate *mantras*, he had smilingly asked, "has your husband not been worshipping Kali goddess and you Krishna of Vrindavan all your lives?"

As a contrast to this, I met many, who claimed or had such a claim put on their behalf by their disciples. But one of them proved to be an absolute fraud in Nagpur. He nearly landed in a jail. The other, in another eastern state, had a set of nine *mantras*, which he gave to his disciples, to some, two, to some, three and to the "more deserving", all the nine. I got all these nine from him in writing. I found six of them to be totally distorted. But this Guru, who has some supernormal powers is neither conscientious about the correctness of the *mantras* he gives, nor has the decency to get the Sanskrit grammar of those *mantras* checked by some Sanskrit pandit.

But my own Guruji, like many others I have seen, initiated many, till I protested strongly. Then, he explained to me ....

I have seen Gurus and Gurus giving *sanyas* to their disciples as though it was like distributing carrots. One of them, who does not even know how to initiate a disciple into *sanyas*, takes the help of a Sanskrit-knowing householder. When one of his *sanyasi* disciples asserted himself, on some point of difference, he not merely turned him out of his *ashram* but, even said that he had never initiated him into *sanyas*. I do not know what is the truth. But such cheap *sanyas* is what I have seen in many places in India.

My Guruji never initiated anyone into sanyas because he was clear about three points:

(a) Pure *sattwick*, vegetarian food was primary for spiritual life.

(b) Worship being a secret dialogue between a devotee and the Lord, no outward symbol like a garland, a *tilak*,[4] a rosary or a *ganda*[5] should ever be displayed.

(c) And when it came to *sanyas*, he was of the opinion that only the worthiest should be initiated. Such persons are very rare. S*anyas*, being a death-like existence in the material world, was not an easy vow for mortals, to observe.

But then why did he initiate so many? His answer was that over a period of time, one improves, spiritually. Initially, I had after many bitter experiences with my Guru-Bhais and Guru-Bahens and great difficulty in accepting this argument. Later, I accepted this as some of them had become very calm, composed, meditative and excellent human beings, after a rather turbulent period of a "wild-oats-youth".

All that has been said here forms the background for the discussion of the horoscope of my Guruji, late Swami Paramananda Saraswati. He was like any true and genuine saint of India, encouraging study of astrology not for any mercenary motive but, for the twin purpose of keeping alive a great Vedic heritage and seeing practically, through the planets how God controls, regulates and guides the universe. I would have given up astrology long ago but, he insisted that I should not, for the sake of my own *sadhana*. My straying into astrological writings and becoming a predictor, for many is what he had foreseen and told a *guru-bhai* more than thirty years ago, and, more than twenty-two years before, I wrote the first article on astrology. He was a seer in the truest sense of the term and, the greatest I have met, though others, who too are lucky like me, to have genuinely great Gurus, must be having the same regard for their Gurus – and such feelings, sacred and pure as they are.

Now see in the horoscope the three striking sanyas yogas:

(a) Four planets in the eleventh house with the tenth lord and none of them combust. The conjunction being in eleventh house gave him his spiritual attainments very early in life and brought him donations for his *ashrams* in lakhs, not merely when he breathed and lived amongst us but even ten years after he left

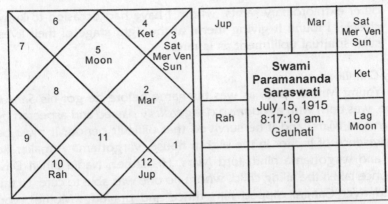

Lagna	Sun	Moon	Mars	Mercury	Jupiter	Venus	Saturn	Rahu
15°21'	28°51'	00°06'	13°32'	09°26'	05°49'	12°40'	15°25'	24°45'

us.

(b) In the navamsha, Moon in the rashi of Mars aspected by Saturn, is another *sanyas* yoga.[6]

(c) Jupiter, in the eighth aspected by Saturn, was good for yoga *sadhana* but, it had a sinister implication for him. I had once discussed it with him and he said "that is God's will". I will discuss it, later. But it happened as I had feared ... and that is the haunting pathos in my story of spiritual ecstasy.[7]

(d) Ketu in the twelfth, alone, without the aspect of the fifth or the ninth lord or of the *deva-guru*, Jupiter, cannot be treated as a spiritual combination, my Guruji told me many times, when he had asked me to work on the horoscopes of many *sadhakas*. I can say now with confidence that when spiritual promise exists, Ketu's presence in the twelfth house, is an indicator of steady to spectacular progress in spiritual life. In the horoscope of three

59

other extraordinary saints, whom I have had occasion to know closely, I found it giving them, at the right stage of their lives, such spiritual upliftment as is rare.

Early Childhood

Young Mrinal Kanti, as was his name before he got his *Sanyas* name, was born with a *Moon so dangerously placed* and aspected by Saturn and Mars, and if he survived that difficult period, it must be the presence of Jupiter in the eighth house, vargottama Atmakaraka Sun, and vargottama ninth lord Mars. His father, Nadia Bihari Das, had once taken the ailing child, whom no one was able to cure, to the sacred river Ganga, dipped him thrice and prayed, "Mother, you decide either to save him or kill him." Thereafter, the child Mrinal recovered but a damaged liver which was his lifelong companion. *Karakamsha* in Mithuna with one malefic and two benefics, Mercury and Venus aspected by Jupiter saved him without allowing him to have a normal liver.

Chara Dasa

The Chara Dasha sequence up to Vrishchika, was neither helpful nor damaging. Rashi by rashi, it was Simha (1915-17), it was the period of his babyhood. Kanya (1917-20), was the period of sickness continuing, with Rahu in fifth, aspected by Mars affecting the stomach region.[8]

Tula Dasha (1920-28)

He had become a pleasantly tolerable child at home. In a family of non-vegetarians, he was a strict vegetarian. His mother had to cook vegetarian food for him separately, with separate utensils kept apart for the purpose. He had an inborn habit of never speaking, while eating. From Tula, the ninth house, perhaps brought to the fore the habits, outlook and the puritanism of a born *sadhaka*, which in East Bengal, Sylhet of those days, was accepted by families, not as a "freak", as modern pseudo psychologists would have us believe, but as a *sadhu*, born in the family and needing some conveniences for his *sadhana*. The entire family accommodated him and his idiosyncracies but, with keen anticipation. For, it was in the Tula dasha that he came to know of a great Muslim Faqir of Tukur Babar, whom he met quite often and, who told him certain things : "*Never discuss Krishna-Leela, openly as most of the vulgar minds cannot see the spiritual sublimity of the highest order.*" A Muslim Faqir saying it – and he remembered it all through his life. A well known psycho (sexo) analyst has written about Radha-Krishna Leela, betraying the limitations of his understanding of these *leelas,* as the fakir or sublime saints know to be the reactions of men, never rising above the level of *"nidra-ahaar-maithuna"* (sleep, food and sex).[9]

The Vrishchika Dasha (1928-36)

Jupiter in the fifth house, and aspects of so many planets on Jupiter, was a very creative, mystical, poetical period with bad health continuing. In Vimshottari, it was the dasha of Venus, the poetical planet. Bengal of early twenties and thirties had the all-pervading influence of the poet, Rabindra Nath Tagore, the only Indian to have won the Nobel prize for literature. Tagore had dabbled in some painting also along with his prodigious poetical outpouring. In East Bengal, it was Kazi Nazrul Islam, whose Shyama Sangeet,[10] sung in classical style, unlike Rabindra Sangeet, ran as a parallel influence. Young Mrinal Kanti wrote lyrics in the undisciplined metrical form, which Shri Narayan Choudhary, a famous literary critic of Bengal, told me personally, were of great merit, great sublimity with a hint or two about his attraction for some girl who seemed to lurk in his imagination. In the late sixties, Shri Narayan Chaudhary wrote a lengthy literary appraisal of the works of Swami Paramananda Saraswati in many journals, particularly one in the now closed *Betar Jagat,* a Bengali monthly of the All India Radio, which many Bengalis believed, was an excellent literary journal.

Vargottama Simha lagna is a sign of redoubled obstinacy. I do not remember a single instance of any mental or emotional flexibility of my late Guruji. Such obstinacy was jarring often in the running of his ashrams, where discipline was violated by one and all, individually and collectively.

Notable feature

The most notable feature in the horoscope is that all seven planets (excluding Rahu and Ketu), occupy four rashis, those of Mercury, Venus, Jupiter and of Sun[11]. There is no influence of Mars or Saturn anywhere. All major planets are in benefic rashis, and coupled with a *vargottama* lagna, helped him do his *sadhana* with such a rare single minded devotion, as would be the envy of many. The same streaks of obstinacy gave him a fanciful idea that he was a painter, like Rabindra Nath Tagore, amateurish, though. He never listened to anyone's suggestion that the cover designs of his books of poems could be done better by others, particularly, by Kanuda, a very good painter, his own disciple, staying in the Ashram![12]

The Vrishchika Dasha, with Vimshottari of Venus, was a case of too many pursuits, poetry, painting and *sadhana* and, the total negligence of studies. But he never gave himself a chance to fail in any examination, because he, after matriculating, just would not appear for any examination, even after attending some classes. A poet has to sit under a tree and do some brooding perhaps! Whether all poets do it or not, his classmates told me, that he did it. He was seen getting lost in trance-like conditions. He was such a votary of truth and, so excellent a human being that if he ever uttered anything, it came to pass. Jupiter, aspecting his second house, gave him *vak-siddhi*. (That state of spiritual progress when, whatever the Yogi utters always comes out true). Whatever he said came to pass. The word went round, but in the cosy, comfortable and cultured days of those decades such a gift was respected and not exploited.

In Delhi, some fellows have it circulated about themselves that they have such gifts which are at their best when a bottle or two of whisky goes down their throats! And any number of black money owners or quick-fortune seekers, are prepared to do it! My friend, and a really gifted astrologer, the late Kanad Rishi Bhatnagar too, had such a canard circulated about himself, though I had seen him giving very fine predictions only when he was saner, on Sunday mornings or, on those nights when he came to meet me, taking care not to booze. He knew that I had turned out a Member of Parliament from my house once, when he came dead drunk and wanted me to predict! Of course, that M.P. never came again. If you know astrology, a bottle or two can still be procured free, in Delhi.

Unlike these petty men, a genuine *sadhak* is required to conceal his gift. The young Mrinal did it so well that only years later, when he was better known as Swami Paramanand Saraswati, some of such incidents were recalled. One of them, I could verify very thoroughly, was that of a woman, who as a girl was in love with Mrinal Kanti and, wanted to marry him. But, he told her, *"I will not marry, but, at some stage in your life you will be very close to me and I will guide you."* She could hardly have known that after the partition of the country, she, as a refugee in Calcutta,[13] would ever go to him and become his disciple, a very ardent disciple, who got so spiritualised, that when she died, she told everyone, cheerfully, that she had got in life what she wanted, the experience of real spiritual bliss.

References

1. It would do lot of good to people to know it. In the USA, I saw mantra, for Herschel, Pluto and Neptune, which are not recognised in Hindu astrology. Such concocted mantras have no divine potency at all but are the haystacks of someone's brain.
2. Guruji would generally listen to me carefully when I pleaded someone's case.
3. For reasons explained later, a real Guru should not initiate many disciples.
4. The sacred mark on the forehead.
5. Can be both a necklace of beads or even a bracelet.
6. It should be in the birth horoscope or the navamsha or drekkana.
7. See in the last chapters the astrological explanation.
8. Remember to apply Jaimini principles of astrology, as discussed in my book, *Predicting through Jaimini's Chara Dasha.*
9. The American theory of abuses is an obsession with psychologists.
10. Exquisitely devotional songs composed to worship the Goddess Mother.
11. To know the sattwick quality of a horoscope, this should be seen.
12. Kanuda had developed leprosy. His great career as a commercial artist came to an end. Guruji kept him in the ashram. All guru bhais, it seems, protested, initially. I liked him and helped him, though he was very irritable.
13. India was partitioned in 1947. East Bengal, now Bangladesh, was formed. Hindus had to flee the country.

...3...
Prabhu Bejoy Krishna Goswami
(Guru's Guru)

A saint with a wry sense of humour used to say, during his bhajans, a *"saint has no past and a sinner no future"*. I am not one of those, who would argue obstinately, that in the money-and-politics-corrupted India of nineties, only the sinner has a future. Here, the saint was referring to spiritual future not the material one, with a limited vision of a big mansion and imported cars, but to life after death.

But to know the biographical details of a saint or, about his past, is never an easy task. A genuine saint neither speaks of his past, with an "I" and, sometimes speaks to some rarest of rare individual or a disciple, *why and how the temptations of the world and flesh must torment him, before he transcends it, if he transcends it at all*. My *Guru-bhais*, some of them even from Sylhet, now in Bangladesh, and senior to me in age, could not help me except telling me more than what I had collected myself, through cross-checking, from various sources. So, I have to grope my way through the Venus mahadasha, and, part of Sun dasha too, in the Vimshottari, and, upto the end of Makar dasha (ending 1946), till I reach a point from where Calcutta based *Guru-bhais* had, something more personal and vivid to tell me.

Dhanu dasha (1936-1939)
Some of his poems were published in some journals and were also selected for some prestigious anthology of poems along with Rabindra Nath Tagore's and others, I learnt!

Makar dasha (1939-46)
It was a period of real change. In Vimshottari dasha, it was Sun's period, his *atmakaraka*, and *vargottama* Sun, aspecting the ninth house from Makar, along with Jupiter. He had got a Guru, his

Tantrik Guru, Swami Suryanandaji, whose Ashram, in Laban, in Shillong, I had seen from outside many times, never entering it. The reason? My Guruji had strong differences with his own Guruji, on two grounds. The first was that he never practised any of '*Ma's*' of Tantrik Sadhana like '*mas*' (meat), or *madira*' (wine). But his sadhana was so intense that he went through all its rigours, including "*shava*" (corpse) sadhana. He had spent many years in the thick jungles of Kamakhya Hill in Guwahati.[1]

The second reason was a terrible point of bitterness. In a cosmic manifestation before him, Prabhu Bejoy Krishna Goswami,[2] a junior contemporary of Ramakrishna Paramahansa, asked him to propagate Krishna cult and, had even initiated him after a Cosmic Manfestation before him. Some disciples of a great saint, Kiran Chand Darvesh, a direct disciple of Prabhu Bejoy Goswami, had often questioned it. Once, they had asked me how and why I could accept it. I countered it thus: *the story of the spiritual initiation of Prabhu Bejoy Krishna Goswami was itself a miracle. He had danced ecstatically many times with Ramakrishna Paramahansa, and Swami Vivekananda knew of the great intimacy that had existed between them, when they were closeted for hours together in spiritual practices.* Ramakrishna Paramahansa had even remarked once: "Bejoy was about to reach the pinnacle of his spiritual life". *He had not taken initiation from the Paramahansa, but from a Nanak Panthi Guru, Swami Brahmananda in Gaya, through a Cosmic Manifestation.*[3] If Prabhu Bejoy Goswami could be initiated in such a miraculous way, through cosmic sudden, and non-physical manifestation of a great Guru, could he not, after many years, initiate others too in a similar way? If Goswami Prabhu could not do it by remanifesting himself, even after his physical death, then his own initiation too could be called a figment of imagination.[4]

But more important for me was the spiritual experiences of the mantra given by my Guruji. Either I accepted or rejected them. *My own experience was best proof of my genuine and blissful initiation into Krishna-worship.* Why should I waste my time in needless controversy? They had not merely no answer but, had been told by their Gurus to avoid discussion with me, as none could meet my arguments, which were too sharp for them. You either believe in the supernormal or do not. My argument was rather bitingly sharp for them, because its logical extension was disbelief in the spiritual initiation of Prabhu Bejoy Krishna Goswami himself, by a Nanak Panthi Saint.

Both in the *ashrams*[5] of Prabhu Bejoy Krishna Swami and his famous disciple, Kiran Chand Darvesh, the *Guru Granth Saheb*[6] was recited and Kiran Chand Darvesh had even done a Bengali rendering of the *Sukhamani Saheb*. Here were some Bengali saints doing the *sadhana* done by the great Sikh Gurus, without either describing themselves as Sikhs or Akalis! *Below its ugly exterior, India is a spiritually integrated nation. It was the great Acharyas from southern India, Shankara, Ramanuja, Madhawa, Vallabha, Nimbarka who had integrated India in so brilliant a way that India retains even today with her a spiritual integrity so firm as to survive foreign assaults, military, cultural, religious and even linguistic.* The recent breed of Indian historians, leftists with their Marx-drunk minds, obsessions with dialectical materialism, and the intellectual distortions, have hardly understood the real India, which is neither the story of kings and conquests, nor of the bourgeoise and the proletariat. It is the story of an eternal quest, individually and collectively, always kept alive, along with all the trappings of all that is worldly and materialistic, scientific and technological. To see that undercurrent of uninterrupted spirituality is, to see the force that always shapes Indian history, throws up the *Alvars*, the *Nayanars*, the Chaitanya Mahaprabhu, the great Gyaneshwar, Narsi Mehta,[7] and more dazzling the great Sikh Gurus, Tulsidas with his *Ramcharit Manas*[8] and the great Ramdas,[9] behind the imposing figure of Chattrapati Shivaji.

A great saint rarely produces many great saints. But he certainly inspires generations of men to do great and good things for the society. *The ignorant critic of Indian saints who describes them as not "serving" society is an ignoramus who does not know that the Indian saint is not a "missionary" converting some from one religion to another, but a spiritual catalyst, who changes a man from within, making the dross sublime to some extent, helping a brute control his barbarism.*

If my entire outlook about Indian history has undergone a change it is because saints have shown to me the unwritten chapters of real Indian history. But it will never be written because "saints have no past" because no biographical details of a saint's life are available.

But in this case, I could see why in Makar dasha my Guruji had to have differences with his own Guruji. See from Makar the concentration of planets in the sixth house, aspecting the ninth house, with both the atmakaraka, putrakaraka and ninth lord aspecting the ninth house, the house of Guru.

Kumbha Dasha

The climax of his *sadhana* came in Kumbha dasha. It must be seen in many ways :

(a) In the Birth horoscope the fifth house has the aspect of five planets including by Jupiter.

(b) In navamsha, from the dasha lord, the fifth house has *vargottam atmakaraka* Sun, aspected by the *putrakaraka* Mercury, a highly beneficial spiritual combination.

(c) But then see *Vimshamsha* the twentieth division.

Here, Kumbha is the fifth house of Vimshamsha, with Ketu, the *gyankaraka,* associated with the Putrakaraka and aspected by Venus and in the fifth from Kumbha there is Saturn aspected by Moon. It is known through fragments of some remarks of my Guruji and the information that I collected from Radhakunda in Mathura district that during this period, Guruji had often visited Radhakunda and had once, kept a vow of silence (*mauna*) for full three years. He had done his *Sadhana* in Kamakhya, the great Tantrik centre of worship and also in Radhakunda the great Vaishnava centre of Radha-Krishna *bhakti.*

In the *Srimad Bhagvatam* it is said that in *Kaliyuga* for success both Tantrik and Vaishnava *sadhanas* should be combined. I have known other examples of some saints doing likewise. Ultimately, different *sadhanas* merge into one single path — the *sushumna marga,* which is why in *Gopal Sahasranaam* one of the names of Lord Krishna is *sushumna-marga sanchari.* At some stage, the differences between different *sadhanas* vanish, if the final goal is attained. It was a path, a bye-way, or the main road — but the goal has been reached by the seeker in his own way.

But the hostility of my Guruji's guru Swami Suryanandji, towards him continued for years because he had deviated from the Tantrik *sadhana,* into Radha-Krishna bhakti, in Makar dasha. In Vimshottari it was the dasha of Sun, his atmakaraka aspected by Mars and Saturn. The Sun being in the sixth house in the Vimshamsha, the quarrel with his own Guru is explainable here.

In a major research, I am getting done on the dashas of different lords of different houses, I have laid down some parameters, tested over a period of time by me, and here I am giving a few. See the fifth lord of my Guruji and the fifth house.

The fifth House

From *Parashari* angle, the fifth house has the aspects of all the four planets from the eleventh house and also Mars, totalling five.

From the *Jaimini* angle, the same four planets and Jupiter aspect the fifth house.

In a series of horoscopes, I have tested career patterns, talents, gifts, normal and supernormal, by concentrating on the fifth house and the fifth lord from Lagna and the putrakaraka of Jaimini. Here, the versatility of my Guruji is so apparent, so jumbled up, so confused and so full of tension that his life had to be what it was: he was agricultural expert, an untrained architect who planned an extraordinarily beautiful Ashram on the hills of Kamakhya, which could be used as a spiritual hill-resort, with a brilliant view of the turbulent Brahmaputra flowing in torrents, down below and such silence as to make audible the musical notes of mosquitoes, the big size Assam variety, like an ethereal symphony of a twilight. He was a poet of extraordinary merit. And he cooked, when once in a while he decided to do it, with a taste so delicious, that we could put to shame some boastful housewives by proving to them that their culinary skills were very inferior!

But that was terrible sources of tension for him, first from his own Guru, and later, from his disciples, some of whom wanted to become *sanyasis* and become Gurus themselves! It created problems for us. Three of them, I know, have become Gurus by now and have been having roaring business in Bengal, where the traditional belief that life without '*Guru-karan*' (initiation by a Guru) is a life wasted, is strong among some sections. So there will always be good Gurus and the fraudulent Gurus. It must have been so even during the time of Adi Shankaracharya — '*Kashayambar bahu krita veshah*' (draped in the saffron garb of sanyasis). My Guruji never wore saffron robes, but there of his disciples, are now in saffrons, collecting around themselves unmarried girls in the age group of twenty-five to forty years. An astrologer without technical and moral excellence and a Guru without effulgent *sadhana,* is like the Indian politician who wants to 'serve the country' in order to satisfy his own power-lust.

The fifth lord

Then the fifth lord is in the eighth house, in itself bad, though it is Jupiter in the excellent rashi of *moksha*, Meena. But Jupiter is aspected by Saturn, a combination for humiliation to be suffered at the hands of his own disciples. That is the lingering pathos of my story of bliss, which I will discuss last.

But a fifth lord, with no planet in the rashis on either side, is spiritually very good for an unattached mind: good for spiritual pursuits but bad for material gains. Such a fifth lord shows the innate capacity in a native to detach himself at will, from what he finds irksome. Hundreds of times, such incidents took place and I have seen him rising above the mire of crass worldliness of others, mostly his own disciples, like the lotus-petal, Lord Krishna speaks of, in the *Bhagvad Gita.*

Vimshamsha

The fifth house and the fifth lord in Vimshamsha are superb. There is an exchange between the fifth and ninth lords and the fifth house has Ketu as well, with Mercury, who is also the twelfth lord, the salvation-giver.

But, see the tenth lord, Moon in Vimshamsha aspected by Mars and Saturn giving the *karma* of a Guru.

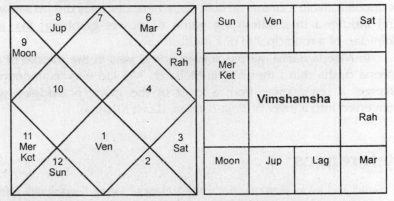

Meena Dasha

The Meena dasha in Jaimini, coincided with his Moon dasha in Vimshottari. Moon, as the twelfth lord, took him away from what was then East Bengal, after the partition of India, to Calcutta and Shillong. Meena is the eighth house from lagna and the sixth house of the Vimshamsha lagna. Here in Vimshamsha, the Moon in the tenth house aspected by Saturn and Mars, led him into his troublesome activity of building up ashrams, at the instance of some rich disciples who hated meeting him in the house of a Guru-bhai who, they thought, had 'monopolised' Guruji and was rude in behaviour. I do not know the truth because till then, I had not met my Guruji. But it was clear that intrigues thickened around him.

Mars in the Tenth

I have not seen a single saint, with Mars in the fourth, ninth or tenth house, not building up ashrams and not facing serious problems of infractions of ethical-spiritual codes. My own Guruji was no exception and having had to look after his ashrams twice, for five years during both of my Calcutta postings, I am inclined to agree with the late Nagari Das Baba of Vrindavan that a Guru who builds up *ashrams*, gets tragically diverted, from the spiritual into the worldly. And with vargottama navamsa and vargottama Mars again in the tenth house, his troubles over his *ashrams* were manifold.

The tenth lord of Vimshamsha, Moon again aspected by Mars and Saturn, here, the fourth lord, showed a story of unending agony.

The sweetest fragrance of a beautiful spiritual flower that my Guruji was, seemed to have been lost amidst the huge thorny shrubs of uncontrollable ashrams he built up, where disciples did no *sadhana* and indulged in pettifogging game of power-grabbing, like any politician of a municipality of a moffusil town.

In Meena dasha, all this started and it was in the middle of the Meena dasha that I met him in Shillong. My life was to undergo a change, a sea-change; from a lover of the game of bridge, I got converted into a lover of *Brija-nandan*. (Lord Krishna).

References

1. Guruji had asked someone that if the ashram of Swami Suryanandji, offered meat-*prasad*, what would he do.
2. Prabhu Bejoy Goswami was perhaps the greatest Vaishnaivite saint in the last two hundred years. His long matted hair stood up like snakes, when he was in divine ecstacy. Prabhupad Baba of Vrindavan, told me that he had met many saints in Radhakund, in Vraj Bhoomi, who had witnessed it.
3. This historical distortion must be corrected.
4. Cosmic Manifestation of great spiritual figures is well known.
5. He had a small cottage only as his ashram.
6 The sacred book of the Sikhs.
7. An immortal saint-poet of Gujarat.
8. The great epic in Hindi of the greatest saint poet of Hindi, Tulsidas.
9. The guru of the great Maratha king, Chattrapati Shivaji.

...4...
I Meet My Guru

On a cold chilly night of Shillong's January wintry blasts, I landed there on the third posting during my career, after what till today, is the most romantic journey I have ever undertaken. A metre gauge train took me from Lucknow to Guwahati, at lugubrious pace, which later proved a terrible handicap in lifting military personnel and material, in the Indo-Chinese clash of October, 1962.

A colleague came to receive me and took me to his house, where he was the tenant of a police officer, whose wife, I later felt, was a mother of some previous life of mine, waiting for me. She was the disciple of Swami Paramananda Saraswati. On an evening, when a 'bhajan' session had been arranged in her house, I was invited to attend, if I was 'willing'. My friend, S. Krishnan, I.A.A.S said that to keep his landlady in good humour, we should attend for sometime and leave. I said a bhajan was not a formal social gethering. I, at any rate, would sit through it and observe everything. My friend slipped out after sometime and I continued, not understanding a word of Sylhetti dialect of Bengali language, in which most of the devotees conversed. I was quite used to Bengalis neglecting a non-Bengali totally and, carrying on conversation in their own mother tongue, without ever feeling that it was a stranger whom they had ignored.

After the bhajan started, some of the disciples began their 'frog jumps', later familiar and sometimes boring, as it appeared. In any Shakti-paat sadhana, when the Kundalini is aroused by the power of the Guru, active Kundalini working in the muladhara chakra, leads to both dadur (frog) jumps and, also, arouses excessive sexuality, as the kaam beeja is there. I saw later in life that those whose sadhana started from manipura or anahat chakra, experienced both miracles and bliss, while those who started lower down, stagnated spiritually, for long periods. I am saying this because I have watched the effects of Shakti-paat sadhana, for over thirty years, in at least six different

71

places, in the country during the course of my postings.

But *Shakti-paat sadhana* is a definite living proof of a very competent Guru, who can pass on to his disciple, his spiritual power, *Shakti-paat* being transmission of spiritual energy by Guru into the body of the disciple. There are many in the country doing it very successfully and, generally it is kept as a secret. It is not one of those gimmicks which was exhibited in Delhi, some years ago, when a group of disciples were asked to raise themselves, by jumping on their hips on a dunlopillo. It was described as levitation, and a photographic trick 'proves' it too! I watched such gimmicks rather closely. Through some physical testing, it can easily be known whether it is a case of *dadur* jump (the disciple begins to jump like frog and is not under his own control so long as the kundalini energy remains superactive) or a contrived jump, individually or collectively, on a soft mattress. Those who have it can go into *dadur* jumps on a solid hard rock without a hurt! These Delhi's showy 'levitation' practitioners should be asked to sit on a rock and demonstrate it. They will land in a hospital.

I was observing my future Guru, all through the *bhajan* — lean, shining face, piercingly yogic eyes. ... The *bhajan* over, he asked me in a chaste Sanskritised Bengali, not in Sylhetti dialect, whether I had any question to ask. And I had, a very genuine question to ask. During the last few months of my posting in Allahabad, I had read many *upanishads* and the description of *atma,* as a thumb ensconsed in the heart, fascinated me. Many such descriptions given in the *upanishads* were more like camphor, I said appearing brilliant and dazzling, when they were read, but evaporating out of the mind no sooner.

The answer he gave me, I remember so fondly, reading of books scriptures stimulates interest in the spiritual; but they have to be realised through *sadhana.*

And then he said "You are not the type of man who would accept anything without testing it, many times. You can never be satisfied by reading scriptures. The best you should do is to take spiritual initiation from any Guru, you like, do the sadhana for six months strictly, as directed. If at the end of six months you do not have tangible experiences, which convince you of the truth of inner experiences, you should go and tell the Guru concerned that you want to give up sadhana and, that you have decided to severe the Guru-shishya relationship."

That night my friend S. Krishnan, had many caustic remarks to make about the *bhajan* and, all that he saw there with those 'frog jumps'. I kept silent. He turned towards me and, asked me what had kept me so engrossed. I told him of my intention to ask him, if he would initiate me. After six months, I would have the right to severe my relationship with him, if my inner experiences did not convince me of the efficacy and truthful substance of the *sadhana*, he initiated me into.

Not merely my friend but, all my colleagues were terribly annoyed with me. They felt bitterly about it because, on the bridge tables in the small town of Shillong, my skill was what they admired. Would I not be available for their bridge-sessions?

Next day, I asked my future Guru and he said he would initiate me but, I should wait for a *Shubha Muhurta* (auspicious time). I had to go on a three-month long tour in the next three or four days. I had wondered if it would be possible for him to do it before that.

I observed in hundreds of cases starting with mine, that in initiating disciples, Guruji mostly followed three astrological principles:

(a) *Brahma Muhurta* (48 minutes before sunrise) was his first preference, if two other astrological conditions were fulfilled. So this was a relaxable first condition.

(b) The second was a *sthira* (fixed) lagna, with the Sun well placed.

(c) The third was either Ketu or Jupiter in the twelfth house. He would not allow unaspected Ketu in the twelfth. It had to have the association of the twelfth lord, or Jupiter or Mercury.

I had to keep awake through the night. In *Brahma Muhurta*, I was given initiation with all the conditions mentioned here fulfilled. The instructions he gave appeared simplest to me:

(a) The *mantra* he gave (mine was a longish one) had to be done once while inhaling and then, while exhaling. It had to be done rhythmically, and the *mantra* was not to be ever divulged to anyone.

(b) Once in the morning, preferably in *Brahma Muhurta*, and once at night, it had to be done on an *aasan* (of wool, preferably) every day, in a closed room with no one seeing you do it.

(c) The food to be taken, which is eighty percent of *sadhana*, had to be *sattwick*, free both from onion and garlic.[1]

I had no difficulty about food. Getting up in *Brahma Muhutra* for a late night bird, playing bridge in long sessions, or reading till late night hours, was a problem. Doing it without being seen by anyone, was possible. One thing to which I have not reconciled even today to is, why were Bengalis allowed to eat fish (but not meat and eggs), with this *sattwick* food. How and how did fish become *'sattwick'*?

In later years, I worked on nearly five hundred horoscopes, to find out the time for spiritual initiation, not those 'herds', who are led like sheep into a camp for collective initiation, but for individual initiation. I chose the best of such Gurus and their disciples for my research. The findings are the following:

Vimshottari Dasha

The Mahadasa will generally be of a benefic or fifth or ninth lord in the birth horoscope. Part of this will be repeated in the Vimshamsha horoscope also.

Chara dasha

The rashi dasa will be the fifth or ninth house from the Lagna or, alternatively, the dasha containing Putrakaraka or with the Putrakaraka in the fifth house, from the rashi dasha. Part of this will be repeated in the Vimshamsha horoscope.

During the course of the *sadhana*, after initiation, if these combinations manifest fully, it is time for *yoga-siddhi*.

Transits

In transit, Jupiter will be aspecting natal Ketu, or will be transiting on it or, will be in the fifth or ninth house

Saturn should be aspecting birth lagna or the lagna lord but not Ketu. Saturn's aspect on natal Moon is excellent.

Cast the horoscope of initiation as it is the second birth, or the 'real birth' as till such initiation one was only an animal, not a spiritualised human being. Cast the dashas etc. as done in a birth horoscope and watch it and, see how helpful it proves.

This was a secret instruction given to me by my Guruji with the permission to reveal it, later. I have watched it very closely for over two decades in many horoscopes where the feedback was honest and genuine.

The birth-details of Guruji, given by him, and the horoscope, as given here, was approved by him. When I say 'approved' I mean not merely this, many other horoscopes approved by him turned out to be extraordinarily correct for many predictions.

His approval was based on his super-sensory verification. In some of my articles, I have referred to such verification by him but let me give here the latest instance.

Once in 1975, sitting in my room in his ashram, I was struggling to fix the proper lagna for the daughter of my younger brother. Passing that way, Guruji looked at me and asked me what I was working on. Since he encouraged my astrological research, I only told him that I was trying to fix the proper lagna for the two year old daughter of my younger brother, K. Vikram Rao.

Without asking for any details, he said, "It is the first navamsha of Mesha." I was not surprised, as he had done such miracles many times before. I worked on it, and in 1991 I told my niece that she would be an engineer and must keep appearing for all the qualifying examinations, as she would succeed in 1991-92. In January 1992, she was finally selected for a prestigious engineering course.[2]

Why I call it a miracle is, that he never asked for any birth details. For a 9th September birth, between 8.30 p.m. and 9 p.m., the lagna had to be either the last navamshas of Meena or, the earlier ones of Mesha. Without asking for any such detail, he told me many times not merely the lagna but also the navamsha. Accepting it with absolute faith, I have not failed in giving correct predictions on a single horoscope.

But when it came to casting a horoscope, he depended on what was given in Bengali panjikas (ephemeris) and, more often than not, prepared wrong horoscopes! And in some cases, he wrote it out in his exquisite handwriting, on thick paper with artistic designs, never missing the opportunity to display his half-blossomed painting skills!

It will take years for the brutalised Indian doctors and the noveu rich to realise that *sattwick* food is not merely the soundest foundation of spiritual life, but of much better health. For me now it was longish tour through the tribal areas of Assam, unbifurcated then, and a pretty long spell of stay in Nagaland, Kohima. Since it is not my story that I have to tell but, my Guruji's, and with an astrological angle, let me refer briefly to three points: pure food, regularity of meditation and meeting minimum number of people (avoiding human contact) was more possible on the tour, when staying in circuit houses, in unknown places and unknown company, gave me enough 'contamination-free' time and seclusion. The experiences which started during this period in meditative dreams – not waking hours – for the next years, has helped me see the limitations of Freudian interpretation of dreams. Carl Jung's '*Psychology and Alchemy*' explains the spiritual phenomenon with better insight, but in the explanation of the mystic and the spiritual most of the western writers are too shallow. Indian saints keep it a secret and, it continues to be *Guru-shishya* tradition of sharing of experiences for valid reasons. The '*swine*' that the educated man is, casting pearls before him is to invite ridicule. I learnt the lesson fast.

Six months before the Indo-Chinese clash of 1962, I had, for full 15 days running, clairvoyant visions about the clash. I shared it with a friend or two only. One of them made fun of me, while the other took it too seriously. When it happened and, we in Shillong, saw the strange spectacle of the Indian Prime Minister Pt. Nehru, in a broadcast to the nation, saying, *"my heart goes out to the people of Assam,"* we wondered why that pusilanimous Prime Minister had not resigned from his post, after the literal Himalayan blunder he had committed in his life. But I did get sneaking admiration from some of my friends, when I told them that the Chinese would not land in the plains of Assam but withdraw – all according to my clairvoyant experiences.

For six years, this phenomenon lasted. Then it stopped, much to my relief, because when the mind is glued to the worldly, you begin to see a little too much of the ugly side of people around. It leads to depression. My periods of spiritual bliss became more continuous only when my clairvoyant visions stopped.[3]

When and how such clairvoyant visions manifest most interested me and I made some research on it. The best illustration must start with the horoscope of my Guruji.

When some of those strange spiritual experiences were experienced by me, it never occurred to me that these were the 'gifts' of Guruji to me, not my own earnings. A Guru does it to show to the disciple what his spiritual potential is or, what he can possibly earn through proper *sadhana*. But artificially, while it could be a source of inspiration for the rest of my life, I have seen many other Guru-bhais and Guru-bahens get swayed by them and land in disaster. Fortunately, none of them landed in a lunatic asylum!

But, recently,[3] I had an occasion to see the horoscope of a boy whose *shakti-paat* was too much for him. His father spoke of the greatness of his Guru and how his son had so many extraordinary experiences. But then, I asked him whether his son had some bizzare sexual experiences, which put him off mental balance. Not merely that, said the father, the boy had become a lunatic and was being treated in Bangalore.

Two astrological questions puzzled me. Who gets more clairvoyant dreams and when, who gets clairvoyant visions in meditation and when, and what can be said to be a 'temporary', one as in my case and the unfailing and durable one, as in the case of my Guruji.

From my research on it, which will remain incomplete, because of misleading feedback, I can give only such examples as I found, genuine or nearly so.

The best combinations for claivoyance, or even siddhis are:

(a) Connection of Ketu with Jupiter, involving the fifth house and its lord, the eighth house and its lord, or the twelfth house and its lord.

(b) The second best is, the same combination as above without the involvement of Jupiter.

(c) The third best is Ketu in the twelfth house without any aspect, Moon in the rashi of Saturn aspected by Mars or, in the rashi of Mars aspected by Saturn, with Jupiter influencing the lagna or the lagna lord exactly.

The best example I have seen to date, though I have not succeeded in collecting the horoscopes of other gifted saints, is that of my own Guruji. Note the combinations.

(a) Ketu in the twelfth house aspected by the fifth and the eighth lord, Jupiter.

(b) In the navamsha, as also in the birth horoscope, the Moon coming under the influence of both Saturn and Mars.

Together with this, since very early in his life he took to *sanyas* and maintained the pure spiritual life throughout, he went rising higher and higher. Clairvoyance was one of his many supernormal achievements, or *siddhis.*

In Vimshamsha, Ketu in the fifth house with the ninth and the twelfth lord, as discussed before, perhaps shows that he was born with this gift. How else could he tell so many people so many things, even before he had formal spiritual initiation?

A good example I have is of a friend who often tells me, when alone, of some events concerning individuals and the nation. He has Mesha lagna with Ketu in the twelfth unaspected, Moon in Kumbha aspected by Mars from the eighth house and Jupiter, Saturn and lagna on the same degree.

Since I have experienced it and I dread the experience, let me cite the small studies I have made of aberrations in clairvoyance. Study of an accurate Vimshamsha chart is an absolute necessity. However, in the birth horoscope what leads to these aberrations is what I am narrating here.

(a) When Mars gets combined with Ketu with fifth and ninth lord, clairvoyant visions are mostly of the ghastly type.

(b) When Saturn, as the fifth lord or the ninth lord, gets combined with Ketu without Jupiter's involvement, the worldly visions cease and divine visions, mostly of lofty hills, pilgrimages, saints giving messages of some future events occur, broken but they are visions.

(c) If Mars and Ketu are in the fifth house, without the involvement of the fifth and ninth lord, such visions are too small and often tragic.

(d) If Mars and Ketu in the fifth have the involvement of the fifth or the ninth lord, such experiences are very dazzling, once in a while.

In the case of great saints for whom *siddhis* become a part of their lives, the period of success of their *sadhana* should be seen. Thereafter, their *siddhis* continue with them.

But in the case of ordinary mortals like me, since I have studied many such cases, I can say confidently, that it occurs most :

(a) In the major or sub-periods of planets in Karka and Meena, preferably in second and third dreshkonas (drekkanas). *What we call sarpa dreshkonas, represents the kundalini power in a spiritual sense. Vrishchika gives this power but with good deal of morbidity. Karka and Meena are the rashis of Moon and Jupiter and, may be because of their beneficent nature, they colour the clairvoyant with sweet divinity. Vrishchika, influenced by Mars, gives tragic, macabre and even ghoulish visions.*

(b) Such visions occur in the periods of the fifth and the ninth lord also.

(c) Planets, in the eighth house having a very substantial role in such visions the range and the frequency almost unlimited.

In transit, Jupiter aspecting natal Ketu or in the fifth or the ninth house from the lagna seems to be the best time for such visions.

I have further noticed that those who have such combinations, mostly in the twelfth house, get these experiences in dreams, while those with the fifth or ninth houses involved may get it, sometimes in their pooja and, sometimes in their dreams. But those who have it in their eighth house, get it in all states, dreams, meditations or even when walking and waking hours.

But I must warn that clairvoyant vision need not be the sign of any spiritual progress. I know many who have clairvoyant visions but, no spiritual discipline in their lives. *Clairvoyance is, more often than not, psychic gift than a spiritual gift.* Saints who have it, only have to close their eyes and see it all. Psychics who have it, go into some sort of a trance which can occur anytime, if they are lacking in spiritual discipline, which primarily is taking *sattwick* food, their aberrations are too many. I have met some psychics in India and even one of the well known foreign psychics, who visits India once in a while. Their 'predictions' are too limited in range, too slippery to be of much value, though I will concede that sometimes they do come out with something startling.

But far superior to clairvoyance is honest and deep work on a horoscope, astrologically. The results are more dependable, substantial and, once in a while, spectacular.

References

1. Ignorant Americans have not been told by their gurus, some of them American gurus now, that as mentioned in the Gita, right food is 80 percent sadhana. In the West, they have the additional difficulty of not getting even vegetables not grown on non-vegetarian fertilizers.
2. Now in 1996, she is a qualified engineer of the Indian Railways.
3. Spiritual progress can become stagnant in the Swadhishtan chakra. It is then that psychic experiences occur most. But is the misfortune of the sadhak, if he mistakes it for achievements.

...5...
Awakened Kundalini

Outside the Hindi belt in the eastern parts of India, a pure vegetarian like me, depending upon a cook to feed him, has to face enormous difficulties if the cook decides to go on 'leave' and never returns, which is more a rule than an exception in those areas! My peon, accompanying me on the long tour in Assam, managed to get a telegram about his mother's sickness and left me half way through the tour. I survived on bananas and milk, if available. It proved a disguised blessing for my *sadhana* and the first of many experiments with food. Later in life, when I met Nagari Das Baba of Vrindavan and Swami Moorkhanandji, I knew why they had for over four decades not eaten rice, wheat or cereals. It is one of the instructions given by the great Bhishma in the *Mahabharat* to Yudhishthira.

In my one month stay in Kohima, in Nagaland, when the hostiles shot down non-Nagas between Dimapur and Kohima, instead of facing such difficulty, I had a very pleasant experience. I was given a hutment in the Assam Rifles apartments, when a Bengali doctor proceeded on a tour. My puritanism irked the army officers, but then forced to play bridge with them, they soon became my admirers. Back from his tour, the doctor not merely shared the hutment with me but sprang a surprise on me by taking out of his box a photo of Goswami Prabhu, my Guru's Guru, telling me that his own mother had taken initiation in that line and that he would look after me well, which he did.

Some months later, the doctor, who had in an impulsive mood resigned from his post, came running to me in Shillong and asked me to help him by destroying his letter of resignation kept in our records, so that there was no break in his service. I did that – the only irregulaι act I had ever committed in my service career. And he told me that he knew that Goswami Prabhu would help him.

I could have dismissed such incidents as 'coincidences', but when they happened almost in a chain for nearly a year, I began to accept supernormal experiences as normal happenings in the life of a sadhak. But this stirred my curiosity to such an extent that I started watching other guru-bhais and guru-bahens, so closely that I nearly did a brilliant research in para-psychology, with not merely a first-hand experience and rare insight but with rare discrimination.

The clairvoyant experiences I have spoken of, are largely the product of co-relating the first hand experiences of my 'subjects' and their horoscopes. Back in Shillong, all my evenings were spent in the study of this phenomena, which included trance, genuine and the fraudulent, practised one.

Astrological Combinations

If there are planets in the eighth from lagna or from Moon, sadhaks can hope to experience 'trance like' conditions in their major or sub-periods. But such a trance can be from unsatisfied sexuality to the genuine one, but mostly it is 'shallow', and an exhibition of a desire to draw attention. Let me narrate some experiences:

(a) A young woman, who sang bhajans at supernormal pitch, more often than, not went into such trances and then, gave predictions of very short range, which came out correct. But, in the 'prediction' she made her own 'desires' get mixed so inextricably that the true content of prediction was too insignificant compared to the irrelevant mutterings.

Years later, when her adoring father gave me her horoscope, I saw the afflicted planets in her eighth house, which had caused it all. My guru-bhais and guru-bahens, who at one stage had extolled her as a 'goddess', later ostracised her when she had an unconventional marriage. They would just not accept my assessment that the family to which she belonged, was excellent, and she herself had rare musical talents. Once a 'goddess' and now fallen! I learnt a valuable lesson. Never even discuss your supernormal experience with anyone.

(b) In the earlier case, of my own guru-bahen, it could be said since she was in her middle twenties, that it could be a case of unsatisfied sexuality, which her horoscope also showed. But my next experience was baffling. Here she was a young girl of eight years, daughter of a milk-man, totally uneducated. In a trance, once she told us to be careful about an earthquake next day, a Monday, at 4.45 p.m., and then at 9 p.m., again.

I did not know whether to take her seriously, but sitting in the office the next day, I had the first experience of an earthquake.

Back home, I had a Professor of Silchar waiting for me to discuss some intellectual subjects, which he liked with his tolerant and pleasant disposition. But he asked me how a 'sane' person like me could be running after the supernormal. I told him of my experience of that day's earthquake and told him that another tremor, according to that young girl was to be at nine that night, when we were sitting and talking! Could it not be tested? Exactly at nine that night, came the second tremor and the professor ran out of the room, with his 'deep' experience of earthquakes, while I remained sitting. When he came back I laughed and asked him what had he to say. He had the decency to say, "You win and I lose."

But my colleagues in the office, for whose bridge sessions I was not available and, whose idle time in the Shillong nights were spent in back-biting, I had to become an easy target. Unfortunately for me, I had a Col. Blimp, directly lifted out of novels of P.G. Wodehouse, as a man above me – and the one who mattered. I ran into difficulties with him but I could not grudge it as I was passing through the sub-period of my eighth lord, then, with Saturn and Rahu in transit disturbing my tenth house!

It was the sub-period of my own eighth lord which gave me such first hand experiences.

(c) The third experience was that of an aggressive and ambitious man, senior to me in age and now a 'successful' guru.[1] He went into trance when positioned near women and, in his 'trance' darted towards them – an act, which instead of being looked upon as a deliberate piece of mischief, was looked upon as a divine manifestation but I had my suspicions and, later, when I got his horoscope, I could see the terrible affliction to his eighth lord, which gave him spiritual experiences, from genuine to contrived ones. But he did pick up the tricks of gurudom, so thoroughly that the success of his later years has not surprised me.

Some Symptoms of Awakened Kundalini

It was in this very company that I met the finest specimens of spiritual gentlemen, who have not merely left an everlasting impression on me, but have been leading fine spiritual life (two of them from Shillong and two from Calcutta), which has convinced me why true devotion to God makes you a superior human being. Let me describe them:

(a) Let me call him "M"[2], a shy and retiring person who in bhajans went into a trance and exhibited classical symptoms of awakened kundalini. He went into spontaneous bhastrika pranayam for hours, together which no one can do even with long hours of practice. In 1979, when I went to Delhi to see Swami Amrit Vagbhava with my friend Anand Kumar Dikshit, the swamiji, even while talking to us, had gone into such spontaneous pranayam with long whistling inhalations and exhalations. My friend, a little surprised, looked at me and I, pressed his hand to keep quiet and later, explained to him what it was.

"M",[3] himself an astrologer, has the horoscope of a pure saint, who must have now run into the best spiritual period of his life somewhere in Assam. In his trances, when he came out with extremely musical loud shouts which could be heard from miles, it inspired all into greater devotion instead of frightening! This was the strangest part of the episode. He was a born recluse and would not talk unless talked to. In the easy mixing which takes place in Vaishnav bhajan groups, he scrupulously kept away from women and concentrated only on his sadhana.

The combinations in his twelfth house are unbelievably beautiful.

(b) I will call the second person "D"[4]. He never got into a trance. Rarely spoke, always concentrating on japam, through his breath, which is our sadhna. In my whole life, I have never met a better nishkama karma-yogi of his class – in the office everyone was happy with him. I could know it first hand from his own seniors, many of whom had worked under me also. His work in the office was done with thoroughness, in time and ungrudgingly, whatever the extra burden thrust on him. Government offices in India have nearly eighty per cent shirkers only. He never expected any rewards, never bothered for his next promotion. Back in bhajan mandalis or in Guruji's ashram, he did the work entrusted to him with the same pleasing thoroughness. From doing correspondence work for Guruji in Bengali, to breaking stones for temple construction or cleaning the drain, in anything he was doing with the same undisturbed equipoise! It amazes me even today to think that such persons exist in this world. I have watched him intermittently for over thirty years.

I tried my best to get his horoscope. Either he has none or

he having surrendered himself to the will of the Lord, wants to know nothing about what will happen to him and when. The salt of the earth, Christ spoke of, I never knew, tastes so sweet!

"Why does Guruji always keep his hands hidden, behind his woollen shawl in winter and behind his anga-vastram in summer", I once asked him.

"Don't you know Guruji's hands are so long that they go far below his knees. He is a ajaan bahu (long arms stretching below kness) – the sign of a great man in our scriptures . . . and Guruji's eyes . . . That was not merely his answer with a rare fire of conviction but also of rare guru-bhakti.

If someone were to tell me someday that "D" has realised God, I would say. "God had no choice."

(c) I would rate "S"[5], whom I saw in Calcutta most closely, as the best example of awakened kundalini. I do not know what Newton would have said if he had seen his levitations. He is a bhajan singer. He lives bhajans, dreams bhajans, sings bhajans. A living Narsi Mehta, if I have ever seen, it is he.

Before thousands and many times while singing bhajans, I have seen him rise, with the harmonium in his hands, fifteen to twenty feet like a tennis ball, come down on hard cemented floor and without getting hurt, recover his balance fast. And within few minutes, he would resume his bhajans as though he never wanted, what happened to him, to happen! He knows and strictly believes in the art of concealing his spiritual experiences. To be loved by so many, Guruji used to say, is to be loved by God!

Since hundreds have seen his fabulous levitations so many times, I accept the law of gravitation with as much ease as the exceptional case of law of levitations!

It is my astrological conviction now that since God has to favour his devotees, he gives to them towards the end of their lives, the best dasha for spiritual blossoming. It is so in his case. His is a case of pristine bhakti, absolute dread of any worldly responsibility, an artist to the core of his being, a spiritual artist. Untainted Jupiter and Venus in his horoscope and, the dasha sequence show the struggles, the later quietude and, now, his God-contemplation. Astrology reveals so much and the dasha sequence, reveals the same story. Spiritual progress is evolutionary, slow, beautiful, and inner experiences sustain them all through life's vicissitudes.

Seeing them, I see the extraordinary truth in the assurance of Lord Krishna to Arjuna. *"Yoga khsemam vahamyaham"* – the Lord takes upon himself the burdens of his devotees.

But one common feature noticeable in all of them is, God never gave them such material success or rise as would have inflated their ego. They are just well-off and they are angels.

(d) "A"[6], closest to my way of thinking, believes in accepting anything after testing. He accepts no claims; he quarrels very beautifully with anyone without bruising anyone's ego.

But he is such a votary of truth, with such talkative habits! He is an enigma to me. Often, men, who talk too much are the worst liars. Even a man, who talks unnecessarily, has to twist truth or exhibit his concealed ego. One has to see "A", to believe that exception to the rule exists.

His horoscope had shown balarishta yoga, he survived it. Later, one day, Guruji told me to see his horoscope closely and told me of a danger that existed. He got involved in an accident which should have killed him but he escaped with a small hurt. Thereafter, Guruji had told me, he would enter the best period of his life. And he is in it now.

In his case, the awakened kundalini manifested in a most artistic way. He would go into trance, his body would tremble and then, with faraway looks, he would get up and bow down before everyone and lovingly embrace males. It lasted sometimes, through an entire night. Sweetness, cloying sweetness, and I am reminded of the shloka of Vallabhacharya – *"Madhuradhipate Akhilam Madhuram"* the sweet being's world is so sweet.

Astrological Combinations

My Jyotish Guru, Yogi Bhaskaranandji, often discussed with me, when I found him alone in Ahmedabad, the spiritual combinations in a horoscope and insisted that the purpose of astrology is cosmic delineation of human destiny, and not fortune-telling. In Delhi, astrology is only fortune telling and sensational political predictions that pass for astrology, and it is a roaring business. Tell about some sexual misadventures and, people in Delhi think that you are a great astrologer; and then prescribe some upaya (propitiation) and exploit those who have enough money to throw it away.

The purpose of astrology is true and cosmic guidance and, is most helpful to sadhaks. He was always pleased when he saw a rare horoscope, but was also clear in his mind that astrology had its own limitations, which could perhaps be overcome, if we knew the secrets of *nadi-amshas*.

The data to be prepared

The data to be prepared for any sound prediction, particularly for sadhakas, is:

	6	4 Ket	3 Sun AK Sat AmK Ven MK Mer PK
7	5 Moon DK		
8		2 Mar BK	
9	11		1
10 Rah		12 Jup GK	

Jup GK		Mar BK	Ven MK Sat AmK Mer PK Sun AK
Rah	Swami Paramananda Saraswati		Ket
			Lag Moon DK

	6	5 Jup Rah	4
7			3 Sun AK
8		2 Mar	
9 Mer PK	11 Sat Ket		1 Moon
10 Ven		12	

	Moon	Mar	Sun AK
Sat Ket	Navamsha Chart		
Ven			Lag Jup Rah
Mer PK			

	11	9 Jup	
12 Sun AK	10	8 Sat Ket	
1		7 Ven	
2 Mar Rah	4	6 Mer PK	
	3	5 Moon	

Sun AK		Mar Rah	
Lag	Dashamsha Chart		Moon
Jup	Sat Ket	Ven	Mer PK

(a) As usual, all the sixteen vargas, but specially birth, navamsha and vimshamsha horoscopes, together with trimshamsha, which has some secret uses.

(b) All Jaimini's karakas with Karakamsha marked prominently.

(c) Vimshottari dasha, a less-used navamsa dasha of Jaimini, (which I have not discussed yet in any article) and, accurate Kala Chakra

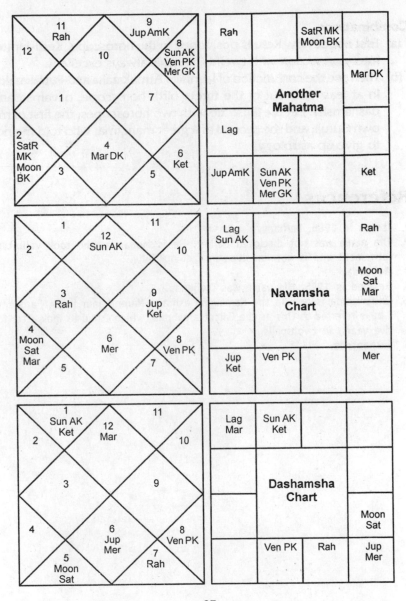

dasha.

(d) The strength of Jupiter, Mercury, fifth and ninth lords, and association of Ketu with them, must be marked out.

(e) Then watch the movements of Saturn and Jupiter in transit, noting down which navamshas they happen to be in when important events take place.

Combinations

(a) First notice how Ketu is positioned in the horoscope. Ketu-Jupiter inter-connection with twelfth house is always excellent.

(b) Then see the conjunction of Jaimini's Atmakaraka and Putrakaraka, in at least two out of the three: birth horoscope, navamsa and dashamsha. Let me illustrate with two horoscopes, the first of my own Guruji, and the second of a great mahatma, who told me not to give up astrology.

References

1. It was in 1986, perhaps.
2. The name was not disclosed earlier. He is Mohanda who took voluntary retirement and is now involved in sadhana fully.
3. Mohanda.
4. He died in 1995. His name was Dwijenda.
5. Dhirendrada is now in the Kamalgazi ashram, Narendrapur in 24 Parganas. I have referred to this as the Calcutta ashram, which I had to look after for five years, in two spells.
6. Sushantoda.

...6...
Astrological Instruction

The language saints use is rarely understood by anyone except the saints themselves. It is here that the astrologer has an absolute disadvantage, and is easily cornered or insulted.

In the case of an important Indian, Satya Sai Baba told him, when he developed an ailment, which is more of a nuisance that saps his confidence than really handicaps him in any way, *"I am transforming you."* But an ambitious man anxious to recover fast, consults everyone he thinks is worth consulting, tries all systems and types of medical treatment available, which he being in a powerful position, can afford. He tries talismans and mantras, with all his rationalistic pretensions intact.

In one case, I told the concerned female relation of a person that the recovery would be slow, prolonged and would turn psychosomatic as the fifth house, though not afflicted still had the association of a benefic sixth lord in the sub-period of a malefic and the major period of an afflicted yogakaraka planet. But to him I told that he should try the best treatment available. But he persisted with the question, "When will I be cured?" Two very good saints had told him to have patience, and he had no courage to ask either of them, "How long?"

The lord of disease, the sixth lord, in the fifth house or *purva punya*, getting aggravated in the sub-period of mild malefic associated with that house. A perfectly appealing explanation was invariably given by my Jyotish Guru, Yogi Bhaskaranandji, as long as he continued astrology, which was till ten years before his death in 1991, on the great day of Shivaratri. And Saturn's movement into the fourth house is fore-warning of the malady deepening, when it reaches the fifth house, I naturally had my own fears of making any definite prediction. I did not want to tell him that what had begun now was going to be a life long ailment and would turn fatal in another sub-period of a malefic, in the eighth house.

But when pinned down and asked to give a definite date of recovery, what should be my answer has always troubled me. It is the beginning of the end is what I cannot bring myself to tell him.

Thereby hangs a tale of a curse-like admonition on me.

On reversion from my deputation to Patna, I was required to do hundreds of horoscopes during my leave, which I spent in my Guruji's ashram in Shri Bejoy Krishna Sadhan Ashram, Kamalgazi, 24-Parganas (West Bengal). The collection of horoscopes with esoteric combinations was vast and a rough statistical checking of spiritual combinations in horoscopes instilled more confidence in me, than ever before in making the out of the way and odd predictions about spiritual life.

But my biggest gain was to learn some do's and dont's in predicting which I had to imbibe without being told explicitly, except in one case by my Guruji.

Let me discuss that case first.

A *guru-bhai* and his wife had come to the ashram one day in the afternoon with their ailing son. Accompanying them was the elder brother of my *guru-bhai,* who played on *khol* (*mridangam*), a persussion instrument, during our keertans and had, later, taken spiritual initiation. The *khol* player came to me and asked me to cast a horoscope of the boy, which Guruji wanted right then.

I did it and kept it. Both brothers came to me and asked me to predict, which I refused to as I never made any prediction on any horoscope which Guruji had asked me to prepare. I made out a copy of the horoscope in the Bengali style for Guruji, which I had kept in my records, in the South Indian style.

But both brothers insisted on my giving a prediction, which I refused to do. But after the father of the boy left, his elder brother insisted on my giving at least a hint.

There are certain relations an astrologer cannot wriggle out of. Between me and Nandida, the uncle of the ailing boy, there existed a deep affectionate relation. Yet, I could not allow him to know what I was seeing in the horoscope was, the worst approaching in about two years.

When it comes to the span of life, predictions should be made two to four years in advance and, no attempt should be made to pin-point the date of death. The astrologer has not merely to do his work in a very detailed fashion but, to suffer the agony of the gloom of morbidity sapping his energy.

"Nothing seems to be good or favourable for the boy", was the

remark I made. Nandida understood it all, in a flash, reacted rather violently and went running to his brother.

They entered Guruji's *kuti*. What happened there I do not know but I was called after sometime and in my presence, Guruji said, *"It is not all so bad as Rao has said"*.

They left, and I wondered what was wrong with my astrological analysis. I looked at it again and saw no reason why I should have a different opinion ... and I remembered, way back in 1962, in Shillong how my understanding of a 'lie' had undergone a change.

The incident I am narrating is of 1976, while what I was recalling was similar incident of 1962. A *guru-bhai* of mine was sick, in the hospital, crying in agony, as his peptic ulcer had given him painful hours. His wife, breaking down, had asked me to request Guruji to do 'something'. Invariably, when such a request is made, the prayer is that the saint should use his miraculous power.

Finding Guruji alone, I told him about the condition of the guru-bhai and what his wife had told me. There was an unusually stern expression on the face of Guruji. Having taken spiritual initiation, he was not following spiritual discipline and was eating meat, onions, eggs – all forbidden. And what Guruji said after that stunned me. "He will come back from the hospital, hale and hearty. But will commit the same mistakes again and die after six months."

The inexorable law of predestination! My *guru-bhai* came back from the hospital and I told him to be very careful about his food habits which, his wife told me, he did not much care about.

I told others who were intimate with him, what Guruji had told me. The others, instead of showing any sympathy, reeled off something of a historical narration of his misdeeds! I was helpless. I talked to his wife through an intermediary but she told me in turn, *"Guruji has assured me nothing would happen to my husband. Everything would be all right."*[1]

So two different versions! One to me and another to his wife! I was confused. Guruji was inscrutable. So deeply engrossed in it, I was sitting in keertan with a crowd around Guruji, who reading my thoughts, as he had done hundreds of times, said without looking at me, *"Shock is what people cannot bear. Poison is what people cannot digest. One must be prepared to face the inevitable and when you know about it, you must help others to prepare for it slowly, gently."*

But I had the insurmountable language barrier. The wife of my *guru-bhai* understood no language except the Sylheti dialect of Bengali and I could not converse at all with her in any language other than

English or Hindi, which she did not know. But then, I had it conveyed to her through a better *guru-bhai* that the food habits of her husband must be strictly kept under control, otherwise the disease would relapse.

But the inevitable happened. My *guru-bhai* was hospitalised after six months and he died. His entire family cursed Guruji and used words which hurt me!

It took me some time to get used to this type of two versions of Guruji, one to the concerned person and the other to me or others and invariably, the other version given to a non-family member was what happened.

Another such incident, the very first I had with Guruji came flashing in my mind. The devout father of a *guru-bhai*, in his eighties wanted to have a glimpse of Guruji, before meeting his end, which he perhaps knew, intuitively, had come. Guruji went to his house with some of us and told the old man. *"No, you are going to live for some more time"*.

Once out of their house, Guruji told that *guru-bhai*, *"Be prepared for your father's death sooner than you expect"*. Two versions, again!

Next day, when I was in office, I learnt that the old man died peacefully the night, after seeing Guruji.

The guru is understood through non-verbal communication. This I understood better than others. I realised soon after my initiation because unlike them, I could not then talk to him in Bengali and he knew only a smattering of Hindi. Put on touring duty by Colonel Blimp, under whom I worked, he was determined to see me out of Shillong as I was not available for bridge parties, for our meetings in posh hotels of Shillong where, in a moment of grace, he had said that I was the best conversationalist in such parties, with my wide range of interests. But, this entire range of new interests added in my life, which opened out a new dimension, irritated him and my other colleagues.

On a tour to Jowai, slightly more than hundred miles away from Shillong, I took the difficult decision to go by State bus everyday there and return at night to be present in the keertans, where I could get the company of my Guruji. Few days after, Guruji was to leave for Calcutta and I was not sure when I would meet him next.

One day, on my way to Jowai, I was thinking of those great symbols of sacrifice, Lord Shiva drinking poison after the churning of the ocean and the great Ramanujacharya disclosing to a crowd a mantra, which his guru had asked him not to disclose to anyone lest he goes to hell. But Ramanujacharya had done it — if others get salvation and he suffers, his rich spiritual life would acquire the content and meaning a great saint's life had to have. Emotions had welled up in me.

At night, that day, Guruji talked only about Lord Shiva and Ramanujacharya, a noble life was the one lived for others, even if entailed suffering, and suffering too got ennobled, and it was not suffering but joy ... those who know and experience it alone know it to be true.

How many times he picked up my thoughts telepathically and talked about them convinced me that with a spiritual giant verbal communication was not necessary.

I have referred to this because fourteen years after my Shillong experience, here I was again, suffering the mortification of being told by Nandida, in no uncertain terms, that my astrological reading was all wrong!

Few days later finding me alone Guruji said, "Bad predictions must be sugar-coated. Men cannot bear pain. An astrologer who causes pain to anyone through his predictions will have to suffer himself sometime or the other. The laws of karma are such".

But what was wrong with the boy? I saw him and there was a swelling on his left eye. I later learnt it was a cancerous growth and that the doctors had held out no hopes, and so had I, without knowing that disease had already been diagnosed as malignant. Why did then Guruji tell them, "It is not so bad ... ". Nandida met me on Sundays and informed me that the boy had been improving actually. I was happy but was still skeptical. On such occasions I wish the horoscope was wrong. But the parents had assured me that the birth time noted was very accurate.

I had now completed my normal tenure in the Commercial Taxes Tribunal, at Patna. A feeling was given to me at Ashram, where I was given an indication later by my guru, as if I was posted there.

A month or two later, after I had been waiting for my posting order, a guru-bhai from Patna, came running to me and said that Guruji had ordered some special wooden almirahs to be made by the carpenter employed by the ashram for me! "Do you know that your posting has been decided. You are going to be posted to Calcutta. Why should Guruji ask special almirahs to be made for you".

There was no question of my disbelieving it since Guruji has said it and we had the most difficult CAG, in Shri A.K. Bakshi who was a terror to all service officers except to few like me. When he had asked me in an interview whether I had any request to make – prize posting, lucrative deputation etc., I had told him I was happy with whatever I had. Though I never became intimate with him, Mr. Bakshi, till he laid down the office, had expressed his fondness for me and had written two-page long note of appreciation on the report I had produced from Calcutta as "brilliant and path-breaking" unlike other stereotyped reports.

And I was posted to Calcutta in August 1975!

Everytime Jupiter transitted into Makar, my fourth house, I got posted to Eastern India and it happened thrice in my career. When, where and how I would be posted was told to me through hints or sometimes clearly by Guruji many times in my career.

So while in Calcutta, during my second spell of posting I had this conflicting dilemma to face – my astrology revealed that the boy would not survive and Nandi da told me that Guruji had told him that

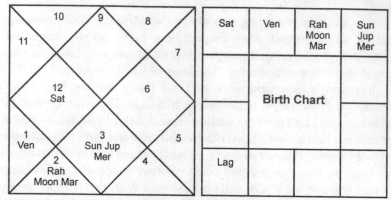

Lagna	Sun	Moon	Mars	Mercury	Jupiter	Venus	Saturn	Rahu
22°38'	01°35'	03°17'	19°46'	22°04'	15°26'	24°00'	05°46'	01°38'

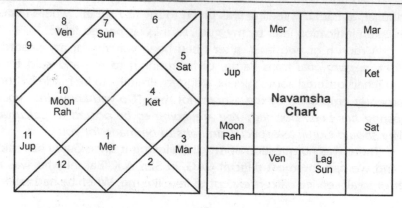

it was not so bad as I had said.

Selfish motives, malice and extreme anxiety of even a good well-meaning householder can create a funny and difficult situation when they take astrological consultations and also take the guidance of someone with genuine supernormal power.

I never want such a comparison to be made with a genuine saint because he can see in a flash the ultimate, that must come to pass. All great saints see what is pre-destined and their insistence that true worship of God and a wise acceptance of the inevitable should be a true tenet of one's faith, creates more controversy than wise reaction.

As an astrologer I concentrate on the intermediate details and see how one would have to face what is inevitable. Even then I do not emphasise the inevitable with vehemence in one laconic sentence which is the privilege of the saint only.

I will give some instances later, but let me refer to my agony that night – here was a *guru-bhai* creating for me a class conflict, my prediction and Guruji's assurance to him – it is not so bad as Rao has said.

(a) Rarely one sees such a terrible balarishta yoga as in this case. The Moon is between Rahu (behind) and Mars (ahead) and has the aspect of Saturn which is rather close.

(b) The dasha is of the Moon, the eighth lord in the sixth.

The tenet that luminaries do not have the blemish of their eighth lordship may not be correct. In fact when such luminaries have heavy affliction, they acquire terrible blemish.

(c) Here the eighth lord is in the sixth house, hardly good for sound health.

Dasha Analysis

(a) It is the dasha of the eighth lord and the sub-period of the seventh lord.

(b) From the dasha lord, the sub-lord is in the second house and also owns the second house.

(c) From the Moon the dasha lord is the third lord, of longevity, heavily afflicted and Mercury is the second lord.

(d) The next period would be of Ketu, in the twelfth house from lagna and the seventh house from the Moon.

Transit

(a) Saturn in the eighth house from lagna was in the twenty-second dreshkona.

95

(b) Rahu in Vrishchika and Ketu in Vrisha were afflicting both the Moon and the natal Rahu-Ketu axis.

(c) Mars transitting in Mithuna was not promising anything in the shape of relief.

Chara Dasha

In Jaimini's chara dasha it was the dasha of Vrischika, which was eighth from the Atmakaraka, Venus.

How long would the boy survive?

Was there any hope, astrologically?

Few days later, they came again to the Ashram and this time the boys's condition had deteriorated. Guruji called me again. I requested him to allow only the father and the uncle to be present and the doors of his kuti to be closed while we discussed his horoscope.

But it did not take much time. Guruji said, "Rao was right but astrologers should not give gloomy predictions. A curse falls on them. They should give subtle hints in subtle language and prepare the person or persons concerned slowly for the inevitable. No one can escape karma".

And it did not take much time for Guruji to say what he had to say. "Treat your son as a guest who has come not to stay for a long time but to depart very soon. He has come to spend his last birth. Have as many bhajans in your house as you can have. Let the boy live in a purely spiritual atmosphere,"

It appeared to me that the parents of the boy and his uncle had already reconciled themselves to it as some doctors they had consulted had held out no hope. Now hearing from Guruji they knew that no miracle was going to take place. Strangely, during the next few days I noticed that the boy was never in any pain and always seemed composed, with a glow on his face as though death was his old familiar companion, or a non-event.

Guruji had assured the parents that boy would have no pain and would die peacefully.

The boy liked me and Sushanto da, our most popular bhajan singer. Once or sometimes twice a week, we had to take part in bhajans in their house and the boy liked my recitation of Sanskrit shlokas so much that I had to keep reciting them till he slept.

May be I owed him a debt from some previous life and was defraying it now. Such calm on his face ... I cannot forget it.

He died in Moon-Ketu period. Ketu is exalted in the twelfth house and aspected by exalted Moon. Is death in such a period the gateway to salvation? I do not know. But Guruji had said he had come to spend his last life. Seeing the calm and composed way he prepared for his death, I have always wondered whether I will face my own death, when it comes, in so beautiful a way.

References

1. Every guru has to suffer such misinterpretations put on their words, by their disciples. While, one group becomes totally judgemental, the other interprets everything as being favourable.

...7...
Pre-destination
The Negative Side

Three, among many, questions put to astrologers elicit different answers from different astrologers, according to their experience or, more often than not, their pretensions. Let me first pose the three questions and answer them in my own way. It being my first hand experience, I see no reason why should I ever change my opinion and I feel no need for anyone to agree or disagree with me.

The Three Questions
  (a) Do I believe in pre-destination absolutely. My answer is not merely yes but I must point out here that I have already given enough instances and am going to give many more here.
  (b) The second question whether astrologers can point out what is predestined correctly is ticklish. Every astrologer has experienced sometime or the other that he insisted with certainty that a certain event, good or bad, would take place and it did. Yet absolute insistence by an astrologer on the inevitable and his talk of 'cosmic compulsions' as a Delhi quack has said hundreds of times about Rajiv Gandhi, P.V. Narasimha Rao etc. is only a piece of arrogance and impudence. The astrologer who has not learnt the art of keeping himself within well known limits of humility, is a menace to the growth of spiritual and scientific discipline in the practice of astrology as a cosmic science.
  (c) Finally the last question – what is it that an astrologer should do, learn and practice to reach more frequently that point of inevitability which we call destiny – is for each astrologer a spiritual self-exploration. And when he reaches this point, he sees God's law prevailing so absolutely that he stops predicting, as my late mother, my first Jyotish Guru, Yogi Bhaskarananda did

in about ten or more years before their death.

Before I discuss it astrologically, let me first give some instances which would stun you less, if as an astrologer, you have the horoscope of the person about whom a saint has said something startling. You examine the horoscope and you can see what the Yogi has seen.

Indira Gandhi

Sometime after Mrs. Indira Gandhi had imposed her emergency in 1975, we were eating prasad in the house of Amiyoda in his Park Street house in Calcutta when Amiyoda, a bigoted Congress man and admirer of Indira Gandhi was praising her. I got irritated and said that she would fall from power in 1977 which is what I had hinted at, inspite of the rather rigid censorship of those days, to my younger brother, Vikram Rao, who was in jail then. George Fernandes and others who knew about it, had asked my brother later, "How did your brother know it all".

Strolling gently in that rather spacious room, Guruji said, "This woman would be removed from power at pistol point." Rai Haranda, who at one stage was the assistant under the well-known Kao of the RAW remembered and when Indira Gandhi lost in election he asked me, "But Indira Gandhi has not been shot dead as Guruji had said that day."

I told Rai Haranda, "Guruji has not indicated any time-frame and astrologically it can be later, after 1982, not before."

Indira Gandhi came back to power in 1980 January and was shot dead in October 1984, 'removed from power at pistol point,' as Guruji said.

One need not discuss the horoscope to explain why astrologers who too predicted the violent end of Indira Gandhi would agree with the prophecy.

Daughter of Nabgopal Khag of Sewri

During the time I was casting the horoscopes of so many men and women for my understanding of spiritual combinations in different horoscopes, Guruji one day asked me if I had cast the horoscope of the daughter of Nabgopal Khag of Sewri who had come to stay in the ashram with his daughter for some days. I said that I was helpless as Khagda did not have the birth details of his daughter.

A few days later Guruji asked me the same question and my answer was the same... again after some days Guruji asked the same question and I had the same answer... and this went on for quite a few days. Everything appeared mysterious... I was confused and apprehended something.

Nabgopal Khagda of Sewri was one of our finest guru-bhais and though never emphatic in his opinions, he was an extraordinary connoisseur of music. His gentle nod of disapproval when someone sang was a very civilized way of expressing his criticism of someone's musical performance.

In Maharashtra, South India, Bengal and Orissa, there are to be seen in the ashram of gurus many talented and melodious female singers of bhajans and the one who comes and sings more frequently, with the approval of the guru, becomes the main singer. In our ashram we had in Jaishree Bhattacharya, better known as 'Maina', the sweetest bhajan singer I have ever heard. If Guruji had not prevented her from joining the more glamorous line of a filmsinger or T.V. singer, millions in the country would have been in ecstacy after hearing that dreamy melody of spirituality which her silken voice created. One day she sang her heart out in the Kamakhya ashram during the pujas. So enthralled were all that no other singer, among many, even dared to touch the harmonium. Singing of great bhajans always depends on the inspiration of the day.

Nabgopal Khagda had approved, only Maina's singing, among so many in the ashram bhajans, but never said so, except to me once, and in undertones.

It was later that I came to know that his daughter (perhaps her name was Namita) was fully trained classical singer and had a very rich voice suiting her classical style. But she always shied away and never sang in the ashram, sitting in some inconspicuous corner as though she knew no music.

Then I heard her one day, singing in a room in the ashram... unbelievable, I thought was her rare voice and her singing.

I wished to have her horoscope for my research and Khagda had the same answer – birth details not known.

A few days later, they left for Sewri and we learnt subsequently that Nabgopal Khagda's daughter was found dead in a pond. Suicide or drowning? We did not know.

Even today Guruji's voice haunts me when I remember the incident ... Guruji had never asked so repeatedly, "Do you have her horoscope. Have you seen it?" I could never guess what Guruji was hinting at. For some days after the incident others forgot it but sixteen years after (1992), I remember it all so vividly. That was pre-destination, which Guruji saw but never disclosed.

The Obstinate Woman

In the ashram, people often talked of an incident which perhaps happened when I was posted in Bombay or Rajkot. It had haunted them all for so many years and I could not collect any chronological details.

For a religious festival many people had collected in the ashram one night and it was decided that at the crack of the dawn next morning, they would all get up, take their bath and go round in *nagar-keertan* (in a procession singing bhajans in the streets). But, suddenly, Guruji got up at two in the night and woke them all, took them out for the *nagar-keertan* for about one hour and came back.

The previous evening, he had told one of the ladies who had come to the ashram not to go near the pond for a bath next morning. After the *nagar-keertan* he repeated the instruction to her and went back and closed his *kuti*.

Next morning, they all went to take their bath near the ashram, and the woman who was forbidden to go near the pond, reached there surreptitiously. Others reminded her of Guruji's warning but she did not want to be deprived of the spiritual merit of a bath on that holy day in a pond and prepare for the festivities of the occasion. Obstinate as she was, she plunged into the water of the pond, slipped and was untraceable. Armed with long bamboo sticks villagers had finally brought her dead body out. Guru bhais and bahens remembered the incident but in and around Kamalgazi, villagers and others criticised Guruji for not being able to avert the death of his own disciple, in the vicinity of his ashram.

Once in a while, when one of the villagers talked about the incident to me, I said, "destiny is destiny. Lord Krishna was with Pandavas yet they had to go to the forest for full thirteen years, after losing their kingdom in a gambling bout."

"Is destiny irresistible", was a question uppermost in my mind. The answer to this question came in a rather unpleasant way.

Often when Guruji got disgusted with the problems of the *ashram*, which were rather frequent, he went and stayed in the house of Tarinida in his Lake Garden house where he was shielded well and very few persons were allowed to see him, though for some of us, the entry was not barred. But I never went there. Only on Sunday evening, Guruji came to the *ashram* for bhajans, I saw him, and then for days together there was no meeting.

One day, Dr. K.S. Singh, who was then posted as Director of the Anthropological Survey of India, came to the ashram after seeing

Guruji and told me that a prosperous and haughty looking woman had been asked by Guruji to come to me and get her daughter's horoscope cast.

She came after sometime and I was prepared. I cast the horoscope and handed it over to her. She asked me to give prediction about her daughter which I refused to do, since the instruction was only to cast the horoscope and not make any prediction. She insisted haughtily, and I refused again and again. The quarrel went on for sometime, and she said caustically, *"If you cannot make a prediction why do you pretend to be an astrologer?"*

It was unnecessary to go into the question and have argument with her, but she was such a cantakerous woman that she even said perhaps my casting of the horoscope could be wrong. It was too much. I said, *"Are you thinking of marrying your daughter to someone outside the country?"* Surprised, she suppressed her emotions in a flash, *"Of course, yes, you seem to know astrology. Anything else?"*

"Do not be in a hurry," I said, and added, *"It will make you very unhappy."*

"You are being stupid. A mother would be happy to have her daughter married to a prosperous young man."

"Soon after marriage you will know who was stupid. I have tolerated so far. Now leave my room and do not argue with me." I said with finality.

She went to Guruji after he had come, complained and described me as 'rude'. Someone present there told me later that Guruji told her that Rao would not retort unless there existed extreme provocation.

Later, after she left, Guruji called me and asked me what was it I had seen in the horoscope of her daughter which made me predict what I had.

There are certain half-hints given in the *Brihat Parashara Hora Shastra*, which a prolific writer of astrological articles who writes very good English, has often criticised in an astrological journal. I never wrote a letter to the editor to say that the attack was irrational, as all that Parashara had said was hundred percent correct. I have tested it on hundreds of horoscopes, and found them giving alarmingly accurate and infallible results. But since Parashara has not revealed how such events are to be timed, some astrologers think that those combinations just do not work.

I discussed those combinations with Guruji and what he said after that was: *"Rao, destiny works mysteriously. I told her not to rush with the marriage of her daughter. But which mother would want to miss such a good son-in-law? Destiny always catches hold of you by your hand and drags you to your doom.* "The favourite Bengali word Guruji used on such occasions was, *'bhabitabya'* (in Hindi it is bhavitavya), meaning destiny.

And then Guruji quoted the Gita, *"Mama maya duratyaya"* (Difficult is the Maya of the Lord).

The haughty lady, I came to know later, was from a very prosperous family in a far off place in Assam and both she and her husband were earning in thousands and their children were very well educated and very eligible for marriage into rich families. Her husband had never wanted her to consult Guruji about the marriage of their daughter but she insisted on squeezing out Guruji's approval, which she could not get. "It would be better to wait" was what Guruji had told her at least two hours before I had cast the horoscope of her daughter and given my negative opinion.

She went away, and got her daughter married off. One week after marriage her son-in-law died in a car accident.

Inscrutable destiny drags us to our doom.

I believe in pre-destination.

I will illustrate it astrologically adding something more ...

I got the horoscope of Samar Chatterji after the event ...

In July 1962, when the ashram at Kamakhya in Guwahati was opened with three day's celebrations, many of my fellow disciples had come from Shillong with me, most of whom from middle class and lower middle class families while from Calcutta had come from all classes, the most prominent of them being the neo-rich. Old Bengali zamindars, westernised Bengalis could outdo the English men but my first experience of Bengali donors to ashrams was very startling.

In subsequent years, during my different postings all over the country, I must have seen at least five hundred of differents ashrams and their munificent Marwari and Gujarati donors who moved in the ashrams of their gurus dressed more unimpressively than lower middle class men and were such pictures of humility! Over a period of years that generation is gone. The new generation of Marwaris eat non-vegetarian food, drink wines of all variety, have MBA degrees.

Bengal which has very few Bengali billionaires, some millionaires but many who are called rich with their varying degrees of opulence, become the disciples of different gurus, mostly, it appears to me, under compulsion of their wives or mothers. And once in the ashrams of their gurus during their occasional visits, they make everyone conscious of their higher economic status.

In 1962 it was my first experience with them. In communism-infected Bengal so much class-consciousness was visible in the ashrams; the bourgeoise, and the proletariat guru-bhai and guru-bahens; a tinier, social group of disciples carved from out of the amorphous social groups outside, wore the garb of religiosity. But at first I was not conscious as I knew some Bengali and could not converse with them in any language other than English or Hindi.

Such a group included many rich Bengalis and one of them was Samarda, who was said to be the biggest donor to the Calcutta ashram, much bigger than the Kamakhya ashram. The proletariats and the bourgeoise respected me for two reasons; in the eyes of the bourgeoise I had a status of my own as a class one officer of the central government and for the proletariat, I was one among them as I did all such physical work with them as labourers may do. In the finest *gurudwaras* of Sikhs I have seen richest Sikhs clean floors, serve others and even do menial service. But I saw no single instance in Bengal of a Bengali rich man doing the same in an ashram.

This background is necessary to the incident I am relating.

Some miracles had taken place in the life of Samarda. For sixteen years after marriage, he had no child. Then after their initiation Guruji told them that they would have a son soon and they had one. This son, when a young boy had developed some disease and was pronounced dead by doctors. Guruji went to their house, put some liquid in the boy's mouth and his life was revived. This was well-known to all and Samarda told me about this incident many times.

Along with Samarda used to come a Chinese friend of his whom I never met but who too, had become a munificent donor to the ashram after an incident. His son had vanished somewhere and he prayed to Guruji to do 'something'. Guruji, as was his habit, said it was 'God's will' but gave him a flower and asked him to keep it. Soon after, his son came back. Guruji's assurance to him, "do not worry" had meant so much to him.

But the same son, after sometime, fell in love with a girl whom the Chinese gentleman, it seems, had disapproved. He again requested Guruji and was told to accept what was pre-destined. And the pre-destined happened, and the Chinese donor cut off all his relations with Guruji and the ashram.

So Guruji had three different images for all of them, a fortune-teller-protector for a majority of the rich guru-bhais and others; a divine inspiration for the better human beings among the poor middle class; some sort of a socialist leader, who brought the rich and the poor together, giving to some of the poor ones the opportunity to cultivate the rich, to solve their worldly, material problems resembling the type of attraction some poor people all over the world have for the Christian missionaries.

I saw more of Samarda, who once was known as the owner of a prosperous rubber factory. Towards the fag-end of 1967, when I was posted to Calcutta on promotion, the CPI(M)[2] and Naxalite[3] grip on the public life of Bengal had increased enormously.

I faced as many as forty gheraos[4] during this period but we had such an excellent Accountant General in Banerjee, that the emotional Bengalis who shouted at us, gheraoed us, never tormented us. Some of them even privately told me, that they had to "do" it because of the Party's order, otherwise, they had liked me so much! I had also seen many of these leaders going to Kali Bari and doing worship there. During daytime they were anti-God, anti-Religion Marxists. At night they were worshippers of Mother, (Goddess Kali).

But what went wrong with Samarda and his factory, I do not know. I saw him grow bitter with everything and becoming more and more hostile towards, first rich gurubhais, then many others, excluding me, and finally, Guruji. Rumours were set afloat by someone concerning what he supposedly had said about Guruji. He had become rich because it was there in his horoscope. Nothing else, no spiritual blessings had helped him! Upto this, it was tolerable but when he started maltreating many gurubhais, and abusing them, I saw Guruji expressing his unhappiness distinctly, sometimes using bitter words. I was present on many occasions when he sent him mild warnings to behave courteously, be polite, and not aggravate his misfortunes. The greater such warnings, the more hostile he became.

The other facts were, typically, Bengal's well known maladies, unreasonable demands for increase in salaries and wages, without increasing production. Strikes were endemic. Factories after factories had to be closed down. Anarchy was mistaken for revolution. Insulting the high placed officers in the central government offices was the cardinal credo of a Marxist faith, which would have surprised Marx himself. A Central Excise Commissioner who had a heart attack during a strike, had to be removed to a hospital. Yet strikes in his office were only intensified. An Income Tax Commissioner was so shocked by all that was happening, that his hair turned white overnight! My own Accountant General, Mr. Banerjee, who was a perfect gentleman advised me to read the books on Ramakrishna Paramahansa and sit under a tap, pouring cold water on my head everyday, to wash off the tensions of the day!

What must have been the condition of Samarda I could appreciate, unlike others. I showed maximum sympathy for him and he knew it but, he knew that I too was a 'brother in distress', in a different capacity, not as an employer but as a co-employee whose fault was that he was in a higher position but not a 'have' in the Marxist sense.

In the ashram there were some inmates, who collected the offerings in currency notes and sent either money orders or utilised that money for their own personal enjoyments of luxuries or necessities. Even the huge slice I paid from out of my monthly salary was misused. Guruji, all the time in Guwahati, not coming to Calcutta, left all the problems – the Marxist-inspired *gheraos* in the office and the embezzlements to me. I had no solution, to a single problem. I was passing through a bad dasha in my own horoscope and, very unfavorable transits of Saturn and Rahu added to my miseries.

Then in December 1969, when I got my transfer to Rajkot, it was a relief and also an agony. The office of the CAG has never shown any common sense in any policy of postings. No CAG, who feels the intoxication of the power of transferring officers at will, has ever shown any desire to introduce an element of sanity in such policy of transfers. We were required to join Shimla training school in January, in the snow-storm ravaged season of wintry blasts. Two years in mid-summer when I was left with no summer clothes I was transferred in the hot-winds tormented Allahabad in June, and again in the chilliest cold season of January I was transferred to Shillong, from where I was transferred in the summer season of 1963.

My Rajkot posting came when all others posted there had escaped it and a bachelor was chosen to be sent as a shuttle-cock for umpteenth number of time to a far-off place.

My Guruji's Instructions

(a) Accept any transfer that comes as the will of God and never protest or represent against it.

(b) Wherever you go, you will get the company of a really good saint and your spiritual insight into the great Indian tradition will deepen.

(c) Till the karma of a man has been exhausted, there is no use his hoping the best in spiritual life to happen to him as it is only when the nishkama stage is reached that the spiritual bliss is experienced as peace of heart, which is God's greatest gift to a living human being.

(d) Siddhis or supernormal gifts are good experiences but they are temptations and distractions from the true spiritual pursuit of life.

Rajkot

Sometimes later I will write about the great Rokadia Hanuman Baba (Prabhu Das Baba) where I saw the real supernormal gifts bestowed on the baba by Lord Hanuman. The difference from the ashram atmosphere was – a peaceful office and a peaceful evening with the great baba.

But came disturbing news in between from Calcutta. Before leaving Calcutta, I had met Samarda after I heard that the union leaders of his factory had made some unreasonable demand, when he was in no position to pay them even their salaries and wages. One of them had then said, *"if you cannot pay us, send your wife to spend her nights with us"*. I do not know if it is true but he was shaken up. When I met him even my artificially contrived words of consolation failed to have any effect on him. I told Batukbhai, my Gujarati guru-bhai and an intimate friend of Samarda, that all the symptoms of suicide had manifested in Samarda. He was not prepared to accept my diagnosis but, I said that I had read enough abnormal psychology to come to that conclusion.

In 1970, I received a letter from Calcutta that Samarda and his wife had hanged themselves on the night of 26th February 1970.

I did not have his horoscope. Later in 1975, when I was in Calcutta, I collected it from a respected professional astrologer, Smanasheshwar, who was consulted by most of the industrialists in our circle.

The horoscope is as follows :

He committed suicide in Saturn-Jupiter-Rahu. Here Saturn is the eighth lord in the third house, Jupiter a maraka and Rahu in the sixth house.

A post-mortem analysis of the horoscope can be done. But on the basis of this horoscope I had made a private prediction that Zulfiquar Ali Bhutto of Pakistan would be hanged. Some similarities between both horoscopes can be seen.

But I am answering the question posed in the beginning.

During that period of crisis, when Samarda had lost all hopes and was using abusive words for us all and Guruji, there was an offer from someone to buy his factory with all liabilities. It would have given him a secure future. I was sitting with Guruji when someone told him that the next day, the deal would be signed and Guruji, as was not his

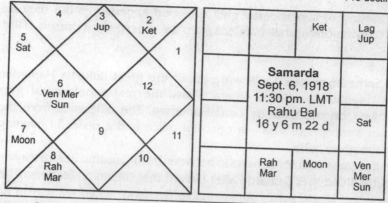

Lagna	Sun	Moon	Mars	Mercury	Jupiter	Venus	Saturn	Rahu
23°01'	19°57'	07°44'	10°57'	13°30'	21°41'	07°50'	02°01'	23°40'

habit, remarked, *"When a man is being dragged to his doom by his destiny nothing favourable can happen."*

That was in the beginning of 1969, one year before Samarda hanged himself. Then I saw in the next few months, till December 1969, till I was in Calcutta, everything going wrong for Samarda, his reaching that desperate end which forces a man to commit suicide.

How many times I have seen Guruji hint at the inevitable! I have hundreds of proofs! Saints see the working of destiny; astrologers can explain it in their own way. But the success-worshippers of our age will laugh at it. Silence is golden and a proof of wisdom, when such question about predestination is debated.

108

...8...
Rokdiya Hanuman Baba
(Baba Prabhu Das)
Pre-destined sadhana

The belief spread by our erstwhile English rulers and India's pseudo-intellectuals, that pre-destination is a source of fatalism, is one of those pieces of perverted logic, which is born both of the ignorance of the preaching of the *Gita* and actual observation of life.

(a) In the *Gita* it has been clearly said:

"No human being can ever remain idle, doing no karma, since they are born of nature (Chapter 3).

All karmas are inspired by nature according to the sattwick, rajasic and tamasic gunas, but the dull-witted mistakes himself for the doer of those actions" (Shloka 27).

Once, I quoted this to an educated lady who came to consult me, and she said, what is pre-destined had to happen, why should she ever do anything to achieve anything. I said that she would do what she desires to do actuated by *gunas* in her, and my or any other astrologer's telling her would not lead to any cessation of activities by her. She was doggedly disagreeing, and then suddenly her child, who was playing in the varandah started crying and, when she got up agitatedly, I asked her to sit down and not rush to her child. Why ? She had asked me. Let the child suffer what fate it is destined to suffer. She looked confused and angry, went out brought the child in and I said, "the *guna* compels you to perform your duty and not leave the child to its fate".

She kept quiet and said that she would not argue further.

(b) Belief in pre-destination never makes you pessimistic. The laws of *karmas* are inexorable. No one escapes them, in this birth or next births, otherwise astrology loses all its base. There are astrologers, who seeing other people prosper through wrong means and not suffer, begin to lose faith in the results of *karma*. Many of them have argued with me in a futile way, forgetting that it is the mahadasha scheme and yogas that show when and how the results of *karmas* will fructify. Those, who are adopting wrong means and prospering must be passing through prosperity-giving periods. When their period of suffering begins the entire picture gets reversed.

(c) To understand the law of reversal, watch a man's thoughts, deeds and behaviour (*aachara, vichaara and vyavahaara*), and see in the case of an evil person how malefic periods become intensely malefic, and how in the case of a man of good conduct, malefic periods remain malefic but lose good deal of their intensity.

(d) To understand the law of reversal, notice that an evil person rises very high and accumulates wealth in his good periods, unlike the morally correct person, who seems to stagnate. The reason is that the evil person sacrifices all principles and norms in his good period and grabs unscrupulously, preparing for the worst to happen to him, when his bad period comes.

Many contrasting instances from the lives of saints will be given first and then shown astrologically.

Rajkot

Within a week of my reaching Rajkot, at the end of 1969, I heard of Rokadiya Hanuman Baba and visited the place, sat down with the Baba, in his evening recitations of the *Tulsidas Ram Charit Manas* and *Hanuman Chalisa*. Invariably, after that the Baba, who got immobilised in blissful ecstasies, muttered something was difficult to understand.

Unlike my Guruji, the Baba had initiated only one person, while all others were devotees who came to his ashram, round the clock because in 1969 a *keertan*, "*Seetaram, Seetaram Jai Seetaram*", had been going on continuously for twenty-seven years uninterrupted.

One day, I asked Baba why he had only one disciple. His answer was that men hardly believed in spiritual discipline, which is rigorous. Most of the people would want lukewarm worship to give them the best results. When it did not happen, as it cannot happen, they would blame the Guru.

What the Baba said was exactly what I had seen in my Guruji's ashram and among the disciples of late Shri Seetaram Onkarnathji, Ma Anandmayee and so many others. In the USA what we call *sadhana*, is a pure mockery.

And then Baba said that most of the people did not believe in right *karma* for lessening the rigours of the *karmas* of their past lives and, when they run into difficulties, they want all their miseries to end in one stroke of worship.

Unlike other Gurus I had seen, who never believed in having restricted number of disciples, Rokadiya Baba made every visitor worship God but never initiated. He never even gave them a private audience much. Worship, worship and worship was all that one had to do.

How did this development take place in Baba?

The answer to this question came in bits, from older visitors to his ashram and his lone disciple. The Baba, who wandered from pilgrimage to pilgrimage in his youth, never getting 'tied' to a place or person, as instructed by his own Guru, had never wanted to settle down in a place. But he was directed by Lord Hanuman, whom he worshipped, to have a temple built for him. The Baba resisted it but Lord Hanuman insisted on his doing as directed, which Baba could not have disobeyed.

Being totally unworldly, he managed to get an idol of Lord Hanuman and installed it in a deserted piece of land, behind the Rajkot railway station but, did not know how to manage the material required for the regular *pujas*. Two days passed, without any offerings from anyone. The Baba said that if Lord Hanuman did not know how to manage his own *puja*, he would throw off the idol into a pond and be a free person again.

But from the third day, regular visitors started flowing in. Gujaratis who are munificent donors, for the regular *seva*, behaved so beautifully that Baba had no choice, except to settle down in Rajkot.

"That is my destiny", Baba once told me. "My Guruji had told me that ultimately I would have to move away from Uttar Pradesh and settle down in Saurashtra, near Dwaraka to spend my last days."

"Even the place where you would complete your sadhana and settle down finally and die is pre-destined", said Baba and said he would live for only ten years more.

I am talking of the year 1970. In December 1980, when a friend of mine from Delhi, on his way to Dwaraka, went to Rajkot to see Baba, told me that the Baba had completely given up eating. All the time he sat on his *aasan* with his eyes closed in meditation. He met none, talked to none. A vow of complete silence maintained was, perhaps, an indication of his preparing to leave the body.

A week later, another friend from Delhi reached Rajkot, after availing of his leave travel concession. Baba was no more. "Ten years more," Baba had told me.

The course of one's life's destiny is not known to us. The astrologer traces it through his knowledge, fairly accurately, fairly accurately for others, even for himself. But I have met saints who told me beforehand, how long they would live and where they would spend their last days.

I would refer to two other saints later, Shafi Baba of Nagpur and Ranga Avadhoot of Gujarat, both of whom told me of their coming end in advance.

Dwaraka

The biggest attractions of my peaceful Rajkot days were the company of the Baba, and efficient office where they sent provident slips two months before time. The staff was amenable to reason and creative planning. And for me of course, the visits to Dwaraka were the blissful experiences the great God had reserved for me. Both great pilgrimages, Vrindavan and Dwaraka are the places I have visited most in my life.

Baba also made trips to Dwaraka once in four or five months, where in Bhet Dwaraka the temple authorities kept the temple open, till our ship crossed the stagnant waters of the sea. We took our bath and came to the temple, which was often beyond an hour, after the scheduled closing time of the temple.

In our first visit, after we returned from the temple, Baba asked us to do Ramayana recitation, after telling how much to do, which took us usually twenty to thirty minutes everyday, in his Rajkot ashram. As soon as we reached the end of the portion allotted, he beckoned to us to do another portion, rather unusual, we thought. When we finished the second part, he asked us to continue further and, we had to do the third part also. All were very hungry by then. We rushed to squat in the kitchen of the ancient ashram where we were staying, and, which was under the charge of an angry Baba, who lost his temper almost every minute! Seeing him so uncontrollable, I quietly asked others to sing "Shree Ram Jai Ram Jai Jai Ram" without stop. Understanding it all, the angry baba of the ashram smiled, waved to us to stop and said to me, "You are very clever, but I am pleased by the devotional retort you have given to us". He attended to us so well, fed us so sumptuously, gave us thick pure cow milk with the remark "Avoid buffalo milk lest you should become dull".

On our way to Dwaraka, we halted at Nagnath, a *jyotirlinga* of Lord Shiva, where Baba quietly pointed to me to meet a person, clad like a *sanyasi* but very youthful, and talk to him. I greeted him. He took me aside and told me, to cut a long story short, that he was directed to complete his *sadhana* in Nagnath, which would take six months more and then move on to different places. He was a Maharashtrian. He emphasised the same point — even the place where one would complete *sadhana* is pre-destined.

In the next six months, when I went to Nagnath, I used to meet him and after that he vanished suddenly. I know nothing more about his whereabouts except the story told there, that he had developed such infallible supernormal powers that crowds started harrassing him and, he decided to run away!

Tapasi Baba

In Dwaraka, Rokadiya Baba one day told us that he would take us to a very fine mahatma, and took us to a mahatma, known as Tapasi Baba sitting under a banyan tree, with two or three small tins in which he kept some potatoes, which was all he ate. He sat on his *aasan* and had nothing to offer us to sit on except some tattered mats.

I have not seen a handsomer saint in my life, handsome in the fullest sense of the term. His entire body had as though golden shining hue, his eyes sparkled with kindness and his talk was so full of wisdom.

I met Tapasi baba many more times later, even when I went to Dwaraka alone. He always welcomed me. As soon as I sat near him, I fell into deep meditation involuntarily, for spells lasting sometimes over forty minutes! Later, when I had met Nagaridas Baba in Vrindavan, such experiences happened many more times.

I am referring to those spells of meditation because I hardly could ever talk to Tapasi Baba, as I did with so many others. Only once, I had some snatches of conversation and asked him why he had chosen Dwaraka and that banyan tree, under which he had sat for over twenty years, without a single disciple to serve him.

Finding me all alone he told me. Every *sadhak* goes on moving from place to place till he reaches a spot, where he finds that *sadhana* is progressing best. That is the place where he is predestined to complete his *sadhana*. This must have been in April or May, 1970. Then he told me that *"Mera sharir to ab pura ho gaya"* (My body's journey has come to terminus now), and in months he would leave the world.

In December 1970, Tapasi Baba took *samadhi*.

Contrast

Like all worldly men whom I had met in Calcutta with their

various worldly problems meeting their predestined ends, which I sometimes saw astrologically and, more often heard from my Guruji, during my Rajkot posting, I met sadhus from Girnar also talked of the pre-destined places for their *sadhana*. And they were men with supernormal powers, which I witnessed. But let me refer to two incidents in the *ashram* of Rokadiya Baba in Rajkot.

"Give him the *sindoor* of Hanuman," Baba told his only disciple one day, when I was sitting alone with him. Before I could ask him what it was, he said if you can get a boy who was born with legs first, from his mother's womb what is known as "breach child", come here on Sunday morning and see the miracle of Hanuman's *sindoor* (vermilion).

I arranged a young boy (the breach case as they call), and took him to the Baba, who applied the *sindoor* of his Hanuman, to the nail of his right hand thumb and, asked him to see our future. The boy gave exact description of my Rajkot residence, Lucknow house and described who was doing what in Lucknow then. I verified it through correspondence and found it vaguely correct, as none could tell me exactly what they were doing on that Sunday morning. But who all were present was a hundred per cent right. But the future predictions the boy gave to many could not be verified by me except one. But my impression is that those predictions were too vague or unintelligible.

Then one day a goldsmith I knew in Rajkot, asked me if I would take him with his six year old daughter to the Baba, and ask whether his daughter suffering from various diseases would be cured. The child looked so normal that no one could have suspected her of being unhealthy. But the moment we entered Baba's ashram, we were told that the boy had not come. Baba said that no more sessions of clairvoyant readings of the boy would be done in his ashram, as he wanted to avoid crowds.

In the evening, when I went to the Baba, he told me after others had left, "That young girl you had brought today will not be cured of her ailments because of her bad *karmas* of her past life. She will also not live long." Baba had known nothing about her. He told me about the entire family with so many details that I was astounded. This was the first of many such experiences I had with Baba, who emphasised 'Karma' and 'Destiny'.

Later, though I could not get the horoscope of the daughter of that goldsmith, I learnt that astrologers had predicted a terrible balarishta in her horoscope. Perhaps she died after some years, but I know nothing about it as, by then, I was transferred out of Rajkot.

But I had asked Baba why should the young girl suffer so much. *'Karma-phala'* was his brief answer. That is destiny.

So the Rajkot posting showed to me another aspect of pre-destination — even in *sadhana* there is predestination.

Then how such is man's free will operate in *sadhana* was the question I had put to Tapasi Baba. He quoted from the *Srimad Bhagvatam*: *it is the physical body that is tied down to planetary influences not the soul. Sadhakas should not take astrological prediction. They should do their sadhana cheerfully, caring for the living today and ignoring the dead yesterdays and uncertain tomorrows.*

My Guruji had initiated so many people's hopes and he suffered so much that he could not live in his own ashrams, for months.

Rokadia Baba had continuous *bhajans* in his ashram. No visitor had any chance to indulge in idle gossip which would attract the attention of visitors to the Ashram. The continuous *Ram Naam* that went on would drive out the thoughts of idle gossip from their minds, very effectively. Every ashram has its own spiritual vibrations, which increase when there is more tapasya done in it, with great spiritual giant like Rokadiya Baba also present in it.

The Real Bank Balance and the Living Today

What Tapasi Baba emphasised is the golden rule followed by all great saints. My Guruji always said do more of the *sadhana* given to you: Mouni Baba of Ujjain told me to predict less for people and ask them to do more *tapasya*.

Majority of the successful people we see in the world are those who have done *rajasic tapasya*, to gain worldly wealth, to increase their opulence, to live luxuriously. It is the crux and motivating force of all powerful countries of the world, exploiting other countries, to become prosperous and arming themselves, to defend themselves from being destroyed. The rich individual does the same in his own way. Morality need not be a segment of such prosperity and may even be totally absent.

The tiny minority or the tiniest minority that believes in accumulating spiritual wealth has a pattern totally different. They do not disturb nature, do not provoke the hostile forces of nature against themselves.

Of both types, the materially prosperous is seeking in the world outside himself, and the spiritually wealthy is accumulating it in his inner world. It is the latter that gets rewarded with peace and bliss,

115

and may live just above the level of wants or, even suffer poverty cheerfully. But such persons must always be few, otherwise no society or civilization would ever be prosperous.

But the majority of ideal house-holders follow the golden middle path, between the material path of prosperity and the spiritual path of bliss. In India, with its long heritage of spiritual experiments, there is the clear division of duties of a *brahmachari, grihasthi, vanaprasthi* and *sanyasi* for this reason. But in a society with such ideal demarcation of duties having vanished, there is an intermixture and confused combination of the duties of one *ashram,* with the other in majority of cases. There is a revival of the traditions of a *vanaprasthi,* who having retired mentally from the duties of a householder, prepares for renunciation. The house-holder has to accumulate material wealth for a decent living. That is being done in India, by giving spiritual initiation with so many relaxations, as done by my late Guruji and so many other enlightened gurus, I have met all over the country or, by Babas like Rokadiya Baba who did not initiate people but made them do *tapasya.*

A successful man should accumulate both *tapasyas,* the material and the spiritual. Some are born with enough accumulated balance of both wealths. They are the famous and successful men of our world.

A Contrasting Study

What interests me as an astrologer is how do ordinary men react to life's situations when they allow their life's energy to flow in a uni-directional way essentially – the spiritual, at the cost of the material or, the material at the cost of spiritual.

"Often when you see contrasting situations, watch the life conduct of the man behind any phenomenon", was what Guruji had said once, when someone had told him about a man with supernormal powers.

When we predict as astrologers we know very little about the moral, amoral and immoral activities of our consultors and, know nothing about their depleting spiritual bank balance, which is commoner, than increasing spiritual bank balance, which is uncommon.

Therefore, the advice of Mouni Baba of Ujjain to me to do less astrology for the majority of consultors and advise them to do more tapasya, has always appealed as the most practical advice.

Over a period of thirty years, I have done these studies, as a very intimate friend, as an astrologer who knows something much more about many – their personal lives, their sins of omission and commission, their tensions, their outer life, so flamboyant and their inner so hollow.

And I know much more about some spiritual persons, ordinary men working in ordinary positions of life, earning ordinary wages or salaries, living within their modest means and even in poverty.

Example of Spiritual Wealth

Born in an ordinary middle class family, with no higher academic qualifications but with sterling inheritance of spiritual wealth from previous lives, this person, whose horoscope has been given below, belonged to a deeply religious family. He got spiritually initiated very early and led a strictly disciplined life. His horoscope shows no benefic in a kendra except Venus, the atmakaraka, exalted in the navamsa and Jupiter in the eighth house, good for yoga-sadhana. But, the horoscope shows suffering, disease and even death in the period of Jupiter (1975-91). Nothing happened except one small accident.

I have seen him, since he often came and stayed with me, get into *samadhi* for hours, when I left him undisturbed. Sometimes it lasted through an entire night. His spiritual life was nearly faultless,

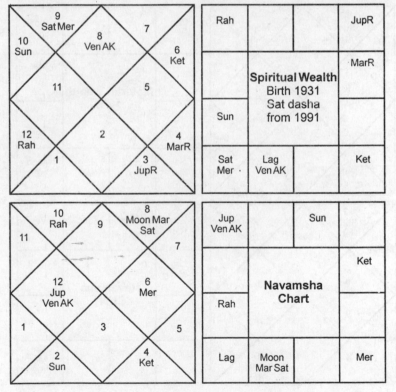

except for spells of sex-torments, which he, as an unmarried man, had to face often and about which, he talked sometimes to some of us.

What we call *graha shanti* or propitiation of planets, is a natural process in the life of a *sadhak*. Tapasi Baba's instruction that a *sadhak* should care only for the living today was hundred per cent true in his life.

Example of Material Wealth

Given below is the horoscope of a person in a prosperous family, whose twin gods were material prosperity and successful career. This person has four children, all very good students, and he himself has earned money fabulously in India and abroad.

At one stage, many years ago an important Indian had asked me to see the horoscope of his wife first, which had shocked me. Later the wife and husband gave me the horoscopes of their entire family. I came to know a good deal about the amoral and immoral activities of the family, the foundation on which they had built their prosperity.

In the mahadasha of Saturn, which started from 1982, he had

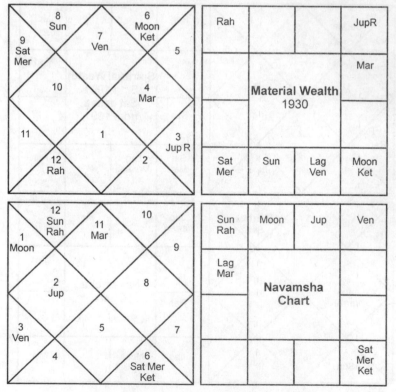

118

been most miserable. All that he and his children have is wealth. The wife and husband live separately in two different countries, outside India, as they cannot come to India for two reasons: they would be arrested for the violation of the Foreign Exchange Regulations Act and, their children have been leading such scandalous lives that they cannot face their society and their relations.

All his children are drug-addicts, their sexual lives are uninhibitedly immoral. The father does not talk to his children and mother keeps away from her children. And all the children hate one another.

"When will I get peace of mind"? This man asked me once.

"Not in this life", I said, even in the dasha of his yogakaraka, Saturn.

The Drawable Lessons

I have seen many examples, studied them astrologically to see the truth of the *Gita's* saying: the wise withdraws his limbs like the tortoise from worldly activities, after discharging them and leaves the fruits of his actions to God, accepts the results, good or bad, as being pre-destined. But he never remains idle. He gets surrounded by a spiritual aura without his knowing. His company gives peace.

The best way of overcoming the torments of life is to serve the grief-stricken and keep in the company of the contented, who have spiritual discipline – the lesson taught in Patanjali's yoga-sutras, works fastest.

As an astrologer, I have seen by now thousands of horoscopes of the materially prosperous Indians and people from the West. Their questions are the same, their sources of unhappiness are the same, their joys and achievements are purely on the material plane and, every shock of their life makes them more materialistic. They maintain a high level of prosperity and others who see envy them, thinking that they would never get the results of their bad *karmas*! It is natural to infer that they are not unhappy, because they have learnt the art of hiding their tensions and crises in family relations. They live under shadows of fear and death, disgrace and material deprivations, with an exterior, so well intact that they are mistaken, for happy men.

In contrast, I have seen those "tortoises", those poor people where moulding of good *samskaras* has been excellent, because their parents were moral, and for them mothers were their true spiritual "*adi-Guru*" (first teacher), goddess whom they respected all their lives, and their fathers were the ideal house-holders, who combined worldly pursuits with spiritual pursuits without sacrificing either their morality or spiritual traditions. I have seen them suffer least in their malefic dashas, and live blissfully during benefic periods. Reverse is the case of the materially prosperous, who accumulate wealth in malefic dashas immorally and suffer most in yogakaraka dashas because yogakaraka dashas create for them such torture as to awaken them to the need to have some spiritual values in life. But it is too late. The example of material wealth given earlier is a typical example of such men. *For them yogakaraka dashas are revelations of the need to mould their lives spiritually.* This man has heavy diabetes, had three heart attacks, has undergone coronary by-pass surgeries. He can only prepare for death in his own miserable way.

The example of spiritual wealth given is of one who has no material prosperity – wants nothing from the world. There is no health complications, no disease. He lives for others and immerses deep inside the recesses of his heart where he has discovered the meaning and purpose of life.

The difference is between the animal, living at the level of *nidra-ahar-maithuna* (sleep, food and sex) and *satyam-gyanam anantham* (the infinite, truth and wisdom) that higher living represents for him the real purpose of human life – the *karma-yoni*, not the *bhoga-yoni*.

...9...
My Jyotish Guru-I

Between the ages of ten and fifteen my mother had taught me numerology, palmistry, aura-reading and astrology, and later, Shri Gaya Prasad Dikshit, a very respected Sanskrit lecturer in Lucknow University and father of my childhood friend, taught me graphology.

But I was never interested in astrology as a subject of serious pursuit as I had to make my own career. I was so keen and successful a sportsman that the occult would not have met my need to make a career. My interest in chess, bridge, in which I did very well and won prizes, and office work kept me so much away from astrology that in my career most of the astrologers, palmists and occultists in the office hardly knew that I could have discussed these subjects with them. Being away from my mother who might have made me do some of her astrological work, there was no occasion for many years for my interest in these subjects to get rekindled.

It was the spiritual use to which my Guruji put astrology, through which my interest in astrology and other occult subjects got revived. My *guru-bhai*, very senior to me in age, and one of the finest inspirations in my life has been Nirmalda, a first class M.Sc (astronomy) from Dacca University and a junior contemporary of Humayun Kabir, the famous educationist-scientist of the Nehru-Indira era.

Once he cast a horoscope of mine and put it before Guruji, who at once said it was wrong. "Rao will have Ketu in the twelfth house, associated with the ninth and twelfth lord, receiving the aspect of the fifth lord, Saturn."

I told Nirmalda that Guruji was right because it was precisely for this reason that my mother, taught me astrology, among all her children.

There is that great astrological truth one has to remember – *one is born to learn astrology.*

Now that many books are available in the market and anyone can pick up some astrology, by reading them or by even completing the astrology courses we run, it is no guarantee that they would become astrologers. Some of them do make successful predictions and many of them make a living out of it, but they are not astrologers in the true and the classical sense.

My Guruji made no comment on my horoscope with Tula lagna and Nirmalda, who wanted to discuss it in my absence, also never tried it again.

Some years later, in another station a friend told me that he had met a very handsome yogi whose address he had and that, he would take me to him. We went there and found his sister, a widow, who told us that yogiji was out of station and that we should come after some days. And when we went to meet him after some days, the very first meeting created an extraordinary impression on me. He was discussing the integrated yoga of Shri Aurobindo, the Gita, astrology and the Himalayas in fluent and very fine English, as he being a Gujarati, was not fluent in Hindi and he avoided Gujarati, which I can understand fairly well.

In my subsequent meetings, which were many, he one day asked me to give him my birth-details. In another meeting, he told me that he had my horoscope, according to Chitrapaksha ayanamsa, which was Tula lagna and correct to degree and minutes as I remembered these details myself. But I was not interested in any predictions nor any discussion of my horoscope, which surprised everyone, who were there because others would have jumped at the opportunity to have their horoscope discussed.

In one of the meetings, I told him that I disliked astrological predictions as it dealt with all mundane problems, marriage, children, career, money, house, death, illness etc. The knowledge of this or predictions about them, some sensation-causing predictions like sexual adventure or misadventure or foreign journey, all these formed a sickening and repetitive pattern in human life.

I was more interested in his talks about integrated yoga, the Gita and other spiritual subjects.

One day he gave me a book, packed in a bag and asked me to take it home, read it, edit it, as I liked. He told me that it was a manuscript of a book he had written. I took it home, expecting it to be on yoga or the Gita but, it turned out to be a book on astrology! I read the introduction, written in Victorian English but containing profound thoughts, on the divine science of astrology. Then came some chapters on Astrology and Karma, Astrology and Destiny, the Philosophy of Astrology, Astrology and Science and the best of all, the wealth of astrological details a horoscope could reveal about the spiritual-emotional traits of human life, the obstacles in the spiritual path and how taking these warnings seriously a spiritual practitioner should mould his life.

The mainstream in my story of blissful inspiration is my mantra-guru Swami Paramananda Saraswati, who opened out before me an entirely new vista of life. It would have been closed to my way of a life, a central government officer, to whom an entirely different way of life was always available and with my skill in the game of bridge. I was always a welcome member of the best clubs, where my play was an attraction. My Guruji had told me when I was transferred from Shillong, that I would meet many genuine saints and faqirs. All of them have been like sweet water tributaries in the mainstream. But Nagaridas Baba of Vrindavan about whom both Angushtha Shastri and the Bhrigu astrologer (I will write about him later) had made predictions became a mighty Radha-Krishna stream of consciousness, later. Between these two, different from both, was the influence of my jyotish-Guru Yogi Bhaskarananda. He talked of yogic observation of the flow of the conscious, unconscious and subconscious not with the cliches of modern psycho-analysts, but based on the eternal truths of the *Gita.*

I read through the book of yogiji. I have never read a better book on those aspects of astrology, its philosophy, its reality based psychological analysis of a personality and the subterranean current of spirituality, with the obstacles known as *yoga-vighnas*. I got the entire book re-typed and yogiji had rung up Dr. B.V. Raman, who not merely consented to write the introduction but had also perhaps sent it. I was transferred by then and Yogiji moved into such a high state of spiritual development that he gave up astrology altogether. I have made vain attempts to trace out the manuscript but his devotees, some very rich persons, have shown least interest in those extraordinary intellectual-spiritual attainments of their Guru, who before his higher spiritual development, was a brilliant speaker in English and a more brilliant writer.

I do not know if anyone else in the world would ever be able to write such chapters. He had the spiritual practices of forty years in the Himalayas where he had spent six months every year, after doing B.A.(Hons) in English, from Bombay University, in pre-independence years. He had studied astrology thoroughly, meticulously, applied it to thousands of horoscopes of all varieties of human beings. He had come to a stage when he avoided questions on materialistic side of human life. He had enough of it. Astrology had served its purpose of revealing to him how the law of *karma* and destiny worked and his answer to the question, how to escape the problems of lust, anger, greed, envy, pride and attachment forming an inner circle within the fixed outer circle of birth, want, illness, grief, and death, was the yogic way of life. In later years, he combined it with pure devotion to God. In the last ten years of his life, his two prescriptions to anyone were drink Ganga water and do *bhajans*.

Sometime in 1981-82, after I had lost touch with Yogiji, one day in Delhi, Mr. G.L. Sanghi, a distinguished Supreme Court lawyer rang me up and asked me, "Do you know Yogi Bhaskarji?"

"Who?" I asked, "From Gujarat ?"

"Yes", he said.

"My jyotish Guruji. But his full name is Yogi Bhaskaranandji."

"Yes. The same person. Today I told him that I consulted a high-placed central government officer for astrological advice and told him your name. I was praising you for some of your unerring predictions given to me and friends known to me. He smiled and asked me to ring you up and ask you whether you knew him".

I went to the Niti Bagh with my younger brother Subhas, house of Mr. Sanghi and in his spacious drawing room, with many top legal luminaries sitting there, I touched his feet.

"That is what is known as sincerity, devotion. Rao could have disowned me and said that he did not know me. I only allayed his arguments against astrology and convinced him why astrology was not mere fortune telling or irrational political predictions, but a complete spiritual-emotional-intellectual portrayal of a man's trends of life with sufficient forewarning, to shape his life properly. Man can make his destiny to a large extent within the orbit of his pre-ordained *karma*, not outside it. A hard-working astrologer can see it, predict it, but cannot prevent it. Only God can prevent it and that is why I have given up astrology and now devote myself only to *bhajans*."

After that, I met him in Delhi every year, till 1990 when one day he rang up from the house of Mr. Pratyush Bharatiya, and said, "Won't you come to meet me. I will be here for two days only. I do not know when we will meet next?"

That sentence went like a dart into my heart. I met him. There was that faraway look in his eyes, total absorption in himself, the grace of a saint who, without saying so was indicating through every act and gesture, "this is our last meeting".

"Come if you can to my ashram for the Shivaratri. This will be the last Shivaratri of my life", he said. I could not go. I received a message from his ashram that Yogiji was no more.

During his visits to Delhi, he told a gathering of prosperous lawyers and businessmen, who had always surrounded him, how he had converted me into a genuine lover of astrology, which I was not, after seeing my horoscope and giving me an analysis of it for my guidance.

They asked me the story and I told it in bits. Let me give a complete narrative here.

The first time when I met Yogiji, he was discussing a horoscope before a small gathering in the small hall, where he sat in Ahmedabad in his own house with his sister serving us tea. He must have noticed my cool indifference to it all. After sometime he stopped it and came to the subject I wanted to hear him discuss. No man can ever give up *karma*, it is the *guna* in him, *tamas, rajas* and *sattwa* that will impel him to do what he must, what he has to ...

It was brilliant. So brilliant that sometimes I went to meet him during lunch time and spent two hours, came back and took the office files home to complete the unfinished work. I have not met any other saint who could treat the snobbish anglicised Indians through such proper doses of brilliant English speech, choicest diction and combine the best of western philosophy and thought, with eastern religions and mysticism with razor sharp logic, in which there was always the anticipation of the questions they could have put to him. He gathered round himself the cream of intelligentsla and made them sing *bhajans*, which he argued was the best and the only purpose of life. I have never seen in Delhi, of all places in Niti Bagh and Jor Bagh, where live Delhi's top lawyers, among India's topmost, and the richest industrialists, such a gathering of persons. These were the people who would charge about twenty thousand Rupees for one appearance in the Supreme Court of India or who did business in millions of dollars all over the world.

So much of distilled wisdom was contained in his introductory chapters of that manuscript on astrology that for many nights I wondered why I had neglected astrology, even after having learnt it. My Guruji had re-kindled my interest in astrology and Yogiji lent to it, the effulgence and radiance of his astrological wisdom.

How he did it, I explained to my astrologer-friends, by citing the example of my own horoscope, from which he once predicted that I would do astrology in a very original, innovative way, do fundamental research and later give predictions to the high and mighty (exalted Jupiter in the tenth). I would then withdraw from this, reduce my astrological activities and devote more time to spiritual practices.

Examples of His Predictions

Ketu

(a) He took up my horoscope and discussed it on some occasions thus: Ketu in the twelfth house with Mercury in its house of exaltation with my atmakaraka was the combination of the ninth lord with Ketu and atmakaraka.

This according to his rating was the best.

(b) The second best was Ketu in the eighth house aspected by Jupiter or with a benefic, preferably Mercury. He praised Mercury in the eighth house, next to Jupiter.

(c) The third best was Ketu in the fourth house with the conjunction of the fifth or the ninth lord or with Jupiter or aspect of Jupiter on it.

(d) He called the fourth house as the "esoteric" house in the *moksha* (salvation) triangle, good for astrological pursuits and allied

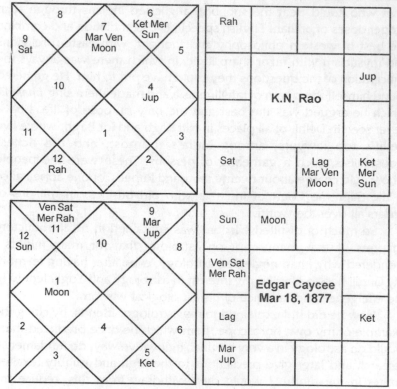

126

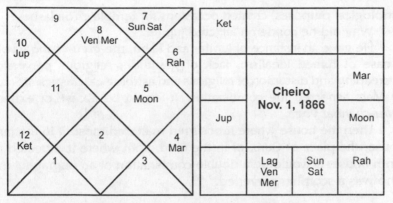

astrological sciences; the eighth house was the "occult" house which would enlarge an astrological vision, with high intuitive gifts and clairvoyance.

I give here the horoscope of Edgar Caycee, the famous American psychic-healer which illustrates it.

(e) Ketu in the fifth house with Jupiter aspecting it, preferably from the ninth house or Jupiter in the third, aspecting the ninth house was a case of extra-sensory perceptions, as in the case of Cheiro.

(f) Jupiter, Mercury and Ketu's association in any house was good.

(g) Jupiter, Ketu and tenth lord's association with Jupiter aspecting the second or the tenth house was very good for astrological pursuits.

(h) Jupiter aspecting Ketu and ninth house helped deep and original astrological research with hard work.

Jupiter

(a) He always preferred untainted Jupiter in the tenth house as the best. "Adviser to royal families" was the classical astrological meaning of it, according to him, a person whose house will be like a temple. Aspect from here to the second house (speech) and the fourth house (heart, according to Sarvartha Chintamani) lent idealism to karma, speech and heart.

(b) Next position for Jupiter was the fourth house. From here he aspected the eighth and twelfth houses, the occult and spiritual houses.

(c) Jupiter in the twelfth house similarly covered the esoteric house and the occult house.

But did he prefer untainted Jupiter? His answer was any malefic associated or aspecting Jupiter (Ketu was not malefic for spiritual or astrological purposes) created occasions for terrible ego-clashes.

Why did he condemn afflicted Jupiter?

He gave an instance of Jupiter and Rahu, the *guru-chandal yoga*, a case of ruined idealism, lack of gratitude, religious perversion, misreading and distortion of religious and astrological classics. If Saturn or Mars aspected the combination, it would be a case of extreme *guru-chandal yoga*.

Then the house where it occurred mattered most. If in the ninth house, the place of Guru, or in the third, from where it aspected the ninth house, it would be a double combination of an ungrateful man who was a scorpion perverted.

Mercury

Briefly, the best was the fourth house for Mercury, second best the eighth, the third best the tenth. (In my case Mercury was more favourable for spiritual pursuits than for astrology.)

He preferred the kendra positions for Mercury. What about the fifth house for Jupiter and Mercury? His answer: good for writing books, business, accumulation of wealth etc. Such persons need not be good predictors.

Saturn

Planet of concentration, Saturn in the third, fifth or ninth was capable of conferring detached view in most matters. But again, he insisted an untainted Saturn, like Jupiter.

Saturn in the eighth was the worst, as it made one caustic in speech, aspected the tenth house from the house of intrigues, the house of speech (the second) and the fifth house, the intelligence which harboured malice.

Then he told me that Saturn in the eighth house gave a prolonged disease, brought on the astrologer the curses of his consultors, which would fall on his children.

The Lagna

(a) He preferred Mithuna, Tula and Kumbha the intellectual rashis for quick grasp of subtle astrological principles, provided other conditions were fulfilled, as stated in the case of Ketu, Jupiter, Mercury and Saturn.

But these people should have malefics in the third or sixth house or both or more planets in fixed rashis, to make them work hard.

(b) His second preference was Kanya lagna, which had Mercury's rashi, Mithuna as the tenth house or Dhanu for similar reason.

(c) What about other lagnas. He said all lagnas could be good provided the four planets, Ketu, Jupiter, Mercury and Saturn were well placed.

Benefics in Kendras

Sometimes, it appeared that he gave topmost priority to benefics in kendras: one, two or three. A horoscope without any benefic in kendra would get compensated to some extent, if benefics aspected kendras. The *Vishnu sthanas* (quadrants) showed nobility and benefics reinforced such noble approach to the divine subject of astrology.

An astrologer with only malefics in kendras was a malicious, ill-equipped, dishonest and poor scholar with either no sound knowledge or ill-digested knowledge, in which he would combine inferior siddhis more, and astrology less. This is known as *shoola* (thorn) *yoga*. They have unhappiness in their families with their children and wife etc. revolting against him and create enemies, out of sheer malice. If there was one of the malefics in such kendras without a single benefic, it was the *shoola yoga* at its worst. Aspect of a benefic on any of the malefics in kendras could at most slightly reduce it, but they are born astrological frauds.

Benefic Rashis

He preferred, whatever be the lagna or position of Saturn, Jupiter, Ketu and Mercury, the rashis of Jupiter and Mercury for the placement of planets most. He would count how many planets were in Mithuna, Kanya, Dhanu and Meena. Next, in preference were the rashis of Venus, Tula, in preference to Vrisha and that of Moon, Karka.

He insisted that the moolatrikona rashis had a deep influence Mesha, Kanya, Tula, Dhanu, Kumbha. Planets in these or lagna in them had their own strength and vigour.

Navamsha

He told me some secret rules and asked me never to disclose them, as without examination of navamsha, the bare analysis of the horoscope could be misleading.

Some general principles are:

(a) Benefic influence on the fifth house, fifth lord or preferably of Jupiter, next, of Mercury and then, of Venus.

(b) He praised sky high Mercury influencing the 10th or the 10th lord.

Nakshatras

He singled out Mercury's nakshatras as the best. It had to be either the tenth lord in the nakshatra of Mercury or a planet in the tenth house in this nakshatra. In my case, he pointed out my tenth lord in the nakshatra of Mars kept me more busy in office while, my Jupiter in the tenth in the nakshatra of Mercury would turn my hobby of astrology into a serious pursuit, not though full time pursuit. It is true, as during my entire service career, I had to stop astrology for some months in a year, when the pressure of office work increased. In 1990 when I authored two non-astrological books, I could not contribute a single article to the *Astrological Magazine.*

He told me that he encouraged me because of my tenth Jupiter, twelfth Ketu with Mercury aspected by my fifth lord and aspect of Jupiter from Kumbha in my navamsha (Mesha) on the fifth lord (Sun) in Simha.

Dasha Sequence

Doing astrology in the dashas of benefics in kendras or malefics in the third, sixth or eleventh would be fruitful. Withdrawal from astrology in the dasha of benefic in the twelfth, and spiritual pursuits gaining precedence, was inevitable and would happen in my case. It is why I would stop my astrological consultations, he predicted. I have already reduced my astrological consultations down to ten percent and on the advice of Mauni Baba of Ujjain I am concentrating only on writing, research and week-end teaching.

This has given me tremendous relief.

Similarities

The spiritual combinations told by my Guruji and by my Jyotisha Guru were more or less common. Why they stressed on these they explained in their own way. An astrologer had to have idealism and spirituality. Malefics in kendras or *guru-chandal yoga*, were ruinous both for astrology and spirituality. The dasha of a malefic in the tenth house, or a malefic in the eighth house was the beginning of disgrace, aggressive malice and self-ruination.

My Testing

I have tested these combinations on more than hundred horoscopes of astrologers who themselves passed them on to me and wanted me to give them predictions. My own addition to them are:

(a) All the combinations given by Yogiji work hundred percent in the birth horoscope.

(b) Navamsha reveals much more or confirms it. But he asked me not to disclose them.

(c) The dasha an astrologer is running is important, as an astrologer in bad dashas would commit more mistakes.

(d) But all this has to be combined with intense worship.
The advice of saints to astrologers has been:

(a) My Guruji insisted on *sattwick* life, with *sattwick* food and *japam*.

(b) Yogiji stressed it, along with hard work on hundreds of horoscopes and vargas.

(c) Mauni Baba insisted on giving consultations to minimum people as, it was a waste of *tapasya*.

(d) Moorkhanandji said that every astrologer must worship the God Sun, through a *Surya Mantra*.

(e) But Yogiji advised me to examine navamsha to find out the *antarayas* or *yoga-vighnas* (obstacles), whether for astrology or spiritual life. What he taught me has proved brilliant. When foreign disciples of Indian gurus come to me, I pin-point, what exactly is going wrong with them, when, and they are surprised.

And then I quote from *Patanjali Yoga-sutras* to drive home my point, which impresses them more as today more foreigners seem to have read the Yoga sutras than educated Indians, except those who have to do some preaching or teach them to their students. Other *sadhaks* in India immerse themselves in their *sadhana* without bothering for these *sutras* and go to their Gurus, when they face difficulties.

So who will make a good astrologer and who will not can be tested by many on their own horoscopes. At any rate, do not get involved in discussion with astrologers who have two or three malefics in kendras, without benefic association or kendras void of benefics or benefic influences.

Astrology reveals both the results of *karma* and destiny, reveals both *karma phala* (fruits of *karma*) and *karma-samsakaras*. Both of them should be examined separately first and then synthesised. Which is why astrology is the most difficult subject in the world, practised more by charltans and cheats than any other branch of human knowledge.

...10...
My Jyotish Guru-II

Can everyone learn astrology? Should so many learn astrology which is possible now with all major classics available in translations in almost all regional languages? In Hindi, Bengali and Telugu I have personally seen huge voluminous translations of these classics. In Gujarati and Marathi lot of work has been done; all south Indian languages have been having such books for over seven decades; in Oriya I was told, when I was in Bhubaneswara, that a very experienced astrologer, Baikuli, had done monumental work. The Maharaja of Kashmir had done a very great service to the cause of astrology, when he got produced in Hindi, encyclopaedic books both on astrology and ayurveda, his astrological classic known as *Ranvir Jyotirnibandha*, is a collective work of a group of scholars, not of one individual and when these scholars reached unanimity of opinion about the meaning of Sanskrit sutras they were 'passed' and included in the book.

In English, such classics have come to us from many excellent Sanskrit scholars who had good command over English language or through such scholars, whose knowledge of Sanskrit was fairly good. Their ability to test the correct meaning of a sutra on many horoscopes was so scientific that their translations are more helpful than mere 'wooden' translations available now.

Revolution through Translations

De-Latinisation of Europe through the translations made available to average European the ancient learning of Greece and Rome and now, without the knowledge of Greek and Latin, great scholars have come to hold their own place of pre-eminence among the writers and scholars of the world. Some of the translations of Tolstoy, Dostovsky from Russian and of Andre Maurois, Andre Gide, etc. have made available to the lovers of literature, the best of the classics of the world, without their having to learn these languages. The finest example of such a very remarkable revolution may be of India itself when *Ramayana*, the *Srimad Bhagvatam* and so many Puranas have been made available from the middle ages to the modern. Some Maharashtrians claim, perhaps rightly, that the *Gyaneshwar* is the best creative commentary on the *Gita*. Now available in Hindi, this classic of that wonderful saint prodigy, Gyaneshwar had met the need of *yoga-sadhakas* who see in the translation, particularly of the sixth chapter of the *Gita* (Shlokas 6 to 21), some of the greatest secrets of the Nath gurus, which was either not known to an average reader or, was known to yogis in the Nath-Panth hidden in the hills of Gujarat, Maharashtra, Rajasthan and U.P. and perhaps in other parts of the country.

The De-Sanskritised

And Yogiji, very rightly, drew a fine distinction between the de-Sanskritised but highly spiritual Indians and, the de-spiritualised Sanskrit scholars; between Sanskrit scholars, who were unsuccessful astrologers and de-Sanskritised successful astrologers; between successful astrologers who read books of astrology only in English and, Sanskrit scholars who memorised *shlokas* and quoted profusely but given a horoscope, did not even see ordinary exceptions to the rule and proceeded, with their dogma-obssessed analysis to arrive at very outmoded meaning and hence wrong conclusion.

Drawable Inferences

Since I am confining myself to Yogiji's observations about astrology, let me clarify here that sometimes he expressed opinions and sometimes he asked us to draw inferences from what he said: Let me give some of them here.

Knowledge of Sanskrit

Knowledge of Sanskrit was useful not at all as a pre-requisite for learning astrology as enough translations of astrological classics were available now. In fact, so many were available now that reading them and remembering them was as difficult for a Sanskrit as for non-Sanskrit scholar. Only through constant repetitive exercises of these principles to actual horoscopes, the meaning of sutras could be understood. Most of the Sanskrit scholars had totally deviated from that highly scientific tradition of *manan*, which is repetitive exercises to arrive at the correct understanding, with good deal of flexibility.

He showed me once the horoscope of a child in which a lot of

133

balarishta yogas were present. A Sanskrit knowing astrologer had pronounced 'death sentence' on the child, on the basis of a *shloka*. Yogiji pointed *arishta* is not death necessarily but ill-health or, other handicap. That child has not merely survived but has made a highly successful career.

Role of Sanskrit Scholars

What was the role of Sanskrit scholars then? Sanskrit scholars will always have a great role to play because there are, according to his estimate, more than two billion Sanskrit *shlokas* lying scattered in manuscripts in different parts of the country. It is the Sanskrit scholar who can translate them. The quality of his translation will of course depend on how accomplished his own astrological ability is.

So his division of translators naturally fell into three categories; literal translation without any intelligent understanding; liberal translation with alternative interpretations left open to the reader to try and examine on different horoscopes; enlightened translation which would be very rare as here the Sanskrit scholar had to be highly spiritual also, besides being a competent predictor.

Who Can be an Astrologer?

He was very clear in his mind about who could be an astrologer. Only one percent among those who study astrology deeply would be sound. Once he explained it on a horoscope he was discussing. The event related to the father's death of the consultor, who had told none that his father was no more. He marked the Lagna, Sun and Saturn and then marked the third, ninth and tenth houses. The second step was the interpretation of the Vimshottari dasha in which he marked the major and sub periods which would prove bad for father. We quickly worked out the periods and asked the consultor who confirmed the date of death of his father.

Interlinking

Yogiji's method was very appealing. He took up the principles from *Parashara Hora Shastra*, given in different places (not in one chapter) and showed how to read a classic. He once discussed the horoscope of Indira Gandhi and showed something remarkable. Those days she was having a lot of problems with the Syndicate of Nijalingappa, Atulya Ghosh, Sanjeeva Reddy and others. He examined her sixth house and said whatever was being written about Indira Gandhi having become 'weak', was totally wrong. Indira Gandhi's horoscope showed spectacular victories over her opponents with very few defeats. Someone had asked him to write about it and send it to the press and he got annoyed. He was teaching us how by inter-linking different factors the prediction should be arrived at, without seeking any publicity.

Every prediction he had made about Indira Gandhi came out correct in the next few years. But once, he pointed to us that Indira Gandhi was making most of her important announcements at a particular time and in those nakshatras which tantriks use, for some *kriyas.* If she did not avoid it, it would boomerang on her and her family. That is history now.

Once he inter-linked six points in a horoscope to portray the quality of the married life of a woman which all of us only heard without, perhaps, confirming or denying, as we knew nothing about that woman. Later, the information that we gathered proved him correct.

Secrecy

Sometime in 1990, a friend of mine from eastern India, a Sanskrit scholar, government servant, astrologer, householder, 'sanyasi' (since he wears saffron robes and has disciples) stayed with me. One day he described the horoscope of his daughter and I said that there was tension in her married life and unless it was closely examined it would be difficult to predict whether it would lead to separation or not. He told me that he had talked to his wife on phone and had learnt that his son-in-law was driving his daughter out of his house!

Then he asked me why was I not writing a book about such inter-linked interpretations. I told him that my yogi jyotish Guru told me that spreading astrological awareness was very good, as it gave to astrology the prestige of a fully developed super-science, which it is, yet keeping some secrets and teaching them only to very deserving ones, was necessary lest it fell into the hands of unscrupulous astrologers who were many.

Astrologer's Own Horoscope

Yogiji examined the horoscope of persons coming to him for learning astrology. Some of these combinations I have discussed already. He told me many more and asked me not to reveal them.

Guru-Chandal Yoga

Jupiter-Rahu together, which caused *guru-chandal yoga* was in itself not so bad in the changed times in which we lived, he said once, unless another malefic aspected it or joined. Here also he called aspect or conjunction of Mars as the worst and of Saturn as bad.

He had his own gradations of Guru-chandal yoga, which could be categorised on the basis of his discussions from time to time.

(a) For Simha and Vrischika lagnas, when Jupiter became the fifth lord, the *guru-chandala yoga* joined or aspected by Saturn or Mars was the worst. They, who had this in their horoscopes, should worship Goddess Saraswati both for their sake, to save themselves from mental perversions and to save their children. He asked us to show a single horoscope of a person with Vrishchika or Simha lagna with prominent *guru-chandala yoga,* with one of his children not becoming a criminal!

If for Vrishchika or Simha lagna such a yoga occurred in the fifth or ninth house, it was a family curse carried from generation to generation. In such families deaths of many children and of the surviving children going astray, was common.

(I have by now observed it on more than fifty horoscopes and found it hundred percent correct.)

(b) For Mesha lagna where Jupiter is ninth lord and for Karka it is again ninth lord, the combination of Mars had one meaning and that of Saturn another.

(c) For other lagnas, first examine the disease-producing potentiality of this combination (also for Vrishchika, Simha, Mesha and Karka) and then other factors.

(d) Once he humorously showed us arithmetically how the variations of the *guru-chandal yoga* could be twenty thousand, seven hundred and thirty-six!

(e) Similarly each yoga mentioned in astrology would have so many variations! That is why astrology is the most difficult subject in the world.

Wasted Benefics

Yogiji had done his B.A. (Hons.) in English literature from Bombay University, under the guidance of Englishmen. He was brought up in the orthodox society of Gujarat and liberal society of Bombay. His own *mantra-guru* was Narayana Swamy of Kerala, who had built his ashram in the Himalayas, which is what attracted Yogiji to the Himalayas for decades.

Till his death he spent almost three to six months in the Himalayas every year. I do not remember to have seen in him any streak of puritanism, which I have seen in less educated saints, some of whose demands of do's and don't's were totally out of tune with the structurally half-destroyed Hindu society of our times.

Yet, when it came to astrology, I detected in him some strong streaks of puritanism! His dislike for *guru-chandal yoga* was an obsession particularly if in navamsha Jupiter was with Rahu or opposite to Rahu together with Mars or Saturn or their aspects! Here again he worked on many variations with a rare subtlety, all of which I found correct.

Next to *guru-chandala yoga* he disliked crowding of benefics in the sixth house which he often described as *"jewels thrown into a garbage heap"*. He invariably examined navamsha in such cases very deeply and gave very startling interpretations. In the case of a person whom I had taken to him he told that he would neither have a change in job for any professional rise nor would he prosper in his own job, unless he 'reformed' himself! Later, in his absence he told me that benefics in the sixth house were good only for earning money with all scruples thrown to the winds. But navamsha and the dasha should be seen. Such unscrupulous behaviour showed most in the periods of second and eleventh lords which in most cases would be followed by the periods of malefics placed so badly, as to destroy *karma, dharma* and *buddhi* (deeds, religion, and mind).

Interpretation of Vimshottari Dasha

His was the only sound and correct method of interpreting Vimshottari mahadasha. Whatever is given in different books is very misleading. Once when most of the astrologers had predicted disaster in the career of a student, he said it was the period of very great distinction! He turned out to be stunningly correct!

I worked on his method and have more than sixty percent success. He taught it two of us, perhaps. But he put us on an oath never to discuss it , but to teach it to some deserving one, in course of time. To illustrate his point, he showed some special charts given in detailed horoscopes of earlier generation and explained how and why they had to be used!

Invariably, every discussion of his concluded with the remark, *"Astrology is the vastest ocean and must be given up at some stage or the other for higher spiritual sadhana."*

He did give it up and never touched a horoscope after that. But then he did not need to do it, as he had told me, when alone, seven or eight years before his death, many things about many persons through his siddhis.

My *mantra-guru*, Swami Paramanand Saraswati did not need a horoscope. Whenever he wanted to avoid answering anyone he told him or her to get their horoscope made and then while discussing it with them, often left the unpleasant part out through very thin sugar-coating! I understood it. Others who knew astrology too understood it! But it created a lot of misunderstanding and even criticism of Guruji! The great saint that he was, he accepted it all. Once the disciples of another Guru in Calcutta whom I would call Swami "G" said or published something harsh against Guruji. He did not react. Later, when Swami "G" fell ill seriously and doctors called it the beginning of his end, he sent word to my Guruji. I went with him with two or three others. In my presence Guruji told Swami "G", "Let doctors say whatever they think according to their diagnosis, you will live for at least five years more and as a healthy man."

Swami "G" lived, after recovering, for six years and his disciples became ardent admirers of my Guruji.

In the case of Yogi Bhaskaranandji when such criticism was heard he never even retorted. Once he only told me, "Mercenaries will always criticise missionaries in spiritual and astrological field."

...11...
Pre-destination and Divine Bliss

Hindus are conscious of pre-destination, transmigration of souls, results of *karmas* and efficacy of penances to overcome bondages which are many.

None of these drives anyone into fatalism. I have seen none who became a fatalist and stopped efforts. Those, who are mistaken for fatalists are those indolent people who would in any case make no efforts to improve the quality of their lives.

Since 1962, after I had completed the fifth year in my career as a class one officer of the central government, in the Indian Audit and Accounts Service, I have studied a thousand cases first hand, both astrologically and otherwise.

My own pre-destination has trapped me thrice into such mistakes as did damage to no one but halted my spiritual progress which when repaired, has deepened my sense of detachment (*vairagya*) and made me wiser.

The best definition of pre-destination I quote is from the *Valmiki Ramayana* when Lord Rama explained the working of destiny to Lakshmana:

"That which we come to know of only when it happens – joys or sorrows – is the result of our karma; that which can be nothing else except the results of our karmas is destiny: who can fight that destiny?"

"Happiness and unhappiness, fear and anger, birth and death and like these so many other events whose reason is not known, is the working of destiny".

"Even rishis doing severe spiritual penances, give up their practices, stricken by lust and anger and fall from their ideals which is a result of the working of destiny."

"That which happens for which we are least prepared, and suddenly upsets work which was well begun is destiny and its working".

Lord Rama also showed the way one should face destiny: accept it, let the working of destiny come to its logical end, yet never leave the path of virtue and never give up spiritual practices.

All the great saints I have met have followed the path shown by Lord Rama. All good *sadhakas* like Batuk Bhai have moulded their lives after this ideal of Rama but after getting a lot of knocks in their lives.

But the most optimistic and wise way to meet the pre-destined is to accept the truth given in the *Srimad Bhagvatam*:

"Destiny controls the body. All physical and mental actions are prompted by gunas (sattwa, rajas, tamas). In the act of the performance of those deeds or even self-abnegation, the ignorant fancy themselves to be the performers of those deeds. It is this pride that creates bondage".

A self-examination of what one has done – how he was prompted to do it, leads to the exploration of something deeper and destroys the pride of his being the performer. It is a difficult process for the less spiritual persons. In the material culture of our times, the pride of performance is the crux of every 'success' story, which we astrologers know to be the result of planetary influences.

But then astrologers should also know their limitations:

"If planets were to be the cause of happiness or unhappiness" says the Srimad Bhagvatam, "how can they affect the soul which is eternal? Their (planetary) effect is only on the body which is subject to birth and death. The pain caused by planets is only on the body. The soul is beyond the effect of planets. Why then should anyone be angry."

Malefic influences on the basis of which astrologers make their dire predictions and make their fortunes, do not affect the happiness of a truly spiritual person.

Spiritual persons, spiritual in deeds, conduct and thoughts, lose their body-consciousness. While others think that they are suffering, the consciousness of their own physical suffering or mental agony is the least because of their spiritual strength.

I will come back to my story of Batuk Bhai not before discussing two fine instances I have seen of loss of body-consciousness.

The Sindhi Saint

In 1963-64, I used to meet in Nagpur a Sindhi saint who had to be carried on a stretcher because he was paralysed upto his neck. His face was always radiant and he always spoke of devotion and destiny, saying the true devotion made one unconscious of the strokes of destiny! He was always surrounded by many Sindhi men and women in his Sadar Bazar satsang. Everytime I saw him, I reminded myself that soul-force is what a human being must keep on developing more and more through right devotion.

Sister-in-Law of Mrs. Batuk Bhai

In a street in Rajkot, near the Panchanath temple, lived a couple, husband and wife with their children who were related to Batuk Bhai. I often went to their house to see the sister-in-law of Mrs. Batuk Bhai who, like the Sindhi saint of Nagpur, was paralysed upto the neck and talked only of the divine theme, with the fervour which some Jain women of Saurashtra have. She had to struggle to express herself in Hindi but Gujaratis can communicate to Hindi-speaking persons fairly well, if they speak in their own mother tongue slowly. In 1970, her husband had been serving her for full twelve years. Next to the Rokadiya Baba it was her company which I found so divine.

Both the Sindhi saint of Nagpur and this lady of Rajkot had lost their body-consciousness and they talked only about divine themes, admitting that they had to suffer their destiny but they were never conscious of their sufferings is what I and many others who met them always felt.

Rokadia Baba's Accident

In Rajkot, once Rokadia Baba fell during his morning walks and got a deep hurt on his left thigh with his skin getting peeled off and the flesh showing prominently, since he wore only a loin cloth. In the evening when I went to his ashram, I learnt about it and also learnt that a doctor devotee who had tried to dress his wound was not allowed to do it. After our *Ramayana* recitation, I told Baba that his wound was becoming a pain to me and that he should get it dressed up. He said he would suffer his *prarabdha* (destiny) since it must have been some misdeed of his past life. But then why should he cause pain to me, I had asked him.

Next day when I went to the ashram I learnt that Baba had not got it dressed up but had only put a cloth on the wound to hide it from our eyes. Again I told him that since I had learnt that he had not got it medically treated, it was causing me pain.

The Baba had to yield and the doctor bandaged it properly.

My Guruji's Suffering

In 1974, when I was in Patna I learnt that Guruji was very ill, suffering and *guru-bhais* were very nervous. When I went to Kamakhya during the Dussehra festival, Guruji had not come up to the hill till the third or the fourth day and everything suddenly seemed to become lack-lustre. Then he was brought to the ashram after being taken on a car to the Kamakhya hill and then, in a stretcher, brought down into the ashram. I was keeping up everyone cheerful to the extent possible by doing *stotra* recitations (Sanskrit) for six to eight hours every day. Guruji was pleased when he was brought and no one was allowed to meet him.

I had redoubled my recitations with a microphone so that the people who gathered there on the hill did not feel gloomy. One day, after I had finished it, a *guru-bhai* came and told me that Guruji had got up and the first question he asked was, "Has Rao not done his *stotra*-recitation". I went back and did it for over two hours.

Two days later, Guruji got up from the bed and went up and down the hill talking to us three or four times! That is the best instance I can ever remember of soul-force overcoming strokes of destiny and physical suffering.

I have referred to the bad liver of Guruji which was his life-long companion. But he never seemed to be conscious during his nearly eighteen hour a day schedule, in which he did so much writing, speaking and attending to the problems of the construction of the ashram.

Nagaridas Baba's Suffering

At the age of ninety-four, Nagaridas Baba of Vrindavan had developed severe prostate trouble which obstructed his urination so much that bladder seemed to resemble a football. Dr. R.K. Caroli who often asked Baba to come to Delhi, could not persuade Baba for nearly one year and the Baba had all the agony of such physical suffering. One night Dr. Caroli and Manoranjanji, a medical representative turned manufacturer, were repeatedly requesting Baba to come Delhi, while I, knowing that Baba would not agree till he was directed divinely to undergo the treatment. I gently press their hands and asked them to keep quiet.

Baba then pointing to the ceiling of the hut in which he was lying all alone, without anyone having to attend on him, said, "Is he dead? Whatever happens, happens according to His will".

One year passed, one day when I and Dr. Caroli came back from Vrindavan in 1981, the doctor remarked that Baba's bladder could burst anytime and become fatal. Next morning, Manoranjanji heard about it and went in his car running to drag Baba physically to Delhi!

When Manoranjanji reached Vrindavan, he found Baba with a small bag ready to come to Delhi! Some of Baba's devotees told him that Baba had said that Radhaji had asked him to undergo treatment and some arrangements had been made already!

Baba came to Delhi and instead of going to hospital, went first to the house of Dr. Caroli and told his ailing mother about the Radha-Krishna worship, for two hours, then went to the hospital where from his bladder bucketfuls of urine was removed! Baba at no stage was conscious of his suffering. One night, when I was with the Baba attending on him he said, *"These fellows think that I am suffering. They do not know what inner bliss is"*.

Once, when I was taking two boys of Taroli, both with supernormal powers, in a *parikrama* of Vrindavan, I met Baba on my way and on seeing a lot of allopathic capsules in the hands of his rustic devotees of Vrindavan told him, "Baba, never take these medicines. There is an expirty date for all such medicines. It can be dangerous to take them".

On the third day, after dropping the boys in Taroli when I came to meet Baba, his entire body was swollen. He told me smilingly. "A rusted nail injured my thumb and one of these fellows asked me to take a magical allopathic tablet. My body swelled up and I nearly died. Then a young doctor came rushing in the night and gave me some injections". Baba laughed his silvery laughter and said, "See that is how destiny works inspite of the forewarning God had given me through your advice day before yesterday".

During the treatment of Baba, many persons met him in the Moolchand Hospital where a south Indian doctor had operated on him. Raja Dinesh Singh too called on him along with other politicians, whose names I do not want to disclose. Baba told me later that Raja Dinesh Singh had a future in politics, not the other 'wretched' ones! Raja Dinesh Singh became a Minister in the cabinet of Rajiv Gandhi, after being in political wilderness, for full seventeen years, in February 1988.

Our friend Jayadeva Trivedi obstinately told Baba that he should spend sometime in his house to recover fully. Baba repeatedly declined the offer but Jayadeva Trivedi had his way. I had told Trivedi, "A free bird of a jungle will not want to be caged in the asphyxiating domesticity of his house." He disliked me for this remark and took Baba to his house.

Later, when Baba went back to Vrindavan he told me, "That fellow Jayadeva wanted me to bless him with a child. He does not know how long he will live to look after the child, even if, he had one". Jayadeva Trivedi died in February 1984!

Dr. Caroli, the heart specialist tried his best to save Jayadeva, but the heart stroke turned out to be fatal.

Loss of Body-Consciousness: Types

An important *shloka* in the *Gita* (chapter xii, sh.5) speaks of the difficulties faced in the worship of the Formless by such worshippers as are tied down to the body. The greater the body consciousness, the greater are the miseries of old age; the lesser such body consciousness, the greater is the enjoyment of bliss, solitude and inner peace in old age. It should be the subject of a seminal sociological study in India by Indians, who should now realise, that fitting their studies into imported sociological models is un-Indian and basically a de-spiritualised view of Indian life.

The types of persons whom I have seen losing body-consciousness to a remarkable degree as they advanced in age, men from all walks of life, not saints, are many. Were I to give them as individual case-studies with their identities, a lot of unpleasant details will have to be brought in. Their lives generally moved through stages!

(a) Sometime or the the other they were totally tied down to body-consciousness, which was absolutely necessary for them to achieve, whatever they achieved, in the materialistic world's competitions.

(b) At some stage in their lives some incident, some tragedy, some illness but mostly some saint initiated them into the art of delving into the recesses of their inner life. A big mark of interrogation that loomed before their eyes now was – what was the meaning and purpose of life and what was the secret of true happiness in life.

(c) Some of them found out their own answers through their own methods. One common element in their answers was a sense of larger identification with either society outside, in which some worthwhile social service allowed them to forget their own personal problems or, their identification with that cosmic element in their own lives which made them realise, that life is much larger than their own physical bodies, which are subject to disease, decay and death.

The Induced

The first type of loss of body consciousness is not an attainment of the person concerned, but was induced by a guru or through drugs. In these days of drug-addicts it can be seen, understood and appreciated.

In *Patanjali Yoga-Sutra* attainment of such a spiritual state as is attained through consumption of intoxicants (*bhang* and *charas*) have been approved but described as inferior. Here the quantity of drugs to be taken has to be increased and the intensity of experience begins to diminish.

But let me refer to *mantra*-induced loss of body-consciousness. I have seen many *guru-bhais* and *guru-bahens,* who in our *bhajans* got into a trance or trance-like conditions, which lasted from some minutes to many hours.

In our Calcutta ashram one *guru-bhai* who used to get into such trances often lay prostrate outside the ashram temple, in the verandah even in winter, with barely any clothes on his body. Though Calcutta winter is not severe yet, for a Bengali of Calcutta a warm, woollen clothing becomes necessary in winter. This man was not conscious of hunger, thirst clothing or bedding for many hours sometimes for as many as eight hours.

There can be seen in many *bhajans* all over the country of such induced loss of body-consciousness.

Induced states of loss of body-consciousness end in the inevitable anti-climax when the person returns to the normal state when his body-consciousness, as normal or deep as generally all human beings.

Definition of loss of Body-Consciousness

The classical portrait of loss of body-consciousness is that of Lakshmana in *Ramayana* and Arjuna in the *Mahabharata,* who could control *nidra* (sleep) *aahaar* (food) and *maithun* (sex). Along with this, there is generally bodily neglect in the sense of not being dress-conscious, ill-kept hair, social non-conformism, though there is nothing anti-social about this.

A Rare Variety

A rare variety of such induced loss of body-consciousness is of my own life. It happened in 1968-69 when in the Calcutta ashram I had asked Guruji what was it that helped one conquer sleep. His answer was that intense *japam* and purest *sattwick* food taken lightly, helped in the conquest of all the three, sleep, food and sex.

For somedays, I analysed my own problem. An office-goer with all the problems of the office needing food and normal sleep – and not a full-time devotee like the young sanyasis. Could I ever experience it?

In my self-analysis I did remember that I had never been dress-conscious, have been a non-conformist in a social sense, and sex-life, as a bachelor is what I did not have. Was I half-qualified to experience it?

Sometime then came to stay with me Shafiq Ahmad Khan, a close friend of Subhas, my brother, unemployed those days, Guruji liked him and Shafiq remembers till today the time spent by him in the Calcutta Ashram in 1969, with the company of Guruji available to him. He had Guruji's blessing. Later he joined the National Institute for Public Cooporation and Child Development, New Delhi.

One night, when both Shafiq and I were sleeping in the verandah in the summer, we heard the voice of Guruji in midnight "chor chor" (thief, thief). We got up went running to his *kuti,* whose door he had kept open. Guruji got annoyed with other ashramites and asked them why were they sleeping like logs while we two only came running at his very first shout. Gopalda, Subroto and others came slowly rubbing their eyes.

Who was the thief and what had he stolen was our question, but Guruji would not answer. He refused to give even the description of the thief whom he, it appeared, obviously recognised by face. He expressed his annoyance at ashramites sleeping like logs and not doing their *sadhana* at night. Next day, we came to know that a pocket watch which Guruji had kept was stolen. Guruji would still not disclose the name of the thief whom we all felt he knew.

Some months later, from Karimganj came a watch-maker to Calcutta to tell Guruji that his watch he had repaired many times was brought to him for sale. All the way from Calcutta to Karimganj in Assam the thief had gone, not to be caught in Calcutta and try to sell it to the family watch-repairer of Guruji!

"Was he ..." asked Guruji.

"Yes", said the watch-repairer.

So our guess was right. Guruji knew the thief but did not want us to know.

But from that night onwards we were instructed by Guruji to take lathis in our hands to go round the ashram, turn by turn, keeping vigil and doing our *japam* walking.

The ashramites, who could rest during the day time should have been in a position to do the night duty better than myself, who had to spend eleven hectic hours in the office, including four hours of hectic movement to and fro everyday.

Shafiq did the duty but, being young, needed good sleep every night. The other ashramites who never believed in any discipline even during Guruji's presence did not care for the instruction.

So almost for the entire night, except one hour, I had to keep the vigil, doing my *japam*, moving up and down. I never felt tired. When Sunilda came to know it, he protested with with the *Guru-bhais* since the burden of such duty should have been minimum on me and maximum on others.

No one followed Guruji's instructions and I did the duty for many months. Sunilda feared that I would collapse with only one hour's sleep for days, then weeks and then months. More than four months passed in this manner, but they made no difference to my mental, physical efficiency or normal reactions. People were surprised. My eyes did develop a deep meditative sleepiness during that time. But I was in a state of constant bliss and I felt very cheerful and light all the twenty-four hours.

Four months, my sleep was as normal, six to eight hours, and I realised, when Guruji had withdrawn the instruction, that he had induced in me a state of lack of body-consciousness by showing that conquering sleep was possible.

I was always a light sleeper. After that, I became even lighter sleeper with maximum four hours' of sleep sufficing, even in my thirties then.

Therapeutic Value of Japam

I will now come back to the case of Batuk Bhai with whom I shared my experiments of fighting at the mental level, my tensions, and he told me that he had done exactly. Then I found that many other *guru-bhais* had done it, each in his own way.

Every time a tension comes up, it should be treated as a blessing, because it is a challenge to you to fight it out spiritually.

There are three methods of fighting it, the first and most effective being japam. Fortunately the *sadhana* given by our Guruji is one which has to be done while inhaling and exhaling. The *mantra* given by guru should be done gradually thus:

Sitting, walking or lying, concentrate on your deep, deeper and deepest inhalations, doing the japam once while inhaling and once while exhaling. Do it at least for an hour or more till you begin to experience a vacancy in the mind.

1. During the course of my induced loss of body-consciousness I

discovered the maximum value of doing rhythmic breathing deeply chiming in with the entire movement of my body, particularly with measured steps.

2. While lying on bed, it can be done better. Lie straight, with either a very thin pillow under the head, or none and after closing your eyes, mentally concentrate between two eyebrows and do it for a continuous spell of at least forty minutes.

3. Now stop this and watch the natural flow of your breath. It may now flow very thinly and very lightly. Enjoy it as long as you can and you will notice that you are not moving the pupils of your eyes and, the sense of vacancy in the mind gets reflected in vacant gaze also.

4. Now again start breathing deeply, for at least half an hour and then stop this and again watch your breath in a similar fashion.

5. Do it for long spells every day, sitting, walking, lying, whatever you may be doing. The concentration must be rhythmic breathing with the *guru mantra*.

6. Over a period of time, you notice your middle part of the spine known as *sushumna* throwing up waves of current upwards. It is an excellent sign, the rousing of the *kundalini* which moves up actively.

7. This habit should never be given up. It must become a life long habit. "*Yagyanam Japa Yagyah Asmi*" said Lord Krishna in the *Gita*. The Sikh Guru, Teg Bahadur sang it in a *bhajan*, "*Swas Swas Sumiro Govinda*".

Batuk Bhai did it while sitting and while lying. In my younger days I did most while walking, particularly doing the *parikrama* of Vrindavan, which I have done more than two hundred times.

The neurotic condition of the mind comes under control, very effectively, even totally.

Experiences

There are five *gyan-indriyas*, or doors of perception – breath, sight, hearing, taste and touch.

Now what *mantra-jaap* does in this manner must do is:

(a) *Breath:* when controlled stills the disturbed mind very effectively. So do it till you tire yourself out in the beginning, and never forget to do it for at least four hours a day.

(b) *Eyes:* closed when the *japam* is being done shows, strange sights. First they can be frightening but continue doing it. The frightening sights get replaced with the sight of hills, seas, distances, familiar faces and past memories.

At a later stage, all such sights vanish and different lights appear, first bright white light, sometimes green, sometimes red. If you stand in the early morning facing the Sun, close your eyes and do it even for half a minute, these lights appear. But later, in the stillness of the night and in the darkness of your room these lights glow.

Blue colours of all varieties appear later. This is Krishna jyoti, representing Lord Krishna and resembles the "eye" with its golden orb, within the blue peacock feather, which dons the crown of Lord Krishna.

(c) Sound: There are twelve types of sounds described in the *Hatha Yoga Pradeepika*. The roar of the sea, sound of conch shells, jingle of tinkets, sound of veena, the thunder of clouds etc. These sounds have a strange way of rising any time. You may be sitting in a meeting and it may rise. It is what is described as *anahad naad* (the sound, which rises without your having to strike anything).

"Kahat Kabir Suno Bhai Sadho,
Anahad Bajat Dhol Re, Tohe Piya Milenge".

explains this experience in a poetic way.

(d) Taste: You will experience something oozing from your palate, first tasting bitter, but later sweet then very sweet. What doctors describe as a symptom of diabetes is a common experience of *sadhakas*. When this occurs more frequently, the need for consuming food goes down. The diet becomes light and lighter.

(e) Smell: You will suddenly get strange smells, generally of *ganja* which sadhus take or, of sweet odours. It is the sign of the presence of a saint or god in his divine form (*divya deha*) which you cannot see. It happens mostly between two and four in the early hours of the morning, suddenly, but not regularly.

Even when you are walking amidst fields when this happens and you know that it is not that of a flower anywhere nearby, you can be sure that a saintly person is sitting somewhere around.

When these experiences repeat and become a regular occurrence in your life, your spiritual development is good, your efficiency of the mind and body superfine (*dakshak* is the word used in the *Gita* meaning 'efficient') and your concentration is one hundred times greater. You can do the work, which earlier took two ours, now in half an hour.

Now a question arises – does it solve the problem of a wayward child, a bad boss, a strained relationship. No. But it makes your reaction not one of agitation but one of philosophical, stoical acceptance. But in the house where you are doing, the spiritual vibrations improve so much that those coming into its orbit change for the better. So first turn your own house into a pilgrimage.

In doing all this make sure that all you eat is only prasad. In Calcutta I gained twenty or more pounds in weight by eating only rice and cabbages in the first two months of my stay in 1968, because I had such a fine physical-mental-spiritual equipoise in its uttermost perfection, though briefly.

Always remember, it is doing this that leads to the process of experiencing bliss within, waves after waves rising from the *muladhara* (naval region) and gradually, it enters *sushumna* and begins to rise high. It spreads all over the body till you feel that your entire body is engaged in *japam*.

When *sushumna* is very active, do not move out of the house as in that mood of spiritual intoxication, you will ignore traffic lights and signals. Once walking on the streets of Delhi, I ignored the traffic completely and nearly came under a bus. Fortunately, since I did not show any reaction, the bus driver and conductor shouted at me and said, "Must be deaf".

To sum up; breathing rhythmically deeply with your guru mantra is eighty percent your sadhana and can be done anytime, anywhere.

Batuk-Bhai did it uniterrupted for twenty five years. Why he liked my company most and spent so much time with me was that I was doing it myself, and cooperated with him fully. Never even in talking while apparently sitting on a chair with his legs on the table smoking cigarettes he seemed to be fully awake.

When he came to Rajkot and stayed with me in 1970, and again to Delhi in 1978, it was precisely for this reason that he could be away even from his family and he could make use of my house as sadhus make use of a cave for their sadhana. There was no body else in my house even to talk to. It suited him most. In twenty-four hours he hardly talked to me for half-an-hour. He was so deeply immersed in his *sadhana*.

The Awakened Kundalini

It manifests in many ways, one is known as *pulak* (sudden jerks in the body), *kampa* (shiver), *sweda* (perspiration), *ashru* (tears). Tears begin to roll down the eyes when a good story of Ram Leela or Krishna Leela is heard. These are divine ecstasies.

Spells of Dryness

Excessive *japam* creates spells of dryness occasionally. What is the way out?

Loud Keertan

In the *Bhagwat* the word used is '*uchcha swar*', the voice should come out of *nabhi (navel)*. In *Yoga Shastra*, the voice originates from three places, *Vaikhari* or that which comes from the throat. Most of the cinema, T.V. and radio singers sing from *Vaikhari* only and it never touches the heart of a genuine *sadhaka*. Once Meena Bannerji sang *bhajans* before Moorkhanandji, but he said such singing does not touch the heart of a sadhu.

Once, I did the Annapurna *stotra* very loudly in Gauhati Ashram, rather wildly and Guruji had lot of *pulak*. Once, I did *Bilwamangal's Krishna stotra* before Nagaridas Baba and he went into *samadhi*. Once, Chintu and Mintu (sons of my youngest brother, Subhas), did it in spontaneous uninhibited way in Vrindavan before Nagaridas Baba and he went into ecstacies and gave them, *deeksha* in return.

Pashyanti is the second source of voice. The singer sings for his Lord, not for the lord and with his eyes closed, when he does it he sees divine sights. Sushantoda, does It always which Is why he sings *bhajans* for hours like Narasi Mehta of Gujarat.

Para is the final stage. The voice stops because the singer has reached the *samadhi* stage. It is what Swami Haridas of Vrindavan used to do.

Service

When you have the opportunity to serve others, do it cheerfully. It drowns your own miseries and brings cheer to your heart.

Every great Mahatma whom I have talked to privately did it one by one till he reached the stage of silence when he does only *japam*, sitting, lying or walking.

Prayer

If you have reached *Nishkama* stage, as I did in 1968, you cannot pray to God for anything worldly. But that stage is reached late by a house-holder. But when he prays to God from this stage, after this preparation, his prayer is so sincere that God has to respond. I have experienced it hundreds of times. But as I said I have now reached *Nishkama* stage. I cannot pray for anything. Whatever is good or bad for me is what Lord should know, He being the Father and *antaryami*.

Experiences of Siddhis

Do not get distracted, but you experience some *siddhis* also while you are doing your *sadhana*. Briefly they are :

(a) *Clairvoyance or Doordarshan*: Closing your eyes, you can know what is happening elsewhere. To cultivate it, and master it one will have to sit for long hours on an *aasana* in some posture, *siddhasana, padmasana, sahajasana* (normal squatting). I have experienced it but without having control over it.

(b) *Pre-cognition or Purvabhas*: You can come to know of the coming events beforehand.

(c) *Wish-transference of Sankalpa*: An instruction or a wish can be conveyed from a distance without any known means of communication. The Guru sitting in Calcutta wishes it and the shishya in Nagpur does it. My communication with Guruji was of this category, as he himself told a *guru-bhai*. Tulsidas describes Lord Rama as *Satya Sankalpa Prabhu*.

(d) *Telepathy or Thought Transference*: Your thoughts get transferred to the person concerned without any known means of communication.

But *siddhis* are distractions and become cause of halted spiritual progress, as happened thrice with me so far.

...12...
Nagari Das baba

To remember Nagaridas Baba in 1995, six years after he left this world (July 1988), is to take a blissful bath in the cool waters of purest devotion. I do not think that I or my friends, who went to meet him in Vrindavan between 1978 and 1988, will ever meet a saint, who transcended *maya* so completely and so sublimely.

In 1978 I was transferred to Delhi after my second spell of Calcutta posting, which was spent in looking after the ashram of my Guru, in two spells (1967-69) and (1975-78), along with heavy work at the office had given me deep enough insight into the problems of an ashram. I was convinced that an ashram was a good diffuse centre of spiritual radiation but not favourable for intense *sadhana*. This feeling had created a mental turbulence, which was difficult to overcome.

Vrindavan, the great pilgrimage centre, has always given me greater spiritual solace than any other remedy. All I do is to go to Vrindavan and take a full round of the town (*parikrama*), doing my *japam*. On this planet of ours, there can be no greater spiritual place, Vrindavan with Krishna-consciousness. I must have done the *parikrama* of Vrindavan more than two hundred times. As an astrologer I recommend this as the most efficacious remedy to people in Delhi, who can afford to go to Vrindavan on a Sunday morning, do *parikrama* and come back in the evening.

During one of those frequent visits to Vrindavan, I heard about Nagaridas Baba. In the terrible floods of 1978, the river Yamuna had reached right upto the path of the *parikrama* and submerged the small and unimpressive cottage of the Baba. In his nineties already, the Baba then climbed up the bunyan tree near his cottage and lay there for fifteen days, with snakes and other reptiles as his companions. Rescue teams in boats came rushing and asked Baba to move to interior and safe places inside Vrindavan. But he refused. Then the parties organised by rich men to rush food too had come to him but he refused to touch the food offered by them. On the other hand, the food brought by some ruffians was all that the Baba accepted. These ruffians, as we ourselves discovered in the next few years were products of bad upbringing but had good hearts, unlike the rich men, who thought that by offering foods to great yogis affected by the floods, they would be able to wash off their many sins.

The floods receded after a fortnight but the whole Vrindavan which had witnessed many miracles of the Baba during this period found in him the finest example of utter surrender to God.

My First Meeting

In one of my *parikramas,* I found a thin, lean, tall, completely dark baba wearing only a *langota* (an undergarment) in the lower half and sometimes a rag covering his upper half of the body and sometimes not even that. His eyes shining with spiritual light and his ringing laughter did not seem to belong to this planet of ours.

I saw him and sat down near him as he lay on the stone platform using a hard, rock-like cement pillow.

"Gurus make ashrams with great and good intentions. But disciples ruin them. The ideals of gurus are defeated. To make an ashram is to invite trouble, to get involved in *maya,* "Baba said without ever asking me who I was and what was my problem. Other two or three persons who were sitting around may not have known that this was addressed to me and it struck a deep response inside me.

Baba went on talking about the utility and also the futility of making ashrams. He was giving something like a running commentary on the previous two years' life in the ashram of my guru – the ecstasy and the poignancy of it all, so much spiritual splendour within so much worldliness.

At least twice a month I went to Vrindavan and spent three to four hours listening to him, most of the time all alone. Such was my great fortune. Everytime I went to him he picked up the thoughts uppermost in my mind and spoke on them. He knew that I loved his extraordinary method of dealing with my spiritual questions without my having to tell him. To-date those hours I spent with him have been the least lessons in spiritual living. The quintessential lessons of spirituality that flow spontaneously from the lips of a great yogi who never touches money, who cooks his own food and who does not surround himself with anything worldly, which I saw in Nagaridas Baba always reminded me of Jada Bharat of *Srimad Bhagvatam.*

Even after forty or fifty visits, he never asked me who I was and from where I came. This was in sharp contrast to other saffron clad merchants plying their business, from big hotels in Delhi or living in big mansions built with Marks, Pounds and Dollars collected from Germany, England or USA.

But I was not surprised. It was the only correct prediction given to me by the Angushtha Shastri. It was God's grace. I was fortunate to have so many intimate conversations with the greatest yogi I have ever met. He performed no miracles but miracles happened. He never preached but whatever he spoke was classical preaching of scriptures, assimilated after years of great spiritual life. He had no disciples but anyone who spent time with him acquired the true selflessness of devotion in varying measures. In the guru-disciple relationship, there is an element of dictatorial behaviour. The greed of an ashram-building-guru, can be jarring specially, if it is one of the Americanised gurus who thinks in terms of multi-million projects. Baba had no ashram, no disciples. In scorching heat, he could sit on siddhasana on hard stone for three to four hours without changing his legs and talk to us endlessly. His eyes always sparkled with kindness.

Slowly, my friend Manoranjan joined in my weekend Vrindavan trips, then Dr. Caroli, Madangopal Arora, Ramesh Bhandari and others joined. About fifty people came to know of Nagaridas Baba from me and they visited Vrindavan only to see him. Since Indians can distinguish between genuine yogis and the fake ones easily, every friend of mine thanked me for what they thought was a great discovery.

From July or August 1978 to July 1988, almost twice a month, I spent four to six hours per visit. About eight to twelve hours a month, for ten years. It was much more than I had ever spent in the company of any other yogi. Yet what I knew about Nagari Das Baba, the man was so little because he rarely talked about himself or his past.

There was a more important reason why I could know so little about him or his past. In the beginning when I went to him all alone and sat, whether outside his cottage or inside, in front of him, mostly I got into deep meditation, in which I became oblivious to my surroundings. My eyes closed spontaneously and intense experiences of the mystic lights and mystic sounds, once begun continued for hours. After it ceased, I was so in-drawn that I could hardly speak. Those hours spent in the company of the Baba were the most divine moments of my life. To talk of anything worldly, be it the past life of the Baba, or of the present corrupt times would have been a discordant note. Often on Saturday nights, when I was alone with him in his cottage he would, as though wake me up at eleven in the night and tell me to go back to my place of stay. The narrow path I would have to negotiate had often snakes crawling , which I could not see in the dark of the night. And the criminals prowling. Yes, Hindu pilgrimages have more criminals than is widely known. The saffron cloth, the respected dress of saintliness, is also the disguise for criminals.

My best experiences in those ten years were in the presence of Nagaridas Baba. Meditation is not done, is not practised. It *happens*. The presence of a great spiritual personage and place, makes meditation spontaneous.

My elder brother, K. Pratap, went to him once and, as is his habit, talked about our entire family, particularly about father, K. Rama Rao, the founder-editor of the National Herald, who had to go to the jail during the British rule. In turn, Baba told him about his own links with the Congress party of pre-independence days and his days with Mahatma Gandhi, in his Sabarmati Ashram, where he taught the *Gita* to the gatherings. But later, he left Gandhi and immersed himself deeply in his *sadhana* in the Himalayas.

Baba came to know my name for the first time, though remembered only "Rao from Delhi." Yet he knew nothing more and never asked me. *I cannot imagine of a more divine relationship.* He never accepted any money, never accepted any other gifts. If anyone insisted on giving him something, he would ask him to get some grains for the peacocks that flocked under the banyan tree in large numbers. He never wanted any disciples.

It is well-known that even yogis suffer from *Putreshna* (desire to have sons or disciples), *Vittaishna* (desire to have material possessions) and *Lokaishna* (desire to be well-known). The only saint I had seen, other than Moorkhanandji, transcending all these three bondages, the higher bondage of yogis, these three *ishnas*, was Nagaridas Baba.

Slowly, Baba came to know the names of others, Aroraji, Doctor Saheb, Yadavji, Bhandariji – we who visited him so frequently. There was no month in all those ten years spent by anyone of us without a weekend with the Baba.

For full ten years, yes for full ten years, we saw him every month. My average was better, twice a month or even more, never less. Each time minimum four hours. To say that he talked and we listened is to make it look more mundane. He transmitted and we received; transmitted his conviction that pure devotion to God was total surrender to His will, yet performing one's allotted *karma* to the best of one's ability. *"We are the actors on the stage of life, who have to act out our roles without knowing what the script of our roles is".*

"Kaam Kiye Ja, Naam Liye Ja", (Keep doing your work, keep

doing your *japam*). What little we could glean from his talks about his own past can be pieced together. Yet it will be skeleton of a sketch of the greatest hero I have met or known in my life.

He was born in the family of a very rich landlord of the eastern Indian province of Bihar sometime, between 1885 and 1895, in the month of July, with Simha rising and with the Moon either in the last degrees of Vrishchika or early degrees of Dhanu.

Perhaps, he was a Maithili Brahmin but did not eat meat as Maithili Brahmins do. He even converted villages after villages into vegetarians and devotees of Radha-Krishna. As a very impressive Brahmachari (celibate), who had advanced spiritually in his teenage as a result of his initiation into the *sadhana* of *Krishna Bhakti*, his heart was not in the worldly life. The only worldly activity he was interested in was the freedom of the motherland from the British rule.

In those days of early marriage, even before he had passed matriculation, his father had arranged his marriage. Out of his fear of being trapped into the life of a householder, he fled his home. After some months he was traced out in the western Indian pilgrimage of Nasik. His father persuaded him to return home, after assuring him that he would not be forced into the life of a married man.

He returned to his place and passed an examination in law and became a qualified lawyer. But he again fled, this time for ever.

Six months a year, he would spend in the Himalayas and the remaining six months on the plains mostly of the Punjab where women fed the yogis on dry fruits and were very lavish in their hospitality. Some of the women of those times, wanting to have great children wanted to have sex with yogis, clandestinely. It is not known if the Baba too got trapped into some amorous act. But he stopped visiting Punjab later.

In what was Punjab and the North West Frontier state then there were many, pretentious yogis who offered protection to their devotees boastfully. "All their devotees and they themselves were either murdered or had to flee during the communal riots of 1947, when the country was divided," said Baba many times, and emphasised the value of humility.

"God is Time and his Wheel of Time changes life."

My choice of the title the Wheel of Time, in two of my books, *Astrology, Destiny and the Wheel of Time*, and the present book, *Yogis, Destiny and the Wheel of Time*, has been inspired by Baba's reference to the Wheel of Time, always.

During one of those years in the plains, some yogis were sitting in one place and a very argumentative man came and challenged them to revive a tree which had dried up and was dying. At night Baba had a dream in which he was told to recite '*Rama Raksha Stotra*', a great Sanskrit hymn in praise of Lord Rama. Baba did it, as directed and after fifteen days the tree became laden with green leaves and fruits and flowers. The news spread in the villages nearby. Before the swarming crowds could come and surround him, he ran away and never returned to that village. The great guru of the famous astrologer, Hardeo Shastri Sharma Trivedi, always prescribed *Rama Raksha Stotra*, as the best astrological remedial remedy.

Once caught in difficult circumstances in a lonely place, he got nothing to eat or drink (he used to drink a lot of cow milk). Perhaps a week passed. Suddenly he found a young beautiful woman appear before him with a cup of milk. He drank it and suddenly, found that she had vanished into air. Who was she? Baba told me once when I was alone with him that she was Goddess Radha.

After this experience, he learnt the most valuable lesson of his life. He depended on Goddess Radha, totally. He loved human beings, helped them, served them but depended only on Goddess Radha, never on any human being thereafter.

He then went on international tours, particularly to Siberia and Russia. Why when and how and what he saw there, he never told us.

During that period, Mahatma Gandhi met him and asked him to preach in his Sabarmati Ashram, in Gujarat in western India. In close association with Mahatma Gandhi, he came to know both Jawaharlal Nehru, who later became the first Prime Minister of India in 1947 and Subhash Chandra Bose, the great patriot who escaped from British eyes and raised the Indian National Army to fight the British.

In a public meeting, one of the famous Ali brothers was delivering a magnificent speech and Jawaharlal Nehru, who was to speak next, pulled him down by physically catching his *sherwani* (long coat). Jawaharlal Nehru was an ambitious scoundrel was what Baba often told.

In 1938-39, Mahatma Gandhi did injustice to Subhash Bose who inspite of his election as the President of the Indian National Congress, had to resign because Mahatma Gandhi and others did not cooperate. "What type of a Mahatma was he? He was a hypocrite. Both Gandhi and Nehru were hypocrites." Baba never compromised with Mahatma Gandhi after that and he left the company of the so-called patriots, he told us.

His guru, who was alive then, sent him a message that India

would be free very soon, in any case. But he should withdraw from liberation struggle and immerse fully in his *sadhana*.

During a police firing on the crowd of slogan shouting patriots, he received a bullet injury on his right thigh. He became lame and could not walk long distances. But even then he never stayed at one place long lest he becomes known and he is forced to have a crowd of disciples and an ashram.

Those, who make ashrams are slaves of *maya*, he would often say. His own guru never built an ashram. He had small cottages built on the banks of the river and moved from one place to another, never staying long at one place.

Vrindavan was his favourite pilgrimage. Once the queen of a state who became his great devotee asked him to take charge of her palatial temple in Vrindavan. He ran out of Vrindavan, without telling anyone and did not return to the place for nearly ten years.

Now in old age (he was past ninety when we met him), he had no choice as he could not even walk much, with his limp. He would die in Vrindavan – he looked forward to nothing else.

He aroused good deal of jealousies among yogis against himself. He was very biting in his criticism of their acts and deeds. They became his enemies. He was poisoned thrice in Vrindavan, through the milk he consumed. He digested it all through his yogic powers. The last and the third act of poisoning did affect him. He found urination difficult.

A pure Vaishnava saint always washes his hands after he eats or even drinks. Vaishnavas always need a lot of water for their use. Then every time a Vaishnava goes to the urinal or latrine, he would wash himself up, be it the night of a winter or the summer. Baba had to go to a long distance for all this, away from his cottage, in the dark of the night, deep into forests where snakes abounded. But that never bothered him.

A cobra lived under his bed for many years. I saw it crawling out of his cottage once.

When I met Baba in 1978, he had been poisoned for the third time already. It made no difference to him except that he had to urinate more frequently than before.

To an English lady I had given a prediction in 1987 that she would marry someone from out of her country. She, who had visited many countries of the world, had described India as a country with so much peace within so much chaos. She was right. There are families in India which live chaotically and still enjoy peace and love. The reasons for this are:

(a) The relationships of love and affection are preserved, by and large, in so many families through mutual sacrifices and emotional warmth.

(b) Puritanical morality has often been the source of double standards. Yet, it is the social preservative that keeps intact the age old value system, which has broken down completely in the west.

For an Indian to accept the western social values and its psychological explanations for 'abuses', a favourite ploy in the hands of psychiatrists, is to forget the vastly superior cultural and spiritual heritage India has.

I have seen hundreds of families accepting puritanical morality and leading emotionally unshattered lives. Conflicts, phobias and mental depressions are more common among men and women, who mistook unfettered sexual freedom for happiness, instant happiness.

Yet, it must be remembered that there was never a final path to peace within human heart except when the householder decided to become a '*tortoise*'. When he decided that enough was enough and there was to be no more, a life of regrets, half-regrets or self-pitying. It has been possible in the lives of those, who led their early years in a family, which believed in spiritual values, met some great yogi, which is easy in Indian life. Later, even as householders if they suffered, they knew they had a spiritual guide to help them, not materially but through enlightened guidance, and not through the mumbo-jumbo of psychology.

Nagaridas Baba, like my Guruji and like all other great yogis of India, did all this, some of them did it openly while Nagaridas baba did it without your ever knowing anything about it. He lived in a small thatched cottage near the banyan tree where we met him. A sooty lantern inside the cottage lit it with a faint glow. There till late in the night, when I sat with him in the initial years of my meeting him, he provided that spiritual solace which I needed. Many times I went into *samadhi*. Once I saw the entire cottage vanishing. There was nothing, no Baba, no friend around, no cottage except blue light resembling the sheen of the peacock feather, which crowns the head of Lord Krishna. Like me how many benefitted from Baba, in their own ways cannot be narrated, unless they like to reveal their experiences themselves.

In the early years, when I went to Baba all alone from Delhi to Vrindavan without telling anyone where I was going, people coming to me for astrological guidance on Sundays, were disappointed. Some of them found out where I was going, why and to meet whom. Others too joined me, Manoranjanji first, then my younger brothers K. Vikram Rao and K. Subhas Rao and their wives Sudha, wife of Vikram, and Vijaylakshmi, the wife of Subhas and their children. Then Satya Prakash Yadav and his wife Asha Yadav and their children, Smriti and Prashant. Most frequent to join me was Dr. R. K. Caroli. *The greater the crowd from Delhi that went with me from Delhi, the lesser became Baba's talks about subtle spiritual experiences.* But each one of them benefitted from Baba's company. If all that long string of events were to be narrated by each of us it would become a volume of over one thousand pages. Baba guided each according to his background. In India alone exists such a thing as the *double walk of a house holder,* one leg on the *Pravritti Marg,* the path of worldly duties and the other on the *Nivritti Marg,* or the path to salvation.

I have seen Baba do exactly what my Guruji did. Like my Guruji, Nagaridas Baba quickened my inner experiences with one remarkable difference. There were no tensions of a mismanaged ashram under my charge, no problem of petty minded *Guru-bhais* unable to drown their egos in the pursuit of spiritual ideals. Life in the ashram was like sitting in an air-conditioned room, with the terrible heat of summer outside. But I had to come out of the cosy room into the heat and dust of atmosphere oftener, than was good for me. It often shocked me and shattered me. My Guruji took me through the fires of life in his ashram. Nagaridas Baba provided the balm of the lyricism of spiritual bliss. Both experiences showed me the two unavoidable sides of human life.

Sometimes there was a sense of revolt against my Guruji in me and one day, when I was alone with Baba, he must have picked up my thoughts and said, *"A disciple can turn his bitterness of his experiences with the ashrams and Guru-bhais against his Guru also. Your Guru has given you a powerful mantra. Your duty is to do it and not think of what all happened in the ashram."*

And in softest tones he would say, *"Respect for the Guru is the essence of sadhana."* When I thought that my spiritual life was getting shattered, Nagaridas Baba restored me back to my original state. I went into *samadhi* in his cottage one night, when all alone. Later, it happened many times between 1978 and 1980. He restored my faith in my *Guru Mantra* and repeated that ashrams did not fulfil the wishes of the Guru.

The Yogi works through the psychic-spiritual power he generates from within. Outwardly, he is like any other human being. This has been my experience with all the great yogis I have met. How do they work in the case of householders, with their double walk, has to be experienced to be believed. *They solve no domestic problem or encourage material greed. They transform persons from within. This and this alone is India's undying spiritual heritage.*

The Case of PM

Let me call them the PM couple of Vrindavan, whom I often saw sitting near Baba, when I reached there on Saturdays or Sundays. Quite well behaved and devoted, I never knew what they discussed with Baba. Brought up in Vrindavan, they were pure traditionalists. All traditionalists have the usual traditional domestic problems which reaches its unhappy climax when the mother-in-law and daughter-in-law clashes take place. One day Baba told me that while all other children of the PM couple were outside Vrindavan, one son with his wife was with them. In this case, it was the reverse of the traditional clash in which the daughter-in-law dominated. The old couple were tortured. Often, the PM couple were not even given food to eat. But they had been coming to Baba for years and had been guided in their spiritual life with rarest affection. Often, I stood at a distance when I thought that Baba was giving them some personal instructions.

During my subsequent visits, I found the couple very cheerful always. Once or twice they talked to me. I asked Baba whether there had been any improvement in the behaviour of their daughter-in-law.

"No," said Baba. She had become more devilish. Yet the face of the PM couple glowed with radiance. They had changed their food habits completely. No rice, no wheat. Only some boiled vegetables was what they ate and their entire time was spent in *sadhana.*

A year or two after that, Mr. PM had sat on his *aasan* meditated in his puja room and remembering Goddess Radha, whose worship is described as the highest form of worship, died.

I was very unhappy. Will Mrs. PM be left alone suffering torture at the hands of her daughter-in-law in her old age, I wondered.

"She has a very small spell of suffering", said Baba to me.

In my next visit, a week later, I learnt that Mrs. PM also had sat in her puja room on her *aasan* and meditating on Goddess Radha, died.

I had seen the radiant faces of the PM couple reflecting their inner cheer. Their outer conflicts had remained unresolved. The daughter-in-law had become more devilish. Baba had told them that when *God bestows grace, He cuts asunder the last bondage of Maya.*

They knew the value of Baba's instruction – the living moment of today devoted to God, with no worldly distractions, was all that they should do and prepare for their departure.

They were transformed. The radiance of their faces haunts me till today.

ಋಞ

We, a group of persons from Delhi, Dr. R. K. Caroli, Satya Prakash Yadav and his wife Asha Yadav, the younger brother of Satya Prakash, Anand Prakash Yadav and the children of Asha Yadav, Smriti and Prashant were regular visitors, at least a month. The cavalcade of the cars that was lined up in the small lane behind the place, where Baba stayed had aroused the jealousy of some neighbouring ashrams, where one of the chiefs even sent a message, that part of the crowd should visit him also!

My youngest brother, Subhas and his wife Vijaylakshmi and their children, Gautam and Gaurav, too visited but having to attend on my sick mother their visits were less frequent.

A living yogi of Vrindavan, now associated with Vraj Academy, Sripaad Baba, has been a very good influence on me. He did say once that we were going to the best of the yogis in Vrindavan. Once he took me to Barsana, the place associated with Goddess Radha and gave me *Radha Kripa Kataksha stotra* and asked me to recite it in the temple. It was a great day because it was Radhaashtami also. After that I brought it to Delhi and introduced it among my friends, composing a tune as I do, for my own worship, though I am not trained in music. The tune became very popular and the young children of Subhas remembered it by heart. Once, when they went to Vrindavan and were with the Baba they recited it in their own way, with all that purity that comes bubbling out of the hearts of children. Baba was in ecstasies. He called them closer, asked my brother and his wife to move away, and initiated them. Later, when I went to Vrindavan I asked Baba why had he chosen my nephews for initiation. His answer was very cryptic, "If children are initiated early they get so much time to do *japam* that they blossom out well spiritually."

As I have said, Baba rarely initiated people and if he did, he never maintained *Guru-shishya* tradition, which more often than not becomes an irksome dictatorship of the Guru.

Madan Gopal Arora and his elder brother had an exhilarating experience. Their father was ill in Mathura, only five miles away from Vrindavan. They requested Baba to see him. Baba went with them on a scooter! Later Madan Gopal and his brother experienced ecstasies in long spells. Baba had aroused their *kundalini* through his touch or will power.

Asha Yadav and all of us were sitting with Baba sometime in 1987, which was a drought year. Swami Akhandanandji, one of the greatest living scholar-saints of his time, took his *samadhi* that year. His body encased in fine silver basket with gold studdings, was immersed in the river Yamuna. But soon, the urchins jumped into the river and collected all the silver and the gold. Baba told the villagers who used to come to him, "Don't worry about me. When I leave my body there will be so much water in the Yamuna that in one mighty current my body will disappear in the water. You will not even have to raise any money to have a *bhandara* (the_feeding of saints)."

Some days later, Baba gave to Asha Yadav his lovely idol of Krishna and asked her to keep it in her home temple and worship properly. It was in 1987. Why had Baba done that?

In July 1988, when we received the message from Vrindavan that Baba had taken *samadhi,* we rushed to Vrindavan. Baba's body was taken round Vi.ndavan by the crowds that had come wailing. Never before, they told us, had such a crowd ever collected in Vrindavan.

The Yamuna was in floods, 1988 being the year of torrential rains. When Baba's body was put in the water, in one mighty current the river took his body away beyond our sight.

Back to the place where the Baba stayed, people collected his belongings, a broken tin box in which there were currency notes, which Baba never spent. He threw them into that box when someone left some money, inspite of the Baba protesting. The money was fourteen thousand or more which met the expenditure on his *bhandara.*

We sat in Delhi often and recollected those great moments.

1. He had said that there would be so much water in the Yamuna that there would be no problem in immersing his body. He took his *samadhi* in July 1988, when the river Yamuna was in floods.

2. He had said that no money would be required to be raised for his *bhandara.* All the money that was needed was there in the tin box in his cottage.

3. He had given to Asha Yadav his idol of Krishna few months before his *samadhi.* Was that an indication of his inviting his end which he had foreseen?

4. He had forbidden a friend, who had decided to marry a second time and was very categorical in saying that his first wife was a spiritual woman. The friend nevertheless married, and soon his business was ruined. He is Manoranjan, who died in June, 1996.

5. He had told Dr. Caroli, when the then vindictive prime minister of

India, the late Indira Gandhi, had forced him to retire from government service prematurely and when he thought, that he would be required to vacate his spacious big house too, "How can she snatch away everything." That was in 1981 and even now in 1995, Dr. Caroli lives there.

6. But he refused to perform miracles. They *happened*. We who sat near him knew that we would never meet another yogi who made no demands on anyone, at all and gave to us all rich inner experience and bliss.

7. "You have not to ask for it. The moment you come near, you get my blessings for pure devotion to God," he said once, when one of us asked him to bless us that our devotion to God should be pure.

8. "There is no such thing as any auspicious moment for spiritual activity", he said once, when we were discussing astrology.

9. Some astrologer had told him in 1987 that Saturn was on his Moon in Scorpio. Later, when I asked Baba he said, "Planets must perform their functions." Next year, he took his *samadhi*.

10. In 1985, when I was transferred to Orissa, a Goswami of Vrindavan was sitting with him. Suddenly, Baba asked people there to clean up the place and spread mattresses. Why all that, they wanted to know. "*People from Delhi would come and do their wailing,*" said the Baba. Soon, Dr. Caroli, the Yadavs and others were there and told Baba that they were missing me. "These are the laws of nature, meeting and parting. He will be with you again."
Ten months later, I was transferred back to Delhi!

A question one must ask after one has crossed the age of forty five and has enough experience of life is, if there is even in the life of a saint a point of sublime spiritual climax. Has he transended *Maya*? It is a rigid test, a very painful test because then you begin to search in the life even of a truly great yogi, traces of *Maya* which cling to him, become visible in the surroundings he lives in.

A Guru, who builds up an ashram invites *Maya*. An author, a philanthropist, a publicity hungry man and such Gurus often seem to be no different. Nagaridas Baba, Moorkhanandji, Tapasi Baba, Shafi Baba and hundreds of great yogis I have seen in the country transcended Maya. What have been their struggles is the story they reveal sometimes because the modern mind cannot understand those intricacies of *sadhana* as well as say an illiterate man of Vrindavan, or of other great Hindu pilgrimages who have watched yogis after yogis,

165

for generations.

The company of these greatest human beings removes many of those cobwebs from the mind of the sadhak. Briefly, let me recollect some of them.

1. It is not uncommon in India particularly in Punjab, Haryana, Delhi, Himachal Pradesh, Uttar Pradesh, Madhya Pradesh and many other parts, to hear people that have fallen victims to someone's destructive spiritual power. Baba said once that he was maintaining strict rules of *tapasya* (spiritual practice), when someone claiming to have such powers created panic in Vrindavan. The fear and agony of people had increased. Someone succeeded in taking Baba to that evil person who threatened Baba with dire consequences. "I sat down on *siddhasana* and asked him to do what worst he could," said Baba. That man tried everything known to him, got frightened and ran away from Vrindavan.

   "But remember *tapasya* increases anger when, if you curse, the man on whom such curse falls suffers, but you are the loser because you have wasted your spiritual energy."

   In September 1981, I did a severe twenty days *tapasya* at my house, after taking leave from the office. Few days later, when I went to meet Baba he told me straight, "Such severe *tapasya* in the atmosphere of the city, where one had to interact with many evil persons creates, more irritations. Those, who live in cities should do it all harmoniously and regularly but, never rigorously."

2. It was amazingly true in my case. I had become highly irritable for the next six months though my spiritual experiences were many.

3. "Those who lead honestly spiritual life will find planets becoming *anukul* (favourable) not *pratikul* (unfavourable)," he said often when people talking of propitiation or *shanti* of planets on the advice of astrologers.

4. Once, a pig was surrounded by many dogs who barked in a chorus. That is how dogs kill a pig we learnt. It was becoming a distraction, Baba shouted at the dogs who, left that place at once. The anger of a *sattwick person* strikes terror, was the explanation of Baba.

5. A rich man of Delhi left a mad dog in Vrindavan. The dog came and sat near Baba and became a vigilant watch dog literally. No one dare enter the *kuti* of the Baba at night and remove anything. Vrindavan, like many Hindu pilgrimages has many thieves and dacoits whom the policemen cannot easily detect and catch.

These thieves would commit theft anywhere. Baba had nothing except one or two untensils. When once, a thief tried to enter his *kuti* he was hounded away by the dog.

In the famous Tripura Congress, Subhas Chandra Bose had won in spite of Mahatma Gandhi's opposition. Gandhi was partisan and not a mahatma at all, said Baba often.

How many such incidents and my friends I can recount. But we never went to the Baba for that. What we saw was mayaless divinity in its pristine form.

In July 1988 when Baba took his *samadhi*, I felt that it was the most agonizing moment of my life.

Recollecting those Blissful Preachings

What were the lessons I learnt? I cannot answer except quoting something divine. Baba quoted from scriptures and explained them, in the day to day context of the lives we lead.

1. The person, who grieves for the dead can neither die nor join the dead. When such is the natural condition of the world, why grieve at all? The Lord of Time drags everyone to such an end. TIME has no favourites nor does He hate anyone.

2. We have been born a thousand times and have experienced the love of thousands of parents, women and children. But to whom do they belong now and to which of them we belong?

3. Worry springs from thousands of places. Fear too have hundreds of reasons. They influence the dull-witted, not the wise one.

4. Man should overcome his mental worries through his own intelligence and physical ailments through medicines – this is the power of science. How can man do it ?

The answer given by Vidura is:

A wise person should practise only what frees him from the duality of happiness and unhappiness. (Dharmaadharma Parityajya Tvameva Bhajato Nisham), *even the distinction between* Dharma *and* Adharma *is duality which must be given up and time spent in God contemplation*
— *Adhyatma Ramayana, p.90*

5. ...what difference can you see in terms of greatness, fame or achievements when you see dead bodies all of which look alike? The body is compared to a house, which gets destroyed. What is immortal is the soul... Man lives and does not live in this world according to the *karmas* of his past life. When such is the natural condition of the world, why worry?

6. The wise, who becomes sattwick, wishes well of others,

167

understands the arrival and departure of mortals as being regulated by the laws of *Karma*, attains to the state of liberation.

— *The Mahabharata*

7. No one is the cause of any other person's happiness or unhappiness. It is the *karmas* of a man's past life that are its causes. There is no one else that gives happiness or unhappiness. To say so is ignorance. The very thought "I do it" is ignorance. Everyone is in the bondage of his own *karmas*. It is man himself, who through his different types of behaviour creates friends, enemies, indifferent and envious persons. Therefore, man should remain blissful in all conditions whether he is in a happy condition or an unhappy one, accepting it all as his prarabdha. As far as I am concerned I have neither the desire to have worldly enjoyments and the desire to give them up. Whether these enjoyments come into my life or not, I will not be in the grip of these. In whatever place and at whatever time auspicious or inauspicious deed has been done that has to be suffered inevitably. So when auspicious or inauspicious results spring up one should neither be elated nor lament over them because no one can violate the laws of God. Man is always surrounded by happiness and unhappiness because human birth is the result of the mixture of sins and holy deeds. Happiness follows unhappiness and unhappiness follows happiness. Inside happiness there is unhappiness and inside unhappiness there is happiness. These two are intermingled like water and mud. Therefore, the wise never get elated or depressed when their desires are fulfilled and when they are not, saying "all this is *Maya*".

...13...
Ranga Avadhoot

My guruji had told me that wherever I would go I would have the extraordinary luck of meeting real great Yogis. That is the only part of my life in which I must say that I have been luckier than most of the other *sadhakas* I have met in my life.

In the last quarter of 1967, I had gone to that extraordinary hilly pilgrimage in Gujarat, known as Girnar, and had spent two nights on the hill top in the ashram of a great Yogi. There most venomous snakes crawled in friendliest of moods. That ashram is known as Kamandulu Kund, where the Yogi never allowed anyone to stay overnight. But he gave me and my companion permission to stay, and even spend some hours on the seventh peak known as the Datta Paduka, the sandals of Lord Dattatreya.

Lord Dattatreya is worshipped only in some parts of the country, particularly in Gujarat, Maharastra and Karnataka.

Since the days of my Nagpur posting (1963) I had got into the Dattatreya worship. I had heard of a great saint, Shri Vasudevananda Saraswati, whose instructions to his disciples were almost like those of my own Guruji: pure food, without onion or garlic, and not to eat food before making offerings to God. So much spiritual purity as my Guruji had insisted on was totally impracticable for many persons including me. I had stopped going to all parties, though a high ranking officer of the central government, and was an unpopular man till I retired, in 1990.

Right in the office, where I was number two man, there was one Joshi who was a Dattatreya worshipper. His father was a real fine saint, with his Yogic powers well-concealed.

My next posting to Bombay (1966) took me deeper into Dattatreya worship. Near Matunga where I lived, there is a beautiful temple of Lord Dattatreya which I visited almost every evening in Dadar.

At the earliest opportunity I visited the place of Lord Dattatreya at the Girnar, in Gujarat, the seventh and the last peak. I have seen many persons, who used the *yantras* of Lord Dattatreya and had attained supernormal powers.

I was passing through the sub-period of Rahu, which is always an excellent period for meeting saints, Yogis and going to pilgrimages as given in *Bhavartha Ratnakara* of Ramanujacharya, a great astrologer. I found it correct in almost all cases of *sadhakas.*

On my way back, our train halted at an unknown destination in what looked like a village and very surprisingly two women, younger to me in age, accompanied by a young man entered our compartment smilingly.

From their reaction it was clear that they knew that the train would stop at the unscheduled station and they would be able to get into the train. Very pleasant they were, and as it happens in India, we meet friends in a railway journey, as though, we had known each other for many incarnations, and then we forget each other. It was not so in this case. I came to know them, the Sarpotdars.

"Somewhere here is the ashram of a great saint, Ranga Avadhoot. Do you know anything about it?" I asked them.

They looked at me, surprised, and smiling, said that they were coming from his ashram which was at Nareshwar.

When and how I could meet him, was my next question.

They gave me their Bandra address in Bombay and asked me to visit them, which I did for the rest of my stay in Bombay. They told me that their father was staying in the Nareshwar Ashram of Ranga Avadhoot and that they could arrange my stay and meeting easily but told me that the Avadhoot hardly gave two or three minutes to persons as he avoided human vibrations as much as he could.

The trip was arranged and I reached Nareshwar where I spent perhaps two days.

After my bath, I was taken straight to the Avadhoot who, looking at me, told the inmates of the ashram that I could go to meet him whenever I wanted to, and that no restriction of the ashram should be placed on me.

Flattered, I had asked the Avadhoot, whether that decision of his would not create jealousy in the hearts of many multi-millionaires whom he gave less than a minute only.

"Do we Yogis not know who is coming to us with what motive?" he answered.

I had a long conversation, which I recorded in the shape of a letter, on the insistence of the Sarpotdars.

Handsome, till then the handsomest saint I had seen, though later Tapasi Baba of Dwarka took number one position. But I do not go to meet Yogis for their physical beauty.

Ranga Avadhoot was the best conversationalist among the Yogis I have met, with fine command over English, Hindi, Sanskrit, Gujarati and Marathi. If he had visited USA, he would have created the largest-ever following.

Later, when he wanted to visit Naimisharanya, near Lucknow, and Bithur, near Kanpur, I arranged it. He stayed in our house in Lucknow and blessed my mother, about whom he had said that she was a saintly woman, spiritually advancing very fast.

I had met him last in Bombay where he came and a two mile long queue of cars had been parked outside the house of a billionaire in whose house he was staying. I had gone to meet him with my younger brother, K. Vikram Rao. Seeing me in the crowd, one of his disciples who recognised me, told the Avdhoot about me and I was allowed to enter that house through back door, sit near him as long as I liked.

Again favouritism, I thought. Reading my thoughts he said that others were coming with pure selfish motives, not with any spiritual urge. And someday I would write about Yogis, I had met. Ranga Avadhoot would find a place in my portrait gallery of Yogis he said, with all that dignity and solemnity, which was always winningly impressive.

It was not surprising that I found in my old papers that circular letter to some of those friends of mine, who wanted to know my impressions about Ranga Avadhoot. All other old papers including twenty thousand horoscopes, with events noted, have been destroyed as a result of irrational policy of postings and transfers of the Indian Audit Department in which I served for thirty-three years.

"I am going to Africa on the insistence of some of my disciples. I will come back from there and soon after, I want to leave my body," he had said. It stabbed me, that sentence, uttered so casually had all that sharp piercing quality which the words of Yogis have.

At the end of 1967 I was transferred to Calcutta where I received no mail because of the communist movement which aimed at a revolution by destroying letters addressed to so many.

In my next posting to Rajkot, which was very near the Nareshwar ashram of the Avadhoot, I asked someone about him and was told that he had taken *samadhi* in Rishikesh in 1969, few months after I reached Rajkot.

I wrote to the Sarpotdars and almost blamed them for not

informing me about it. They wrote back telling me that they had written to me a long letter while I was in Calcutta and got no reply from me.

Back from his African tour, the Avadhoot went to Rishikesh and there told a disciple to wait outside his room where he sat down on his *padmasana* and gave up his body, as only Yogis can do.

Ten years later, the great Yogi Devaraha Baba gave up his body in a similar way and it was witnessed by many of his disciples.

The circular, with notes given after it, will show what the Avadhoot had to say about spiritual matters. He had blessed a tree in his ashram to have curative powers. Ailing persons sat under it and reported lot of relief.

The desire to visit the Nareshwar ashram vanished from my heart when I heard that court cases were going on for the possession of the ashram.

☸☸☸

My dear Joshiji,

This morning I returned from Nareshwara where Shri Ranga Avadhoot has his ashram. I spent nearly eight hours hearing his stimulating talk on many subjects on which I put questions and in that sense I was the luckiest of nearly two thousand visitors that visited the Ashram during those days, Saturday and Sunday. I owe this extraordinary piece of good luck to the kindly interest taken in me by the Sarpotdar family about whom I told you once. More about this family I will tell you later. Avdhootji once encouraged me to continue with my questions as he said he was pleased by my desire to know but you will well appreciate that my meeting a spiritually enlightened person is dictated by reasons other than mere questionings as I am in more placid waters now than ever before. Yet in the smooth gentle way those hours were spent with him glided, as if it was a communion in which words were of least significance. But the bondage of words being terrible and being too much with us, it is through them only, that I can convey to you something of a fragment of my rapture.

Avdhootji lives in Nareshwara, which was a jungle of cactus before he chose the spot for his Ashram. A cobra, befriended by two peacocks was seen frolicking under a tree by him, and he instantaneously realised that only a Tapo-Bhoomi could have removed the sting and blood-thirst of inborn hostility of those creatures. A Shiva-temple nearby, desolate and concealed in the overgrowing foliage of the dense forest confirmed his impression. To cut the long story short he decided upon establishing his Ashram there. Even today without that Ashram, Nareshwara will be no more than an unrecognizably obscure spot in the *Padma Purana*. Nareshwara's re-emergence into our history is of significance, its great spiritual effulgence apart, in the most mundane historical fashion as well. In that sense Nareshwara is a vindication of the historicity of Puranic narratives. My heart leapt with joy when I came to know of it.

I can go on indefinitely recollecting and writing but let me be brief. A little disorder that the letter is bound to contain can well be sorted out later. So with my eyes on the wall-clock and fingers on the typewriter let me set off, luckily next two hours are work-free, like a long distance runner.

ಬಿಂಚಿಬಿಂಚ

At 69, Avadhootji is handsome enough with his black goggles on to make many a woman miss more than a heart beat. With his goggles off his personality is bewitching, his gentle compassionate eyes speaking of fathomless depths within. The black goggles he wears is to avoid the glare of sunlight ever since some overenthusiastic photographer flashed a bulb one night some years ago on his eyes causing some damage to the retina of hiseyes. His skin glows like the mellowing leaves of a scorching summer – the golden sheen and the gentle curl and all that. He speaks softly in musical undertones with no drawl, no affectation no conscious artistry of some of the westernised Indians. There is the essence of wisdom distilled into those words forming themselves into orderly sentences, euphonious — no harsh expression but a mild raillery served his purpose when such purpose had to be served. I was throughout conscious of being in the presence of a superb conversationalist who spoke with consummate ease in Hindi and English (which I understood) and Marathi and Gujarati with others who interrupted our conversation sometimes, but only sometimes.

ಬಿಂಚಿಬಿಂಚ

Avdhootji greeted me with a question: How I came to know of him. Joshiji of Nagpur, I said and before I could even proceed to describe I saw an affectionate smile play on his lips and his face was beaming with joy. And then I told how I came to know the Sarpotdar family and how through them I seized this chance of meeting him in his Ashram.

I asked him why no literature was available on Lord Dattatreya in Hindi and why the worship of Dattatreya remained confined to Maharashtra and Gujarat only. And what was the significance of this worship. The pamphlet on *Datta-Upasana*.

Let me give very briefly what he said on *Datta-Upasana* as I propose getting his pamphlet translated into English to do better justice to the subject. So please be ready with your study of *Datta-Purana,* etc. I have many questions for you and not being a Nagpurman I will give you very little time to answer my questions.

కుసకుస

In the beginning there was only "OM" (A U M). All men worshipped without any conflict. But modes of worship multiplied as men multiplied. Then arose the conflict between *your* God and *my* God. The Unannihilable Unity of God seemed, in our illusory world, disintegrating. The Puranic legend has it as the triple manifestation of the Lord in the forms of Brahma, Vishnu and Mahesh. A farmer preparing to till the land is Brahma, the farmer protecting the growing crop is Vishnu (armed as defenders should be armed with Sudarshana Chakra, etc.) and the farmer harvesting the crop is Mahesh whose acts of destruction are divinely creative. All the three manifestations fuse into one unity in Dattatreya as the *Puranic* story goes. Even otherwise the emphasis on the unity of Godhood becomes apparent in the *Datta-Upasana*.

DATTA consists of two letters, both dentals, pronounced alike— even the name symbolises the *Advaita* element. And *Datta Upasana* is symbolic of re-reaching the universal truth of the oneness of good human tradition of man as contrasted with the multiplicity of gods and modes of worship.

Krishna of Lord Chaitanya and Meera, Rama of Tulsidas wafted into the hearts of millions of their readers in this country as the ecstacies of those great devotees. In Maharashtra Narasimha Saraswati, Vasudevananda Saraswati, Akkalkot Swami and scores of others sang of Lord Dattatreya in similar style. This did not happen in other states. That accounts for the popularity of Datta Upasana in Maharastra. In Gujarat it is becoming popular only now. Though Girnar and Guru Shikhar in Mt. Abu are there, Gujaratis have not had the benefit of much literature on Dattatreya. Now that gap is being filled gradually.

Ranga Avadhoot in his sadhak days

His heart pines for the solitude of the hills, the celebrated Himalaya which has been our Tapobhoomi through millennia. To reach there and never to come back was an ambition worth cherishing and he cherished with all the intensity of a *sadhak* for a life of Himalayan quietude and beauty. His prerigrinations took him in those years to the great saint of that era – Dadaji Dhoonivale

Dadaji's name evokes tender emotions in Avdhootji. No other saint he has seen in his life had such an *Unmatta* state. Crowds pursued Dadaji wherever he went and the police and rulers drove him out – it was a story of unending migrations till the end of his days. The young Ranga went and stayed with him for a few days. A Sardarji, retired from the army, used to come to him and became a very good friend of Ranga. The Sardarji was hefty, strong, hardy and devoted to Dadaji. But once he was in a great dilemma ... he had lost all money and had only five hundred rupees left with him ... and with a huge family to support, he came to Dadaji to beg for mercy. Dadaji asked him to stay for thirty days, later asked him to stay for twenty eight days and then asked him to stay for eight days. What was he to do? He explained his difficulty to Ranga who advised him to pray in his heart quietly and not argue. There was no such thing as contradiction in these differing instructions, only a test. On the day on which the Sardarji was to depart, he kneeled down before Dadaji and Dadaji took his hefty baton and mercilessly smote the Sardarji on his outstretched palms. Sardarji bore it with equanimity, and that was the end of the miseries of Sardarji. This was quite characteristic of Dadaji ... he smote, abused and drove people away from him and yet they collected round him in thousands.

Dadaji advised Ranga to give up the idea of going to the Himalayas as he was destined to work around the Narmada only – a field carved out for him.

Later, Ranga came to Omkareshwara where he wanted to do an Anushthan for eight months in the presence of a Mahatma who also advised him to work near and around the Narmada. And the Mahatma took Samadhi earlier than Ranga expected.

His wanderings took Ranga to Nagpur where the great aulias, Taj-ud-din Baba was his chief attraction. Like all aulias, Taj Baba abused and smote people but people collected round him exactly in the same manner as he had seen people crowding round Dadaji earlier. Taj Baba respected Brahmins very deeply. And he always addressed Brahmins as *Pandats*. Taj Baba, called Ranga, *Are O Pandot Idhar Aa* and allowed him to sit by his side for good many hours. Remarkable was the affection shown by Taj Baba for the young Ranga.

The Narmada

Ranga then went round the Narmada, the religious circum-ambulation (*parikrama*) to be done for the spiritual efficacy it gives.

The Narmada is the most unique of the sacred rivers. I asked him why Yudhishthira was told that a mere sight of the Narmada confers spiritual boons on devotees while a dip in Ganga and three dips in the Saryu become necessary. The Rishis, he said, had the foresight to see that the Ganga would begin to decline spiritually, five thousand years after the onset of the Kaliyuga. The Narmada would remain unpolluted all through ... both at the source and at its termination there are Shiva temples and she skirts round the sacred forests and temples in this part of the country.

Narmada Maa is very kind and some lucky men even get a *darshan* of her. There was for example a fat huge Gujarati, so fat that one could not have reconciled to his walking even a few miles. But he undertook a *parikrama* of the Narmada, running out of stamina, tired, fatigued, once he was dying for food. An old lady appeared before him in the thick of a jungle and directed him to a village nearby where she said her four sons resided and who would feed her. The pilgrim went to the village and found that no old woman with four sons ever lived in that village. In making enquiries about the old woman and her four sons, the pilgrim reached a temple where a priest came to his rescue. The priest went to the spot where the pilgrim had met the old woman and after hearing the full description, the priest burst into tears—Narmada had after all blessed the pilgrim with a *darshan* while he having spent whole of his life was not yet lucky to have a *darshan*.

The fat Gujarati pilgrim later went to Ahmedabad and opened a tea stall whose tea became so famous that customers used to come to him in unprecedented numbers. The secret of it was that in each cup of tea he used to mix a spoonful of Narmada water. Narmada Maa did the trick by giving to those cups of tea the unusual flavour they had become famous for.

The Ashrama

It was during the Narmada-*parikrama* that the young Ranga saw the unique friendship between creatures known for their inborn enmity for each other and decided to choose that place for his abode.

(My question about his spiritual experiences and his idea of institutionalising, etc. he forestalled and answered before I even put the question to him)

A small cottage was there. Few days were spent under a tree. Then came a *bhakta,* who had a building erected in the vicinity of the temple. Activities increased, a Trust was founded and strangely they first tried to put a clause in it by saying that the buildings would be placed at the disposal of Avdhootji. That is exactly what was not liked by Avadhootji as that would become morally binding on him to stay there. Not merely has the clause been deleted from the Trust Deed but even his name does not find a mention in it! Strange are the ways of the saints—in his own Ashram Avadhootji is living like a helpless tenant, who has been allowed to live there through the tender mercies of others to retain his rent-free quarters.

Some Personal Questions

I put some questions about his spiritual experiences in Nareshwara after the *parikrama* of the Narmada was completed. He modestly evaded the question–why *Aatma Purana?*

Still, I put some personal questions and he was kind enough to answer them realising that I was not the scoffing type but the worshipping type of questioner.

1. Why do you still wear the sacred thread? You are a Sanyasi.

    He smiled and answered that his mother being alive, he would be required to perform some religious ceremonies still as a son and to perform them he should not put aside the upanayanam. At any rate his upanayanam did not interfere with his Sanyasa.

2. The origin of his 'Avadhoot-hood' was uppermost in my mind but before I could put the question, he read my mind and answered thus.

    "When I came to stay in Nareshwara people around predicted that in less than a week I would run away. Weeks passed, months passed and yet they persisted with their prediction. When I did not leave the place, they started coming to me with their problems and ailments. I tried to drive them away. I even kept a baton with which I started beating them. But as they got beaten, they started getting cured. So now they started to throng to my place to receive beating from me. I had to stop even that—and like that the institution grew round here. Those days I tried to put on a stiff appearance artificially, which becomes necessary to keep the crowds off. So they called me an Avadhoot."

"Getting cured like this is a matter of faith. A woman from Bombay, who is perhaps a school mistress in some school was down with TB. In her acute sufferings when doctors pronounced almost a death-sentence on her she wrote to me. I wrote back to her that she would be all right. She overcame her fatal ailment without medicines."

3. You not merely do not allow people to offer money to you but even fast for the whole day if money falls from the pockets of devotees kneeling before you. Why all this?

"Well the simplest explanation is I do what I have been asked by my Guru to do. Guru's instructions must be carried out unquestioningly.

"And then there is the taint that money carries. When you accept the money of others, you also accept the *samskaras* of others. Your own spirituality declines."

"I fast for the whole day only when the coins falling from the pockets of others touch my body, my feet. Not otherwise."

After hearing the above answer the natural question in my mind was that the Ashram after all represents the accumulation of others' money. Why this then. But before I put, he straight away came to the question himself.

"Unselfish acts progress smoothly. Acts motivated by *Aadesh* remove from such acts the "I" ness inherent in acts. So my passive participation in the Ashram construction etc. will go on unimpeded. The authorship is not mine, even the ownership is not mine. I am free to leave it when I choose. Even my name does not find place in the Trust-deed."

4. Here in this Ashram I find what I have also noticed in pilgrimages and Samadhi, Mandirs in Vrindavan, Puri etc. The trees bend down gracefully from all their sides making a shady bower as though in a spirit of humility. Is my observation correct?

"Yes. In a place of worship where deep and intense faith reigns this happens. The neem tree you speak of which does not have bitter leaves, the tree which gets arched on all sides is not the only one of its type here. Watch the tree we happen to be sitting under, for instance. It was erect a few months ago. It happens. Where there is *tapa*, it happens."

5. My younger brother is a journalist and writes well. I wish he begins to write about all such spiritual phenomena and about you. Will you bless him?

(Avadhootji raised his hands in a gentle blessing posture.) I heard about someone coming to meet you but not finding enough inspiration in his heart, has not written about you though he took all the material from here for a write-up. I realise that without an inspiration one should not even entertain the wish to write on such subjects.

"Yes, some people have written about me and some people want to write about me. Once a journalist came to me asked me to tell him something so that he could write about me. I told him that I was leading an uneventful life in a place in the depth of a jungle and could not be interesting enough for him for a newspaper write-up.

(Here I interrupted him and spoke about the brief justification George Bernard Shaw gave for his "sixteen self-sketches". A journalist in his senses should find a saint most remarkable for his story. But because of the Northcliffian definition of news journalists they could not help their adoption of a perverse definition of news.)

"Yes. But some Sanskrit scholars have written about me. Sanskrit scholars are usually age-drunk individuals. Still they have written about me as Sanskrit scholars do not do usually. Then someone mentioned me in thesis on the influence of Gujarati saints on Hindi literature and quoted some of my songs. Research scholars often come to me for guidance and a student in his thesis on the *Origin and Development of Datta Upasana* has also mentioned me."

"But mostly they write about such subjects with good deal of ignorance. In the Marathi newspaper someone wrote about one full-column, all of which was unintelligible stuff."

6. Has not the time for Ashok's (the yongest of the Sarpotdars) initiation come yet. I told him that *deeksha* would do him immense good.

"Well he is my man. I have known him long before his birth. The fates of so many (*prarabdha*) are tied up with me. Ashok is a pseudo-communist (he laughed). He is not confident. It is all right. Things take shape.

7. In telling me about your experience during your Narmada *parikrama* you told me about some very hospitable jungle folk, even dacoits feeding you. I hear that in Naimisharanya also there are such people. (Where exactly is the place? he asked me). Naimisharanya is few miles away from Lucknow on the Lucknow-Sitapur railway line, the railway station Nimishar is Naimisharanya.

A good friend of mine, who stays right from where the Parikrama starts likes to play the host to saints. If you bless me, I may succeed in making some arrangements for you. (I do not know if I will move out). Your movement at the moment is uncertain perhaps. Or perhaps you will not leave Gujarat. (No such thing. My mother is here. I will not move as long as she is with me).

Miscellaneous Questions and Answers

1. Lots of works written in non-Sanskrit languages, like Hindi or Marathi are said to have *Mantra-Shakti* in them. Does it mean that power inherent in them is imparted by the person in this case, the saintly composer concerned.

   Yes, it is the power of the saint. Such power can exist in any language. It is not the language but the spiritual power of the composer that is material.

2. In Girnar when I sat near the Datta Paduka I experienced something. But people asked me to sit there at mid-night. What is your explanation?

   Pilgrimages have powerful vibrations. As they get polluted, they get diminished but new pilgrimages grow up. This country is the most fortunate in this respect. Other countries also have some mystics. But outside this country we have very few instances of great spiritual achievements. Neither such high ideals nor such great achievements are witnessed elsewhere. It is the land of saints.

   Dattatreya has for his abode almost inaccessible places. Their purity remains intact. About Girnar a monk wrote a book, which was published by the MacMillan & Co., and the introduction to the book was written by W.B. Yeats who introduced Rabindra Nath Tagore to the western world.

   Our *Rishis* and *Munis* always explored a thing in all the three ways, physical, emotional and spiritual. So what appears as *nirgunatmaka* to one may become *sagunatmaka* to another. There can be exceptions. The same Girnar, which is the place of powerful vibrations for one can be the place of actual sight of Dattatreya for another. In Mahur, the monk had obstinately wanted to see Lord Dattatreya asleep at night. First night he heard the sound of footfalls, second night the sound of someone walking, opening the door, sleeping, rolling on the bed etc. and the third night even the bed-sheets etc. were thrown off the bed as one does after rising up. Nothing is strange. There are exceptions and exceptions.

3. You retire at 11 a.m. in the day and come out after 3 p.m. Similarly at night. What is the purpose?

    In certain hours when peacefulness reigns around introversion is spontaneous.

4. The Peepul, Banyan and Goolar trees are supposed to be very sacred. Why?

    In religion-oriented times everything was given deep religious meaning. All these trees spread coolness and help introversion of energy. And then the blessings of the Lord are there. Medicinally they are extraordinary trees.

5. Some of the *stotras* have some *phala-Sruti*. Is it not encouraging *Sakama Bhakti*? If I do not do the *phala-Sruti*, will it be all right?

    There is nothing wrong in it. Children are induced to do things on the promise of some reward. It is the *Sakama Bhakti* that spread the fame of a saint and thereby helps the cause of devotion in the world. *Sakama Bhakti* is not bad. It is at any rate better than none.

6. In your Ashram you do not allow people to smoke or use tobacco etc. Why?

    Addiction becomes distraction. So I discourage it.

7. Why are you against cards?

    It ruins *ekagrata*.

8. Chess was a compulsory game in Buddhistic monasteries. Why?

    Chess gives *ekagrata*.

9. What is the importance you give to food.

    What is nutritional need not be spiritually good. A French scientist dipped a magnet in the juice of onion. It was demagnetised.

10. During your Narmada-parikrama you took gur-water. Is that enough. Did you continue with that when you were doing *pranayama*?

    Gur-water was all right for *parikrama* but during *pranayama* the appetite is keen. You have to consume more food.

11. In Shahpur Khed, (Kamar Ali Darvesh Dargah) there are those magical stones how do they lift? (He had not heard of them, I had to explain).

    Well the Darvesh may be there invisibly. He lifts it. It will continue so long as he does not fall into some trap.

12. But we tried the same in Kamalja Mata's temple in Bhimashankar. I succeeded there also.

When you believe, two things happen... your own power gets enhanced and the all-powerful God does not let down one, who believes in him.

13. I do not know whether I should ask you about your spiritual enfoldment after you came to Nareshwara?

Why talk, Why not realise! It is not a matter for talk.

14. What is this Jai Manushya here in Narmada. Is it an enemy of crocodiles?

Jai Manushya is a small creature and never lives singly. Wherever it lives, crocodiles leave that place and run away. I do not know if it preys on crocodiles.

ಬಂಞ

Explanatory Notes

Lord Dattatreya

Goddesses asked once, who was the greatest *pativrata* woman on the earth humans inhabited. The answer given was, Sati Anasuya, who like a true *pativrata* woman treated her married life as a sacred and spiritual aim of her life.

Could it be proved, asked the goddesses.

Then the Trinity of Gods, Brahma, the creator, Vishnu, the preserver and Maheshwar, the destroyer, visited the house of Sati Anasuya in the disguise of Brahmins to be her guests. In keeping with the tradition of treating guests as god (*athithi devo bhava*) she asked them to have their bath and have the *prasad*, sacred meals.

The guests laid down a condition that she should serve the meals without any clothes on her body. Her husband, Rishi Atreya told her that with her great spiritual powers, which she had being a *pativrata*, she could transform her guests into small children before whom, if she served meals, she would not feel embarassed.

Days passed by in this manner and finally when the testing Gods decided to return, the goddesses having been satisfied, they were allowed to return to their original form.

Before returning, the Gods asked her to ask for a boon, which she refused. But when Gods persisted, she said that since they had stirred her maternal instinct, they should be born simultaneously as her children.

That is how Lord Dattatreya was born, with one body and three heads.

I have talked about the supernormal powers gained by the Angushtha Shastri in 1978, when he met me last. He had told me that I would meet in Vrindavan a great Yogi resembling Jada Bharat of the Srimada Bhagavatam. I have met many such worshippers, who had such supernormal powers. But Dattatreya worship is even now confined only to some parts of the country.

The worship of Lord Dattatreya emphasises the one and the only God which men, with their differing creeds and religions, forget.

The River Narmada

It is said that worship along the banks of the river Ganga gives *gyana* or divine wisdom; along the banks of the river Yamuna, *bhakti* or true devotion to God; worship along the banks of the river Narmada, gives *mukti* or salvation.

Aatma Purana

He meant auto-biographical, which could sound egotistical.

Sacred Thread

Though corrupted in use, the sacred thread the Hindus are required to wear are constant reminders of the worldly sacred duties they are required to perform. One such sacred duty is to give a religiously sanctioned cremation to one's mother, after her death. The mother is the first guru of a child or *aadi guru.*

Serving one's parents is not merely a sacred duty, but no one can expect to get salvation, if such great filial debt as children owe to their parents remains undischarged.

So long as the mother of Ranga Avadhoot was alive he wore that sacred thread. She was a great Yogi in her own right and fed wild animals with her own hands, which I saw during my stay in the ashram.

Money of Others

Different from the house-holder has to be the renunciate or the *sanyasi,* who must not touch other's money at all.

As it is, he who cheats others of his money, actually cheats himself because along with his money, he has to take a share of the sins of the cheated person.

Aadesh

When a Yogi reaches a high state of development his *Ajna Chakra* between the eyebrows, becomes activated as a result of his *kundalini* power. It is then that he does nothing according to his own outlined plan. He now gets instructions directly from God.

When such *aadesh* is got, a Yogi does as directed. My late Guruji, never wanted to be a guru but he was directed to do it.

Ranga Avadhoot never wanted to build an ashram but he was directed to do it.

I have seen both my Guruji, who left the entire burden to me twice, during my Calcutta postings, and Ranga Avadhoot, their ashrams, as nothing more than a wayside tent.

Ashok

He, being the youngest of the Sarpotdars, was loved by all. He had perhaps some communist ideas then which is why in that family he was the only one then left out and not given any spiritual initiation.

Nirguna or Saguna

The worship can be of a *Form* or the *Formless*, each according to his own beliefs and tendencies.

Sacred Trees

Some trees have more spiritual vibrations. They help in sadhana.

Ekagrata

Yogis have one-pointed concentration without which they could not have developed their supernormal powers. Whatever destroys *ekagrata* is ruinous for spiritual life.

Shahpur Khed

There is between Poona and Satara, in the state of Maharashtra, a place known as Shahpur Khed where there is a *durgah* or the cemetry of a Sufi saint, some of whom were devotees with supernormal power. Here in the Shahpur Khed one can see Hindu temples over which mosques of Muslims were built. Who lived there is not known. Whether a great Yogi of the Nath tradition of great Yogis or a Sufi saint, is not known.

Often, when I was in Bombay, if anyone argued with me why I believed in the supernormal, I took them to this place *where if nine persons put under a heavy round stone only the tips of their index finger and said in a chorus, "Kamar Ali Darvesh", the stone lifted nearly five feet above the ground, miraculously.*

Kamala Mata's Temple

In the great pilgrimage near Poona, there is Bhimashankar a great pilgrimage, a *jyotirlinga,* favourite place of Lord Shiva.

In Bhimashankar, there is another famous temple, known as Kamakshi Temple where too there were some huge round heavy stones outside the temple as we had seen in Shahpur Khed. Some of us, urbanites, tried to lift the stone physically and failed. Some villagers who were watching us, laughed at us. Then we decided to put the tip of our first finger and said in a chorus, "Kamalakshi Mata Ki Jai" and the stone rose, as high.

Faith moves mountains and lifts stones.

...14...
The Religion of Yogis

Religion is a human necessity. It helps man regulate his life. In a negative sense it is a fetter, which a society puts on the individual and collective personality of man.

In a positive sense, religion produces a compassionate human personality.

In the highest sense, it takes him to the level of divinity after which, he ceases to belong to the religion he was born in. His is now a universal religion. That is the religion of a Yogi.

In my childhood in Lucknow, I used to go to Hussainganj to meet a friend of mine after crossing a row of dwellings where washermen lived, all Hindus. There in an open, very small, uncovered and windowless room-like structure lived a very healthy person, as dirty as a human being could possibly be, but his skin and eyes shone with a resplendence which attracted everyone.

Women fed him what little he ate. No one ever saw him sleeping.

No one knew who he was and from where he came. I saw him there for two or three years, always in the same posture. People around, called him 'aulia' or a Muslim saint with unconventional habits.

Then one day, he vanished suddenly. I vaguely remember that someone in the family of a washerman was dying, and he went and saved him.

Thereafter he vanished. Now, I can explain it. He wanted to avoid crowds. Once the miracle performed by a Yogi is known, uncontrollable crowds start flocking around him.

In the relation between the washermen, all Hindus and that Muslim Yogi, there existed no barrier of religion. Hindus have such innate spiritual tradition, the spiritual awareness to respect a Yogi because they know that a Yogi is above all such discriminations. It was in those days when the Hindu-Muslim relations were growing bitter, leading, finally to the partition of India in 1947.

Yet a Muslim Yogi could live in Hindu surroundings and be venerated.

The finest divine songs written in the nineteenth century on Lord Rama and Krishna in Hindi have been collected by the late Viyogi Hari in the collection of bhajans of the Gita Press Gorakhpur publications, which when it was in five parts, was in the fourth part. This part had only Muslim saint-poets' contributions.

I have referred to the fakir of Tukur Bazar of Sylhet, now in Bangladesh, telling my Guruji when he was young not to discuss Krishna's *leelas* with people. Viyogi Hari's collection of those songs by Muslim saint poets show that they had reached that high stage when they could see in the Radha-Krishna devotion, the acme of perfection in *bhakti*.

In Nagpur, at the farthest end of the Kasturchand park leading towards the railway station, there used to sit a fakir with two stones in his hand, rubbing them. He was, or had become blind. When I first visited him one night, he asked me who I was. I said a devotee of God. Later, one day I found people asking him what number of a lottery ticket they should purchase. He disposed them of in his own way.

"What do you want ?" he had asked me, after they had left.

"About God", I had said.

He started weeping and shed tears profusely and said that was what people were not interested in. And then said, "You will have to wait". He then told me, that was in 1965, that I would have to go to Delhi and do many things before I could feel that my *karmas* had been exhausted. It was thirteen years later that I was transferred to Delhi without my trying for it.

One day he told me that an eye doctor had told him that he would give him spectacles, but it would cost him twenty five rupees. Would I give it to him? I gave him the amount and he passed it on to a needy person standing near him.

"What will I do with eye glasses. I am happy without them," he said.

He had no needs. God looked after him.

One day he startled me by asking me, "Do you know who I was in my previous life?"

Without waiting for my answer he said, "I was the emperor of India, Aurangzeb," (the last great Mughal emperor of India, generally portrayed as a fanatic Muslim.)

I enjoyed peace in his presence and I used to stand there for one or two hours every time I passed that way.

Shafi Baba

In Nagpur a very strange experience compelled me to get acquainted with an extraordinary sufi saint. For some days I and a friend of mine had decided to go to a Hanuman temple and do the great *Hanuman Chalisa* recitation for six months every morning. One day while getting down from the hill where the temple was, we decided to get down from the side which we had not seen. It brought us to the main road leading to the city of Wardha. With fine open fields on both sides, we decided to walk a mile or two. A strong fragrant smell suddenly bewitched me, but I continued walking. After going about two hundred yards or so, I told my friend that I wanted to retrace my steps. Surprised, he walked back with me. Reaching the same spot where I had experienced that fragrance, I saw on the right side a police station where a fakir, Muslim saint, sat in green clothes. As I walked towards him, the fragrance increased. It was too intense.

He smiled and said, "Give me a Rupee to go to Taj Baba's place."

I gave him more but he refused to take more than what he had demanded. Later that evening when I had gone to a shop, I saw a photo of a mausoleum and asked the shop keeper what was that. Taj Baba's he said. "Who is Taj Baba?" I asked him.

"A great saint who lived here some decades ago and remember, whosoever goes to his *dargah* (cemetery of holy saints in the Sufi order) experiences great peace," he said.

I came to know from someone who used to visit that place that a disciple of Tajuddin Baba, a great living sufi saint, Shafi Baba lived there.

I went there at the earliest opportunity, taking with me a lot of small currency notes, because of my earlier experiences at many such places.

Then a noble friend whom a rich man's daughter loved, came to me and told me of his troubled conscience. I told him about Shafi Baba and took him there.

One day he went alone and before he could say anything, Shafi Baba said, "You are a Brahmin, she is not. This is not proper."

To hear this from a Muslim saint!

One day I heard that my friend was in the hospital where he was admitted after an accident in a vehicle.

I saw him. He was unconscious. I went to Shafi Baba, who told me not to worry. Within fifteen days, he was all right.

After recovering fully, my friend told me that on the day he was involved in the accident, Shafi Baba was addressing only a bird and saying, "You have been saved by Taj Baba (his Guru) otherwise you were sure to die today."

I often talked about Shafi Baba to a Maharashtrian couple in whose house we used to have *bhajans* regularly.

One day that lady whom I will call Mrs. "N" told me that she liked everything about me except my going to a Muslim fakir. It was not necessary to argue with her except telling her that a Yogi had no religion.

"Will you arrange a jeep for me to go to the place where Taj Baba did his *sadhana*?" the one and only demand Shafi Baba had made on me. I did it, and on our way back, I requested him to visit a place. He said that he generally did not, but if I insisted, he would. I took him to the house of Mr. and Mrs. "N". Seeing a fakir in green clothes, Mrs. N came out of her kitchen and touched his feet understanding at the same time that he must be Shafi Baba about whom she had made what I thought was an uncharitable remark.

The Baba looked at her and said, "Why did you ever not come to me with all that trouble in your stomach? I would have given some water to cure you."

I was surprised as I had not known about this ailment of hers. And a Hindu woman would never talk about it with any male except her husband.

I took her there and she was cured.

When I got my transfer orders to Bombay, Mrs. N had wept.

She had come to see me off and had been told that I would not be able to visit Nagpur, as I was posted to the Western Railway which did not cover Nagpur for my official duties.

I reached Bombay and went to the Western Railway Audit Office where the Chief, Mr. P. Y. Godbole told me that I had been transferred telephonically to the Central Railway, where I met that gentleman Muslim, Manzure Mustafa, a beef eater whom I always described as better than the best Hindu Brahmins in our service.

He had demanded me as his subordinate by name for the work of the bifurcation of the Central Railway.

Back home, I saw a letter from Mrs. N, who had written to me that Shafi Baba had told her that I would visit Nagpur officially on duty. It was amazing. I was transferred from the Western to the Central Railway after I had got into the train.

On a Sunday, I decided to see Kanneri caves after getting down at the Kandivali station. May be very foolishly, I decided to walk all the five or more miles through the park in spite of knowing Bombay to be

Asia's most criminal city. After walking a distance, I saw some tough looking fellows, and I felt that I would be robbed though I had nothing except some currency notes and my wrist watch to lose. Suddenly I saw Shafi Baba next to me. I rubbed my eyes to make sure that he was Shafi Baba but he vanished. Some minutes later he appeared again and vanished again. Soon after, those tough looking fellows moved away, and I got a companion who walked with me, a young and lively Gujarati boy. We walked back from the cave, this time I was fully self-assured.

Some days later, a friend wrote to me from Nagpur that some of the Muslim disciples of Shafi Baba had complained that a "Hindu called Rao" was favoured by him in preference to his own Muslim disciples. But ignoring all that, Shafi Baba said that he needed a pipe for his *hukka,* (a pot filled with water fitted to a tobacco container, and attached to a pipe for smoking, to remove the harmful contents of nicotine), and that he would not accept anyone else's money except mine. I bought one and had it sent to him in Nagpur.

A few days later, I went to Nagpur on an official tour and went to Shafi Baba with my friend.

Seeing me he said, "You could not even recognize me."

I explained to my friend what had happened in Bombay when I was going to the Kanneri caves, and told Baba that I wanted to make sure that what I was seeing was correct as I had done once or twice before when I had seen my Guruji also bi-locating himself.

Such are the siddhis of Yogis, who are neither Hindus nor Muslims.

An Assamese woman disciple of my Guruji had acquired some powers very suddenly and had great experience of Radha Krishna *leelas.* It was later that we realized that it was the power, which Guruji had generated through his *shakti-paat sadhana,* and not her own spiritual earnings.

Kazi Nazrul Islam of East Bengal during the British rule was a Muslim and was identified with Shyama Sangeet, which is all about Goddess Durga and Kali.

Yogis have no religion.

...15...
Caution and Warning

Read this chapter repeatedly before reading "Ecstacies Spring From Fires", which follow this chapter. Sadhana is not meant for fickle minded spiritual practitioners.

I
WEAKNESSES OF GURUS

Uddar Nimitam Bahu Kritah Shokah,
Kasha-yaambara Bahu Krita Vesha

Caution

The above is a quotation from the great Adi Shankaracharya's poem, *Bhaja Govindam*. It means that for the sake of one's stomach (to eke out some livelihood, or food), one may don saffron clothes and pose as a *sanyasi*.

In all ages, including ours, there have been and are many fake *sanyasis* or *yogis*. It is not everyone that dons saffron clothes that becomes a *sanyasi*. In the *Gita*, *sanyas* has been described as *giving up the fruits of actions or material desires* (*Gita* Ch.18, sh.2).

Warning

While there are great and true yogis, there are many, who are not.

After the first edition of this book was sold so fast, I thought that I should add this unpleasant chapter without which I may mislead many Indians and foreigners coming to India in search of *yogis*. Given the luck, they will meet some. That depends on God's grace. Gurudom can and has become a business in many places. An American friend asked me if I wanted to be promoted as a yogi in the USA. His arguments were that being brown-skinned I would succeed as a big hit because I could converse in English, recite Sanskrit *shlokas* and predict also as an astrologer, which no *guru* visiting USA has ever done or does. I told him that one could become a Guru after realizing God, which has not happened to me. Even otherwise, if my own Guru Swami Paramanand Saraswati had told me to become a Guru, I would have had to become one even. I was doubly disqualified to be a *guru*. I do the next best thing. Under the instructions from my Guru, I predict for people and ask them to do Sanskrit *stotras,* which Maharshi Parashara and other great *rishis* have given us. It is the inseparable part of the Hindu tradition and Hindu astrology. It is not a business. Therefore I do not allow anyone to pay me for all this. Those, who have taken spiritual initiation suffer no harm because God will reward them for their sincerity. But the fake guru will have to pay heavily for all this.

Caution

Now you can meet many yogis with supernormal powers, who may be having supernormal powers but *may not have transcended Maya.* It is a hard, cruel and very deceptive situation for everyone of us.

How does Maya manifest in the lives of yogis with supernormal powers?

It can happen in many ways but *three well-known weaknesses* of Yogis are:

A. The Desire to be Builders of Ashrams

There is nothing wrong if *gurus* build small ashrams where they could be available for their devotees. It is when they fall into the temptation to build a big *ashram* or many *ashrams* that they create all trouble for themselves. Such *yogis* have to have rich men as their disciples, as the poor or middle classes cannot donate enough money for such ambitious projects. They expect their disciples to keep raising funds for their projects and do all the managerial work, neglecting *sadhana.* Then, when their end comes, they leave behind themselves a chaotic organization in which there is no spirituality. It must lead to discrimination between the rich and non-rich disciples. Many *gurus* and *yogis* have one small ashram with only one or two male disciples serving them. In recent years, some Indian gurus have started having foreign women disciples running their ashrams in India and even staying alone with them. It is risky, to say the least. Then we have women gurus living with males, who run their ashrams. The warning given in the *Srimad Bhagavatam* is thrown to winds by these gurus.

The story given in the *Valmiki Ramayana* about the curse when one becomes the head of an ashram is worth remembering.

The Curse of becoming the Head of a Muth, Ashram or a Religious Institution

After Lord Rama had become the King of Ayodhya, he ruled with great justice and there was law, order and harmony. One day, his younger brother saw a dog barking outside the palace. When asked, the dog said that it could explain its conduct only before King Rama.

Briefly, what happened after that was: the dog, who was injured, said that he had been hit by a baton by a Brahmin. On being summoned, the Brahmin admitted his guilt but said that he being hungry, was going to beg for alms. The dog, standing in his way, was not allowing him to pass by. So in anger he had hit him.

"What punishment should be given to the Brahmin," asked King Rama. The dog said that the Brahmin should be made the head of a religious institution at Kalanjar. Rama did accordingly. *The courtiers thought that instead of punishment, a boon, a reward had been granted to the Brahmin.*

Lord Rama then told the court that they did not know what *karma* yielded what fruits. This secret was better known to the dog, who was asked to explain why he had suggested such a strange punishment, which appeared to be more like a boon or great gift. *The dog said that he was the head of the Kalanjar Muth (ashram) in his previous life and had followed scrupulously and religiously all conduct of good life, yet, he had to become a dog in his present incarnation.* The Brahmin will now, since he was so full of anger and vindictiveness, a serious flaw in spiritual life, which would not merely ruin himself but will pave the way to hell for seven of his succeeding generations. Therefore:

1. No one should ever accept the position of the head of a Muth.
2. If you want to ruin a person along with his family, make him take charge of children, women, cows and holy persons. He will commit some mistake out of the arrogance of his power and hurt the meek and humble people and incur the wrath of God.
3. He, who steals the money of holy persons and women, or who takes back the money donated, gets ruined along with his loved ones.

The dog was a discriminating thinker on divine subjects in his previous birth. He then went to the holy city of Varanasi where by fasts (remaining without water and food), he thus remained in a divine state in his last days.

The Moral: If you are to serve the helpless and the holy, your responsibilities are so difficult that even slight infraction of the rules of spiritual conduct can bring about untold sufferings.

B. To have a Large Number of Disciples

Maya is so irresistible that many gurus believe in having a very large number of disciples, thousands, tens of thousands or even hundreds of thousands through some chosen disciples, who are given the permission to initiate disciples. It is not a spiritual mission but pure and simple business.

If ordinary human beings develop the desire to accumulate wealth, we call it greed. But when a guru wants to have a large number of disciples, it is either a divine instruction given to him by God or his own guru. It is difficult to know what is the truth. It could be their own grandiose thinking. But it creates many problems. The worst problem it creates is: *the guru has no time to concentrate on the spiritual progresss of a single disciple.* I have seen it happen everywhere. After the death of the guru, disciples fight for supremacy and some of them establish themselves as gurus. Then there is a quarrel among these 'gurus'. The disciples form their own groups around these 'gurus'. Then there are court cases, which drag on for many years. The worst example I know of are the court cases between Kriyananda in USA in the SRF movement, who himself told me that he had been fighting cases against the main organization of the successors of the great Yogananda. He had already spent millions of dollars till December 1993. His quarrels with Fay Wright, who is now known as Dayama are, well known. She had met Yogananda at the age of fifteen or sixteen when she had gone to listen to him with her mother. She had come with a Mormon background and later became the disciple of Yogananda and took *sanyas.* She commands sincerest respect from a majority of the followers of Yogananda. Now she heads the Self Realization Fellowship. It is said that Kriyananda was in the ashram of Yogananda in the last two years of his life only. Then, someone in the USA told me that he got involved in a controversial land deal in India. After that, Kriyananda developed his own ambitions, it is said, and he created his own wing, which has grown up well. It is not known whether he was asked to leave the SRF or left it voluntarily. Then he is said to have introduced *OM CHRIST* as a *mantra.* Or, if it was introduced earlier, he overemphasized it more.[1] I met disciples of as many as nine American gurus, who claimed that their gurus were the rightful successors of Yogananda. In India we have hundreds of such cases.

The great advantage of having many disciples is that many people acquire some sort of a spiritual discipline, which they may not have got otherwise. The disadvantage is that there is no worthy successor to the guru after his death.

194

Caution

If you have taken spiritual initiation from a guru, who has a large number of disciples, sit at home and do you *sadhana* sincerely. Do not mix with the crowd of other disciples, who become gossipy and talk over enthusiastically about the great guru, but themselves do no *sadhana* and disturb you also from doing your *sadhana*.

C. To have Publicity

This was not the weakness of the Indian gurus till Vivekananda spoke about his guru Ramakrishna Paramhamsa. After that, some gurus want their Vivekanandas and some disciples become self-styled Vivekanandas of their gurus.

In the USA this craze for publicity reaches maniacal proportions. Americans do *sadhana* for some months and dash off a book on all spiritual subjects including *kundalini*, Indian gods and goddesses, and Buddhism and all its varieties, with all the bookish knowledge they pick up. These books are full of ignorance, prejudices, distortions and ludicrous generalizations. But they are sold in large quantities. The result is a contagious craziness, which became clear to me when many Americans put the most preposterous questions to me. In a country where they have broken families and no social life, they are misled into thinking that in one birth and in one leap they would get *'illumination'*. Some of them, who have six to ten written books on spiritual subjects of Asia, begin to speak arrogantly using the spiritual terms of India like *'karma'*, *'samskara'*, *'kundalini'*, *'ahamkara'*. Americans do not know where to draw the line. Along with it, they have developed what they call past life regression techniques through which they show to their clients their past lives. Like many fads in the USA it will die a natural death and will be replaced by some other fad.

II
WEAKNESSES OF DISCIPLES

It is necessary to know that all disciples blame their guru for their lack of spiritual progress. Even in the case of my Guruji, the finest I have seen doing *shaktipaat,*[2] we have had many *guru-bhais,* never doing self-introspection and finding out themselves why there had been no progress in their spiritual life. The greatest book ever written on the science of spiritual life is the *Patanjali Yoga Sutras.* The most scientific analysis of the obstacles in spiritual life given in the book, which all of us fail to see in our spiritual lives should be kept in the mind by a disciple. It is fruitless to blame the guru even if the guru is of a very ordinary spiritual level as is the case in the USA. In India disciples have always been lucky in having extraordinary gurus, who have always given excellent guidance to their disciples, but according to their spiritual level.

Obstacles

The obstacles to spiritual life given in the *Patanjali Yoga Sutras* are being given here briefly:

Physical Obstacles

1. *Ailments, sickness, disease or terrible physical handicaps*
   This often is the result of some terrible *karma* of past life. In such conditions a great guru asks his disciple not to be disappointed but continue doing *sadhana* in spite of this handicap. I have given instances in the book how some good *sadhaks* have done it.

2. *Unhappiness*
   In the case of Indians it is caused by all their worries with their families while this is not the case in the USA where family ties do not exist except in some sections of orthodox Christians. In the USA the problem is very complex. It starts with the story of a broken home, premarital sex, unhappy relationships and finally the damage done by psychiatrists whose roaring business thrives in 'discovering' complexes in their patients and keeping them rooted in childhood abuses.

3. *Physical unsteadiness* (resembling Parkinson's disease)
   The result of consumption of intoxicants and wild habits like drug addiction leads to this sometime or the other.

4. *Difficulties in Inhalation*
   It can be caused by asthma or some other ailments. It definitely destroys the rhythm of *japam* and *pranayam*.

5. *Difficulties in Exhalation*
   Same as number 4 above.

Psychological/Mental Obstacles

6. *Frustration caused by non fulfilment of Desires*
   In the case of most disciples, whether Indians or persons of any country, one's own frustrations regarding wishes, desires related to their wordly, physical, sexual, material, career or family

life is always the most common obstacle. It is not easy to be non attached, which I know is God's greatest gift to a spiritual aspirant, yet it has to be cultivated intelligently. All the knocks of life teach this valuable lesson, which we forget.

7. Doubts

It can be called the most common obstacle of educated Indians and most of the Americans I have met. In the USA they switch gurus as soon as they do not find an instant pill for illumination. These days when there is so much character assassination of some of these gurus in the USA, whether Indian or American, through mischievous publicity, a disciple's doubt in his own guru can assail him constantly. It is not necessary to treat it as an obstacle. Even if the guru is a very ordinary person, that a sincere disciple has to be rewarded by God is well known to us in India. Losing faith in one's own guru, expecting quick supernormal powers (*siddhis*), or even illumination, the disciple cannot progress.

8. Material/Sensual/Sexual obsessions

Indians are familiar with the stories of their great rishis, Vishwamitra, Durvasa and Narada falling into temptations, suffering their agonies but doing their *sadhana* with greater intensity and zeal. There can be no *sadhak* who does not fall into such temptations. The wiser forget them, overcome those temptations and regain their spiritual splendour. Most of such stories are not recorded. In my talks with hundreds of *yogis,* I learnt from them that these temptations have to come, a *sadhak,* must fall into them. The wiser *sadhak* does not despair. He decides not to fall into those traps again and is ever cautious. In the USA somehow it has not been possible to convince people that these could not be combined with spiritual demands of life. It would be far better to be an honestly married man doing *sadhana* rather than imagining fancifully that one could have many relationships and also a good spiritual life.

Spiritual Obstacles
9. Illusory Spiritual experiences

Like the wish fulfilment Freud talked of, every *sadhak* has many spiritual experiences. They can be very damaging when the *sadhak* mistakes them for real spiritual progress. I have written in the book that my own Guruji's instruction was to test these experiences again and again before accepting them as genuine ones. I know of thousands of such experiences of hundreds of *sadhaks* and *sadhikas,* which did damage to them because it inflated their ego.

10. *Not making expected Spiritual progress*

It is very natural for a *sadhak* to feel that he has not made adequate or expected spiritual progress. It creates deepest frustration. I know of *sadhaks,* who gave up their *sadhana* and took to violent, vulgar or grossly materialistic life after such frustrations. To know spiritual progress is being made and when not, is most confusing. It is well explained in the fifteenth chapter of the Gita which should be read repeatedly.

11. *Not remaining steady in Spiritual progress*

Some *sadhaks* attain early success in spiritual life but fail to remain steady. They lose patience and even give up their *sadhana.* This is the worst mistake one can commit. After attaining some real tangible progress, there should be no need to feel frustrated at all or panic.

12. *Neglecting Sadhana*

This need not be elaborated. The meaning is crystal clear.

13. *Carelessness*

It is the most common fault. Every good guru instructs his disciple in some do's and some don'ts. They should always be remembered.

14. *Laziness*

It need not be explained. It is a common fault. I have been a victim of this repeatedly when during my office work and later load of astrological research, I made no attempt to squeeze out some time for my own *sadhana.*

Ways of overcoming Frustration in Spiritual Life

The remedies, which work most miraculously in overcoming frustrations in spiritual life are four:

1. *Company of happy persons*

A person, who has least attachments, desires and frustrations in life is a happy man. He has transcended dualities of life, if not totally, sufficiently well, to be happy mostly. In his company the astral vibrations of his personality create a diffuse sense of happiness. We have many such persons in India among good *sadhakas.* Remember not to become a nuisance for them.

2. *Showing kindness to unhappy persons*

It need not be elaborated. The unconscious blessings of an unhappy person whom you have helped will always help you overcome your miserable spiritual condition.

3. *Keeping alive your sense of Sacredness for the Virtuous*

Do not become judgmental. A virtuous man may stray from the path of virtue in a bad moment. But he will come back to his sacred state very easily. If you lose your own faith in the sacredness of his life, it does damage to you spiritually.

4. *Indifference to the Non-Virtuous*

In the world we live in, a majority are non-virtuous. Remain indifferent to them. Do not hate them. Hatred is a bad and very damaging emotion, spiritually.

III
ADDITIONS

To all the above, let me add, what great yogis have told their disciples.

1. *Do not invite a Yogi to your house frequently*

A yogi leads a life, which is a total reversal of the life you lead. If you begin to invite him to your house, you give him a chance to go astray and get attracted to sex and money. Then you yourself begin to lose faith in him. If he comes once in a while, uninvited serve him properly but do not allow him to stay long in your house, *for your own sake.*

— Instruction of the great Yogi, Devraha Baba

2. *Do not read too many books on supposedly Spiritual subjects*

It is better to do your own *sadhana* as you have been instructed. Reading too many books can cause more confusion. Writers of books on spiritual subjects may themselves be very confused persons but with a gift for writing. Reading those books can create avoidable conflicts in your mind.

— Instruction of the great Vaishnava Guru,
Prabhu Bejoy Krishna Goswami

3. *Keep alive a sense of Sacredness when it comes to Money and Sex*

○   A person obsessed with sex and money slips fastest from spiritual path. I have met more cheats, who pretended to be spiritual, tried to promote spiritual, religious, ayurvedic and astrological seminars, cheated others and accumulated money or promoted themselves.

Extend these tendencies to all the activities of your life. Without this precaution your spiritual life will deteriorate very fast.

— Ramakrishna Paramhamsa

4. Take bath at least Twice a Day

A clean body and a clean mind are necessary for *sadhana*. In my childhood I remember meeting white men coming to India with their stinking bodies and thick yellowish layers on their teeth resembling paint. The reason why Indians were forbidden to go abroad became clear to me then. But it seems that the westerners have discovered the virtues of daily bath in the recent two or three decades and from an Indian point of view, some glimmerings of civilizations have appeared in the west, which we have always associated with plundering imperialisms.

— All yogis advise

5. Avoid Carnivorous Vegetarianism

The food you consume should be pure and vegetarian. It should be known to you that as stressed in the *Gita* and the *Chandogya Upanishad*, the strongest spiritual base of any *sadhana* is pure food. For better spiritual life, do not consume even the milk of cows fed on non vegetarian fodder. The Mad Cow disease of England must be taken as a warning. It is difficult to get pure and unadulterated food in India. But India's adulterated stuff is better than the carnivorous vegetarianism of Europe and the USA. The dangerously adulterated food of India can ruin health. Our incompetent governments can take no action against this inspite of the Anti-Adulteration Laws.

— All yogis advise

6. Triple Fires of Life

Vishnu Purana states in clearest terms that it is after seeing, suffering and realizing that no man can escape the triple fires of life, that one develops detachment and divine knowledge. They are: the *physical ones* likes sickness and psychological problems: the *natural ones* like victimization by fellow human beings and fear from animal (accidents etc. in modern life): the *spiritual ones* as given in the *Patanjali Yoga Sutras*.

— Vishnu Purana

7. Signs of Spiritual Progress

The *Gita* gives some clear indications, which can be used to see how much spiritual progress anyone has made:

1. To feel that you are not a significant person.

2. To not be haughty.
3. Forgiveness.
4. Non-violence.
5. Simple and honest speech.
6. Serving the Guru.
7. Inner and outer cleanliness.
8. Inner stability.
9. Self control.
10. To be non-attached to life's enjoyments.
11. Lack of pride.
12. To think about the world full of grief.
13. Doing the duties of a householder without any sense of attachment.
14. Equanimity.
15. Unconditional devotion to the Lord.
16. Love of sequestered life.
17. Not to be attached to persons immersed in worldliness.
18. Loving always the knowledge of the divine.
19. Experience of cosmic secrets.

— *The Gita*

References

1. I can believe it because when I met him in 1993 I saw at his place a beautiful idol Lord Krishna placed in a dusty corner. When I asked him, reply was that it was better than being in a museum!
2. I have not seen such powerful *shaktipaat* which made my *gurubhai*, Sushantoda to whom I have referred to as "S" in the chapter under "Awakened Kundalini", levitates most fabulously upto the branches of high trees.

...16...
Ecstacies Spring from Fires–I
(My Story)

Among the disciples of my Guruji, only two non-Bengalis, I and Batuk Bhai, a Gujarati Jain, who had taken spiritual initiation some years before me, alone were noticed. Very few non-Bengalis had taken initiation from him. We two received maximum love and affection from *guru-bhais* and *guru-bahens*.

I became more prominent because I had organized a system and method in the ashram and had fought those tyrants who thought that by virtue of their seniority, they could behave dictatorially in all the matters of ashram administration.

The first was when I came to know that a very senior *guru-bhai* had set up his spies in the ashram and another, counter spies, to know whether the ashram would remain under their control or not.

It is my experience that schemers and crooks working with a really true Yogi fall into the traps they set for others. I have seen it happen many times. The great poet Tulsidas has stated very clearly that the first act of God, before he wishes a crook's downfall, is to take away from him his sense of right decision leading to loss of intelligence and judgement.

These are unpleasant stories but I must recount one. A very powerful triumvirate of *guru-bhais* had become a source of terrible indiscipline in the ashram, when they, in the absence of Guruji from the ashram, interfered so much that those who embezzled money started defying me.

One Saturday evening, I lost my temper with two of them and right in the presence of the inmates told them, "If I come to know of it anymore, I will not allow any of you to enter the ashram."

It was a long, one hour quarrel. Now they understood that their dictatorship had to come to an end. The other group too came to know that they should stop doing what they were, so long as I was posted in Calcutta. A large number of *guru-bhais* liked me for that showdown. I felt that it was unfortunate that I had to tell those old men not to treat the ashram as their private property or a farm house, which it was for most of the rich *guru-bhais*.

All this had happened in the absence of Guruji, who took more than four months to come back to the Calcutta ashram from Gauhati, unlike in previous years.

In the meantime, came Christmas, which was celebrated in the ashram by feeding the poor to which came never less than three thousand persons from the neighbouring villages, many of them Muslims.

Guruji had the inconvenient habit of feeding the rich *guru-bhais* in his own cottage, giving them special treatment. They demanded that they be given the same treatment now. I told them that they should come and serve food to the poor, and if in the end, nothing was left for them, they could go home and eat. They could afford it, not the poor.

I need not recount all those incidents except pointing out that the Hindus had forgotten the scriptural injunction that the donor should, after donating, feel honoured that he has been given a chance by God to do spiritual service. I have heard of similar stories from other religious communities and also other countries.

Yet Guruji could not get out of the stranglehold of such persons ever. The only change was that one group replaced the other. I know personally that it happens in all ashrams of the world.

I remember a Christian woman always dressed shabbily, who attended her church regularly, but after her death, no ceremony was held for her in the church. Later when her will was made known, it was found that she had gifted a very large amount of her hidden wealth, which was fabulous, to the church. The church then held a special service in the honour of that 'great' soul.

It is my firm conviction that all great Yogis, who build ashrams mismanage them very efficiently, and, all those, who manage their ashrams efficiently in the role of gurus are hardly Yogis.

The major difference of opinion I always had with Batuk Bhai was about the mismanagement of the ashrams of real great gurus who, living on a rarefied spiritual level, could never make down-to-earth administrative decisions.

It is one thing to respect a Guru and entirely different to praise his ashram. I drew a line of demarcation between the two. Batuk Bhai knew all about it, and with the extraordinarily sharp commonsense he had, he never took sides in this controversy.

It is a long story, a very long story, which I will condense, recollecting as many relevant details of my thirty years or so acquaintance with him till his death.

The story of Batuk Bhai whose memory inspires me even today.

I perhaps first saw him in 1962 during the founding of the Gauhati Ashram, but noticed him more perhaps in January 1968 during my first Calcutta posting when he used to come to the ashram on Sundays.

Both of us were passing through difficult periods astrologically, I in my service career and he in his business dealings, in which he had trusted some *guru-bhais*, and got cheated.

Both of us experienced what a seer our Guru was, how enigmatic, and what an actor pretending to know nothing about what was happening.

Let me narrate my story first.

The transfer of Col. Blimp from Shillong brought, this time, a pleasant Accountant General, to whom God had not given enough commonsense to crosscheck the information he was given, but had given rare disposition not to damage anyone's career. In January 1963, at the Ramakrishna Mission in Laitumukhrah, Shillong had chosen an elderly Assamese scholar to speak on Swami Vivekananda during his centenary celebration. A Bengali scholar was to speak in Bengali, and I was to speak in English. In spite of so many officers, senior to me in rank and also in age in our own office and in the Indian Civil Service of British days and the Indian Administrative Service in the Assam Secretariat, the local Swami had chosen me to speak. He insisted, after our long and frequent meetings, that I would have something stimulating and fresh to say. I knew the difficulty of the Swami. He wanted his function to be a success. He was bold enough not to be guided by the enormous bureaucratic seniority of all other senior officers in Shillong.

My speech was warmly appreciated, more so because I was a speaker just thirty-two years old, compared to the over sixty years of others. Later I had too many invitations from other organizations to honour. But the entire function was boycotted by all the officers of our office, including the Accountant General.

Five months later, I got my transfer orders to Jaipur in July, 1963. I later learnt that the A.G. had written to our headquarters saying that he did not want a brilliant officer to get swayed by religious fervour at so young an age. My colleagues had their revenge at last.

Astrologically, Rahu had changed from Cancer to Gemini in May

1963 into my ninth house, when this letter was written.

Suddenly then Guruji came to Shillong, the most unscheduled visit. The behaviour of Yogis is irritatingly enigmatic mostly, and most protectively beneficient yet. He was, as though, present to give me a farewell. I had some small worries on my mind then.

Without my telling him, he spoke what still today are immortal words for me.

Guru is not the physical body. The *mantra* given by Guru is always the power of Guru with the disciple.

I need not worry about the marriage of my youngest sister, Hema because as soon as I would reach Delhi, an offer for marriage would come and would be finalised. The marriage would be held in Vrindavan.

The third utterance was rather strange. "Learn how to be harsh, not soft always. Use harsh words both in speaking and writing, otherwise you will find it difficult to face many challenges in life ... and challenges would be many in your life."

It was an odd instruction, as till the age of thirty I do not remember having used any harsh word in speaking or writing.

I had always gulped down all insults hurled at me. What could this instruction mean I understand when both in my official career, and now in the world of astrology, I keep meeting challenges.

I reached Delhi and my elder brother K. Pratap told me that an offer for my sister's marriage was there. I told him that I would do all the talking and that the marriage would be held in Vrindavan. He looked at me and, perhaps, thought that I was being stupid.

But everything happened exactly as told by Guruji. I visited Vrindavan for the first time and after that more than two hundred times.

I reached Jaipur where I was posted for a brief period. Then I was transferred to Nagpur, where the first official letter I received from Bombay, where my new Accountant General, an upstart, was that I had been appointed as an Inquiry Officer to investigate into the cases of N.N. Deshpande and R.L. Shirkhedkar.

A few days after, I got a secret message from M.M.B. Annavi, who was then posted as the Deputy Accountant General, (Administration), to come to Bombay, on a third class railway ticket making it look like a private journey. Fools I thought, sat in our Bombay office who did not know the elementary fact that leaders of office associations could always find it out through their own more reliable links. Why was what was sought to be done, not being done with dignity which officers have to have.

I reached Bombay and Annavi told me that they had sought legal opinion in the case I was required to inquire into. These two, Deshpande and Shirkhedkar, who had won their cases from the High Court could be re-suspended on the same charges. I should prove the charges in such a way as to give to the Accountant General a chance to dismiss them. Then, when I met the A.G., a rather clever opportunist, he asked me whether I had understood the meaning and purpose of the instructions. I did not answer him.

After I returned to Nagpur, Shirkhedkar came to meet me one day. I asked him to come into my room which had surprised him as he had not been able to meet a single senior officer during the last five years. They were literally afraid of meeting him.

Shirkhedkar talked to me rudely in the first meeting, which I gulped down realizing that a man who had been kept under suspension for more than five years, while all his juniors had been promoted, could exhibit abnormal behaviour.

When he told me that officers had been afraid of meeting him, I told him that he would be afraid of meeting me. I challenged him to prove me wrong. He retorted by saying that I had nothing to inquire into as I was already under instructions to give a report against him. I asked him why had he admitted all the charges in the official correspondence. And then, did he expect any inquiry officer to ignore his own written admissions? He kept quiet, met me many times later, but never appeared for the inquiry, which had to be given exparte.

But in my recommendations I stated strongly that since the High Court had given its judgement in his favour, he should be reinstated in service without any penalty.

My recommendations, brought down on me an avalanche of fury from the Accountant General and the then Comptroller and Auditor General, A.K. Roy.

I got three successive bad confidential reports for the next three years. I knew that I would not get my promotion, the best one available.

I never informed Guruji about it. In the meantime, the A.G., pretending to be on a tour to Calcutta via Nagpur had sent me a word to meet him in his railway coach at the railway station. There he asked me whether I knew what would be the consequences of my recommendations. I asked him whether he knew what would be the consequences of his not reinstating Shirkhedkar. What? He had asked me. There would be another court case in which I would be cross-examined and I would speak the truth that I was instructed to prepare the grounds for his dismissal. But my recommendations were based on the principles of natural justice, in spite of admissions in the letters of Shirkhedkar. The A.G. was crestfallen. After that whenever we met, we never talked to each other.

In July 1966, I was transferred to the Central Railway Audit office in Bombay, which entitled me to railway passes and some travel concessions. Earlier I was toying with the idea of quitting the service and either joining journalism where good openings had always been available to me, or better still, doing full time *sadhana*.

I was in Nagpur, not with Guruji, and had not told anyone about all that had happened to cause in me total revulsion, against the debased values of officers in good positions.

I then got the one and only letter in English, obviously written by someone for Guruji, in which I was advised that since my *karma* was not exhausted, I should make no precipitate decision.

It was a miracle. How did he know my thoughts from Calcutta?

Such thoughts did not vanish from my mind still. Availing of a railway pass, I went to meet Guruji for the first time in four years. As soon as I reached the ashram, he came out of his cottage, as though he knew about my arrival. Looking at the sky he said, "God knows that you have fought for truth and justice. You will come to Calcutta on a higher post."

It had never happened in the history of our department that an officer with three successive bad reports was ever considered for promotion.

I had sacrificed my promotion for someone else's family who had suffered for five years and his family had starved. I faced it all and won the sincerest admiration of staff members who knew everything that we had classified as secrets, from the stenographers working under us. But all persons above me who would decide my case of promotion had turned hostile to me.

The subsequent chronology of events is:

In March 1967, Guruji had told me that I would get my promotion.

In June or July 1967, the Departmental Promotion Committee was to have gotten the approval of the retiring CAG, hostile to me, for the promotion of our batch.

For some reason that meeting of the DPC could not be held.

In the meantime, the CAG retired.

The new CAG Sri S. Ranganathan, called for my entire case, I learnt.

He said that I could not be punished for the stand I had taken.

In Bombay I told my batch-mate, R.V. Bansod (who produced the famous Bofors Report which ruined the career of the former Indian Prime Minister, Rajiv Gandhi, in 1988-89) that I would be promoted and transferred to Calcutta. He thought that I was being superstitious and had lost my sanity.

But when it did happen, in December 1967, Bansod had the grace to concede that my Guruji had great supernormal powers.

This was the biggest miracle in the history of the audit department.

The only other such miracle I know of is that of Mr. G.B. Singh, who after two bad reports from a former CAG, A.K. Bakshi, would not have got his promotion. But his old friend, Mr. Gian Prakash, came as the next CAG and gave him his promotion.

A Yogi sees what an astrologer cannot.

My interest in reading scriptures took a most ecstatic turn and helped me overcome whatever might have caused any bitterness. There was so much inward cheer. What I owe to these great scriptures of India is what I can only summarize here, only in parts, and, very briefly.

Incarnations of God and Devatas

It has been discussed why God incarnates Himself in our world of mortals to restore the disturbed equilibrium when the weight of sins becomes unbearable. God's incarnation is to be distinguished from man's miseries when he is caught in the cycle of births. When He incarnates as human being, he behaves mostly like a human being yet glimpses of his Omnipotence get revealed.

The stories of God's incarnations make the Indian religion, the Sanatan Dharma, better known as Hinduism, the most optimistic and most colourful, songsful, joyful, festivities-filled multi-coloured splendour. Every religion leads one on to spirituality, each in its own way. Hindus have many such Paths and many of them are very colourful. The Hindu Paths are all-embracing which is why Hindus have never found anything new in any religion which they did not know already.

There must be a reason for God to incarnate himself. This reason changes from one Mahakalpa (call it the Cosmic great epoch of billions of human years) to another. In themselves those stories make interesting reading and inspire devotion. You then love God as one of your own family circle yet know him to be great, peerlessly great.

For instance see the differing versions about the birth of Lord Rama. (*From Valmiki Ramayana p.56, Gita Press Gorakhpur*)

Incarnation of Lord Vishnu

Rishi Rishyashringa[1] said after he had completed the *putresthi* yagna for the birth of the children of King Dasharatha, "You will have four sons." Just then the gods were telling Lord Brahma that the demon King, Ravana had become too powerful and was devastating the world with all his immoral actions. Brahma said that in asking for the boon from Him, the demon King, Ravana had requested that his death should not be at the hands of *gandharva, yaksha, rakshasha* or *devata*. This boon was granted to Ravana who remained under the mistaken belief that no human being could kill him because human beings were too weak to do him any damage. To maintain the sanctity of his boon and also get Ravana killed, Lord Brahma requested Lord Vishnu to be born in four forms, as the four sons of King Dasharatha. These would be human form in which, if the Lord killed Ravana, the sanctity of Brahma's boon to Ravana would remain unviolated.

Then Lord Vishnu assured the assembled gods and Lord Brahma that he would be born in the family of King Dasharatha, would destroy the family of Ravana and rule the world of men for eleven thousand years. To be of assistance to Lord Vishnu who had now decided to be born as the sons (in four forms) of King Dasharatha, other minor gods too gave birth to brave and heroic children in form of monkeys and bears. The parentage of some famous warriors who fought from the side of Lord Rama in the battle of Lanka was as follows.

	Father	Son
1.	Lord Brahma	Jambavaan (bear).
2.	Lord Indra	Bali (monkey)
3.	Lord Sun	Sugreeva (monkey)
4.	Lord Brihaspati	Taar (monkey)
5.	Lord Kuber	Gandhamaadan (monkey)
6.	Lord Vishwkarma	Nal (monkey)
7.	Lord Agni (Fire)	Neela (monkey)
8.	Lords Ashwini Kumars	Mainda and Dwivid (monkeys)
9.	Lord Varun	Sushena (monkey)

And the greatest and bravest of them was Lord Hanuman, son of the God Pawan.

God incarnated Himself along with many of his divine companions, mostly in non-human form.

The Hindu belief in the divinity of all creatures flows from such stories of incarnations.

Why had Vishnu to Incarnate as Lord Rama?

Behind every story of the incarnation of God in the world of mortals there is an interesting story. In ancient times in a fight between gods and demons, the wife of maharshi Bhrigu was kidnapped by demons. The wife of the rishi actually gave refuge to demons which enraged Lord Vishnu who cut off her head with his weapon, *Sudarshan chakra*. This enraged Bhrigu, who cursed Vishnu that he would have to be born as a human being in the world of mortals where he would have to suffer separation from his wife for many years. Lord Vishnu accepted the curse cheerfully. He was born as Lord Rama and had to suffer the pangs of separation from his wife, Sita twice, first time when Ravana kidnapped her and the second time when he himself asked her to leave his palace. All this was told to King Dasharatha long before the events took place by Maharshi Durvasa.

Even God will not violate his laws regulating predestination.

— from Adhyatma Ramayan

Lord Vishnu assured Lord Brahma that pleased with the *tapasya* of rishi Kashyap He had decided to be born in his family. Kashyap was then ruling as a King by the name of King Dasharatha. He would be born as four sons from the three wives of the King.(p27).

Then Lord Brahma asked *gods to be born in monkey families.*

— from the Valmiki Ramayana

1. Who Was Sita In Her Previous Birth? (p.1496)

Once Ravana, the demon King saw a very beautiful woman doing hard spiritual penance. Seeing her extraordinary beauty, he offered to take her as wife, but the maiden whose name was Vedavati refused the offer. She explained that her father was Kushadhwaja, son of Brihaspati (Jupiter). Since her father recited the Vedas everyday when she was born, she knew the Vedas and was named Vedavati. When she had become youthful many offers came from the high and the mighty for marriage with her. But it was the desire of her father that she should be the wife of only Lord Vishnu. This annoyed the demon King who murdered her father one night. Then her mother too decided to leave her body and entered the funeral fire along with the dead body of her husband. Since then Vedavati decided to get Lord Vishnu as her husband.

This did not appeal to Ravana, who caught the tuft of hair of Vedavati. She immediately cut off the hair which Ravana had touched and entered fire to give up her body. Before dying, she said that:

1. She would be reborn and would become the cause for his death.

2. A woman cannot kill a male with her physical strength. She also did not want to curse him and waste her accumulated spiritual merit.

3. She would be born as an *ayonija* (immaculate conception) *daughter* of a holy father.

In the next birth she born out of a lotus and soon Ravana recognized her and took her to his palace. There a wise minister saw the baby and told Ravana that the girl carried with her all the signs of the destruction of his Kingdom. Ravana immediately threw her into water and from there her floating body reached the Kingdom of Raja Janak and landed on a field. While tilling the land she was discovered and she became the daughter of Raja Janak. In *satyayuga* she was Vedavati and in Treta she became Sita. The line that gets drawn on the field while tilling with a furrow known as Sita. Some people describe the front part of the furrow as Sita. It is how Vedavati became famous in her next birth and became the cause of the destruction of Ravana and his Kingdom.

From the Adhyatma Ramayana

Once the astrologer-rishi, Narada visited King Janak and told him that the Lord had decided to incarnate himself to kill the demon King, Ravana as the four sons of King Dasharatha. Goddess Yogamaya had taken birth in the house of King Janak as Sita whose marriage with Rama is what he has to perform.

2. **King Dasharatha on his Death Bed: Why Did he go to a higher world?**

— Ayodhyakand p.357

Lord Rama had to go to the forest instead of becoming the successor to his father, King Dasharatha. It was in deep agony that Dasharatha lying on his bed remembered the sins committed by him. His condition was like that of Sun covered by Rahu which is the description given by Valmiki. The King tells his wife, Kaushalya

Yadaacharati Kalyaani Shubham Va Yadi Vashubham,
Tadeva Labhate Bhadre Karta Karmaj-atmanah
— sh 6, p.357, Ayodhyakanda
*Whatever auspicious or inasupicious deeds man does, he gets
happiness or agonies accordingly.*

The King recalled a sin he had committed in his youth when
his father was alive. He could hit a target blind-fold on merely
hearing a sound ... Once while going in a forest in the pitch
darkness of the night during the rainy season, King Dasharatha
had heard the sound of gurgling water which was like a pitcher
being filled at a pond. Unable to see it in the night, he thought
that an elephant was drinking water in a pond. Then a human
voice was heard: "I am a *tapasvi* (a spiritual person) I had come
here to fetch water." He served his old parents who were entirely
dependent on him. By killing him the King had killed three
persons in a way, the great son and his two old parents who after
his death, would die in agony. He asked the King why had it
done since he was helpless and could not reach his parents to
quench their thirst now. His father too could do nothing now to
save them just as *'a tree cannot prevent a gust of wind from
snapping the branch of another tree'*. He told the King to go
convey this tragic news to his old, emaciated and blind parents in
order to prevent him from being charred to death through their
curses. Then the injured *tapasvi* told the King that he did not
want to leave his body in the agony of the pain being caused
physically. If the arrow was drawn from out of his body he would
die instantaneously, if not, his physical suffering would become
unbearable. *He told the King that he wanted to do dhyana
(stabilize his mind) to prepare to leave the body in a happy frame
of mind.* He was not a Brahmin. I am born of a Vaishya father and
Shudra mother. Therefore the sin of killing a Brahmin had not
been committed by the King. So the King should free his mind
from the fear of *Brahma-hatya* (the killing of a Brahmin.) The King
drew out that arrow of his which had entered the heart of the
*tapasvi, who now in his exalted and divine state of mind, went to
heaven.*

Nervously the King went to the ashram where the parents of
the *tapasvi* awaited the arrival of their son with water. Then the
father of the *tapasvi* being the great *tapasvi* he was, he said that if
the King had not admitted the sin committed by him, he would
have cursed him and his body would have been torn into a

thousand pieces. Then they asked King Dasharatha to take them to the pond where their son's dead body was lying. The father blessed his sinless son so that he would attain to a higher world. The son then appeared in a divine form before them and said that as a result of his sincere service to his parents he had attained a high divine status and that his parents too should join him soon. The old *tapasvi* then told the King that just as a charity giver gets the results according to the nature of the charity given, he too would die in a miserable condition when his son would leave him and go away. *Then the old couple themselves left for the divine abode.*

Remembering that tragic incident, King Dasharatha died in agony.

But because his son Lord Rama did great virtuous deeds, Dasharatha went to Indraloka (a higher world). At the end of the battle of Lanka, one of the many persons who had descended from the higher worlds was Dasharatha himself (p. 1421). It was only now that Dasharatha came to know that the Lord Himself had incarnated as his son.

Moral — The moral and spiritual deeds of children become the causes of the liberation of their ancestors.

3. **The Divine End of Sharbhang Rishi**

There is the story of Sharbhang Rishi in the Ramayana, who Lord Rama saw during the years he had to spend in the forest. The rishi full of divine splendour was awaiting the arrival of Rama just when he, through the great spiritual merit he had accumulated, was preparing to leave his body and go to Brahmaloka, the higher world. In the presence of Rama whom he had requested to stay for a while, he burnt fire, recited *mantras* and left his body in the presence of God. His body turned into that of a youthful divine being and he ascended to Brahmaloka.

Moral — Those, who lead spiritually flawless lives know of their coming end and prepare for it with their minds absorbed in God contemplation.

4. **The Divine End of Jatayu, the Bird**

Jatayu the valiant eagle had found Ravana when he was kidnapping Goddess Sita. Lord Rama reached the injured Jatayu and told him, those who perform *agnihotra yagna,* fight in a battle like heroes without running away and gift away land, go to higher worlds. If the Lord performed his last funeral rites, he would go to the highest world.

Moral — Towards the end of a honestly dutiful and spiritual life someone who can perform funeral rites properly reaches near that person. Funeral rites performed by a right and spiritual person has its own spiritual significance.

5. **The Divine End of Kabandh, the Monster**

Kabandh, the monster, was very hungry when both Rama and Lakshmana encountered him during their wanderings in the jungle. He was huge and his arms had illimitable strength. Rama cut off the right arm of the monster and Lakshamana the left one. Falling on the ground, the monster realized that he met some extraordinary persons and asked who they were. Then he told his own story. *His strong arms were his real curse-like handicaps in spiritual life.*

He was a very splendrous and powerful person in his previous life but took to the evil habit of frightening the *rishis* in the forest after assuming the guise and form of a monster. One day he tried the same trick on a great *rishi* Sthoolashira who cursed that he should remain in that terrible and horrid form of a monster. The frightened monster requested the rishi to tell him how he could overcome this curse. The rishi said that when Rama and Lakshamana would cut off his arms, he would get back his former form. The monster then told them that in his previous life he had done strong spiritual penances and had obtained a boon from Lord Brahma, who granted him a long life. Now in sheer haughtiness, he once attacked Lord Indra who injured him badly, without killing him because of the boon of Lord Brahma. Now he requested Lord Indra to help him become fit enough to be able to eat food. Otherwise he would starve. He was then given strong and long arms with which he could eat animals in the forests by catching them with his hands. *Lord Indra had also assured him that when his arms would be cut off by Rama and Lakshamana, he would go to the higher world.*

Then Kabandha said that if the Lord performed his funeral rites he would give him introduction to a good friend and also some clues about where his kidnapped wife, Sita was. *Kabandha said that in his present horrible state his divine powers could not function.*

Only after his body was put in a pit and cremated according to the scripturally sanctioned methods he would get back his divine powers and would be of help. When Kabandha was cremated as he had desired, he got his divine form and said:

| Kings have six approaches to good administration ||
The Name of the Approach	The Meaning
1.	*Sandhi*	Treaty of friendship with enemies.
2.	*Vigraha*	To wage a war on the enemy.
3.	*Yaan*	Attacking the enemy.
4.	*Asan*	Waiting for the right opportunity to take action
5.	*Dwaidhibhav*	Duplicity.
6.	*Samaasraya*	Taking refuge under a King who is more powerful.

Rama should therefore strike friendship with a person in a similar plight, who then was Sugreeva, the monkey King whom his brother, Bali had turned out of his house. He was a good and moral person with a lot of personal heroism. He would help Rama.

Then Kabandha got back his former beautiful and powerful form.

Moral — This is a case of no death but the death of an evil state in which one may live. When divine blessings are showered on him he overcomes it. Good spiritual conduct followed by a monster like life but reversion into spiritual discipline before one meets one's physical end can pave the way to salvation.

6. Divine end of the Untouchable Woman, Shabri

As directed by Kabandha, Rama and Lakshamana reached the beautiful Pampa Lake where they met an outcaste woman, Shabri, whose spiritual practice had reached its most beautiful climax. After serving the Lord, she sought His permission to give up her physical body and go to the higher worlds where the great rishis she had served awaited her arrival.

Shabri then prepared a sacred fire and self-cremated herself with the Lord watching. She got a divine form and ascended to the higher worlds.

Moral — God and spirituality are not the monopoly of the high castes. He, who follows the true spiritual path attains salvation.

7. Magical Revival of Lord Hanuman

When it was being debated as to who would jump over the

215

vast sea that separated Lanka from the continent of Aryavarta (India's ancient name), Jambvaan reminded Hanuman the story of his birth.

There was a famous fairy by the name of Punjakisthala. Under a curse, she had to assume the form of a monkey. Her name was Anjana and her husband's Kesari. The lord of winds, Vayu once got enthralled by her beauty and gave birth mentally (through *Sankalpa*) to Hanuman who had boundless strength. Once the child Hanuman (p.1550) was very hungry and his mother had gone away somewhere. To appease his appetite he thought of eating something. He saw the shining Sun and mistook it for an eatable and went to that world. There he saw Rahu. Mistaking him to be an eatable, he rushed towards him. Out of fright, Rahu ran to Lord Indra and narrated the incident and reminded him that the right to gobble the Sun on certain lunar days was his was now challenged by a young child.

Lord Indra got annoyed with the child Hanuman and broke his chin (*Hanu* in Sanskrit) with his weapon, *vajra.* This annoyed Lord Vayu who stopped all winds which created panic in the world. Then gods amended their mistake and bestowed on him all types of knowledge and wisdom. Since then Hanuman became his name.

Hanuman is known for extraordinary qualities which, though not directly relevant to the topic under discussion, should be given here for its extraordinary illumination.

Hanuman had all the great mental gifts
1. To be a good listener.
2. To listen with attention.
3. To retain what was listened to.
4. To preserve what was listened to for discriminating analysis.
5. To weigh the pros and cons of the lessons learnt through listening.
6. To understand the meaning of all the lessons learnt intelligently.
7. To understand the essence of the lessons learnt.
8. To fuse the lessons with the understanding of eternal truths.

Hanuman has all four types of strengths
1. He had physical strength.
2. He had mental strength
3. He had the strength born of experience of getting out of any type of physical or mental tangle.
4. He had the collective strength of his group of good friends.

Hanuman had all the fourteen sterling qualities

1. The sociological knowledge of the times one lived in.
2. Firmness of purpose.
3. Ability to bear all types of pains with great strength.
4. Knowledge of various subjects.
5. Cleverness.
6. Keen enthusiasm.
7. Ability to keep.
8. Not uttering contradictory things.
9. Valour.
10. Measuring the strength of his own and his enemy's.
11. Sense of gratitude.
12. Offering protection to those, who took refuge under him.
13. Lack of jealousy.
14. A sense of dignified solemnity.

But he had forgotten his boundless powers, which gods had bestowed upon him. When the child Hanuman was revived he had acquired immortality as a boon of all gods and Brahma. Being uncontrollably mischievous by nature he disturbed rishis doing their spiritual practices. The rishis however could do nothing because they were aware that the child Hanuman had been give a great boon by almost all the gods, including Brahma. Then the rishis got annoyed with the boy and laid a curse on him that for a very long time he would not be even aware of his illimitable strength. For many years Hanuman forgot his power and wandered in the ashram like a gentle and ordinary boy. His mischiefs stopped. He had forgotten that he without a peer in sheer strength. Blessed by Lord Sun, he had become a scholar too without a peer as he could learn any subject in the shortest possible time. He had divine wisdom which is why he is also referred to as *Gnaninaam Agraganyam* (the first and foremost among wise men). Then after the lapse of a long time, when the right time would come, he would be reminded of it to fulfil his great mission of doing a great work for Lord Rama. On the eve of the battle of Lanka, *he was reminded of his great powers by Jambavan* ... Now assuming his huge form, Hanuman fulfilled the task of finding out the whereabouts of Sita by leaping over the seas with ease.

Note — It is why ·among many other names, Lord Hanuman is known as *Anjani-putra* (son of Anjana) and *Kesari-Nandan* (son of Kesari).

Moral — A reminder of the divinity in you works wonder. But a curse laid on you can cover it under a cloud for sometime till an opportunity to rediscover it occurs.

Immortal Presence of Hanuman and Others

Before leaving for his original abode, Lord Rama told Hanuman to stay in the world of mortals and spread Ram's Name. Along with Hanuman, the others who were asked to stay till the end of Kaliyuga were Jambavan, Vibhishana, Mainda and Dvivida who all help devotees, particularly by giving divine guidance leading to salvation.

These five immortals have with them three others, Ashwathama, Bali and Vyas.

...17...
Ecstacies Spring from Fires–II
(My Story)

So now about Batuk Bhai, who too had faced a similar problem round about the same time, but in Calcutta.

I was posted to Bombay when a gentleman Muslim officer, Manzur-e-Mustafa, had demanded of me by name to do impartially the work of bifurcation of the Central Railway into South Central Railway. He trusted me fully, convinced of my impartiality since he had seen me in Shimla in the very beginning of my career, when I had worked under him. There was no single complaint after that Herculean task had been accomplished.

From January 1, 1968, a new, the first ever, office known as the A. G. Central, to deal with the central governmental offices, was to start in Calcutta. I was ordered to hand over charge, and with no joining time given to, me, was asked to rush to Calcutta on promotion which would have been denied to me otherwise.

It was as Guruji had told me, promotion and posting to Calcutta. If you do not see chaos in Calcutta, you must instantly feel that something is seriously wrong with the city. Yet it is the only metropolis of India where so much humanity is alive. In Calcutta they talk of a revolution. I used to tell them that the day the city of Calcutta begins to look clean and beautiful, it will be a revolution.

When you meet a good Bengali, you should know that you cannot meet a better human being in your life. All my Bengali colleagues were without exception, angelic. It was too good a dream. Too many good colleagues around you make you unfit for handling the problems of bad colleagues in bad offices.

The worst human beings I had met until then were also Bengalis, when I reached Delhi where I met men, to manufacture whom, the Creator must have used only ... what?

In the pollution free atmosphere of the ashram where I was ordered by Guruji to stay, I ate only rice and cabbages and gained twenty pounds in weight. Guruji called his doctor disciple, Amiyo Madhav Chakravarty, and asked him if he could explain this change in me. The bliss lasted, as long as I had not learnt Bengali, after learning which, I discovered that *guru-bhais* rarely talked of spiritual subjects and were as worldly and most imaginative scandal-mongerers. The religious community that forms itself around the Guru is drawn from the same society, which indulges in such talks. It has the additional disadvantage of too much familiarity and intimacy.

Then there were the self-styled Vivekanandas around Guruji as Swami Ramakrishna Paramhamsa had. The rich donors had treated the ashram as their private property. It would not have disturbed me at all but when Guruji asked me to look after the ashram, it was a case of double burden falling on my shoulders. A turbulent office and an unmanageable ashram.

I did the cleaning of the ashram, filling water tanks and. doing what should have been done to keep the ashram as neat as possible. Yet when I performed all this without Guruji ever giving me instructions, no one ever noticed it, except, the late Haridas Goswami. Once he asked Guruji, when they were sitting in a farm-house about a mile away from the ashram, "I never see Rao coming to your cottage and you never give him any instructions yet how does he perform all the necessary functions in the ashram even after such heavy work in the office."

It took me some time to understand that the rich and powerful *guru-bhais* were divided into groups, each wanting to capture the ashram, and have it run as they wanted. The only decent and cultured gentleman in that group was Haridas Goswami.

"Rao has not to be told verbally what to do. I communicate my instructions, heart to heart," Guruji said.

Some of them who had already grown jealous of me, for no fault of mine, disputed the claim. Suddenly on a Sunday morning, some of them came in their cars to see what I was doing. I was cleaning the cottage of Guruji, with Sushantoda and Achintoda. Goswamida suddenly came and rushed to embrace even though I was looking like a typical Indian scavenger.

They had been told by Guruji that I had been told telepathically to clean his kuti. They had distrusted it and had come to verify it themselves.

The jealousy against me increased because I never told anyone of them that it was pure bliss that I had been experiencing. I had to become, some months later, victim of their jealousy.

The agony inside me was such as I had never experienced. before. Were those who were initiated by such a great Yogi and had the advantage of long association with him for so many years, so mean, so intrigue-loving and such scandal-mongerers?

Years later, I am of the opinion that it is not everyone that is fit to be initiated spiritually. The contrast that existed between Rokadiya Baba of Rajkot and my own Guruji seemed to be immense in this matter. He initiated only one person while my Guruji initiated as many as, I guess, over twenty thousand; ten thousand males out of whom two hundred may have been gentlemanly in their behaviour and the remaining serious about nothing, neither the *sadhana* nor the help that the ashram needed from time to time. I was spending all my salary on running the ashram. As a government officer whatever good salary I got was not sufficient for the enormous expenditure. Rich *guru-bhais* who watched it all, seemed to have decided not to contribute any money. Guruji hardly stayed in the ashram. I, a bachelor, felt for the first time how an Indian house holder must be experiencing difficulties in managing the expenditure of his family, with one man in the family only earning and three or four depending on him.

In my childhood, when my father, a patriot, was in the British jail, I had suffered pangs of poverty. There was nothing I could do as I was only in my sub-teens. Such self-imposed poverty as we faced, was father's willing sacrifice for the liberation of the country. Here the situation was totally different. Those who were contributing earlier, withdrew their hands because I took no sides, joined no group.

Miracles take place once in a while. In the running of an ashram, normal human planning has to be done. Raising of money, forming a trust, employing servants to do many odd jobs, but mainly cleaning of the ashram and filling of the water tanks was absolutely necessary. Guruji never allowed it and if the ashram was still running, it was a miracle. I was the sole contributor and the sole sufferer because I had either to run the ashram well or get out of it.

After 1980, *guru-bhais* have now done all that. There is a trust, there are paid employees and there is a system and method in the running of the ashram. My argument prevailed finally with *guru-bhais,* but long after that great and magnificent presence of the Guru vanished.

Then there were thefts, embezzlements. My bliss vanished, and I was waiting to be transferred which was bound to happen sooner or later.

The Central Government Employees' strike of September 1968 was the other crippling blow. The Communist-dominated office unions with no help from the State Government, had created a most dangerous situation for us all. We the officers were the target of those striking employees. An Income Tax Commissioner had many heart attacks. Another big officer had the mortifying experience of seeing his hair turn completely white over night.

Back in the ashram there were all the managerial problems. I vaguely remembered a Sanskrit saying I had read somewhere that if you want to go to hell the best way is to become the head of an ashram.

Guruji, who could do nothing with all his supernormal powers, was mostly away from the ashram.

To date that has been the most valuable experience of my life. In intense spells, the great God showed to me the individual and collective villainy of human nature. All this from those, who had taken spiritual initiation from the same Guru.

I had only two sympathizers, Sunil Chaudhary, who could only have sympathized with me, and Batuk Bhai, who knew much more about them, watched me closely. His office was about a hundred yards away from mine where I was *gheraoed* (a term communists use to surround their superiors to make demands) but not insulted because the office staff had liked me and come to me for personal help.

Batuk Bhai came every day to take me first to his house at Bhawanipur, where he asked me to bathe, eat and then go to the ashram, which took two hours' travel by bus.

It was the recitation of the *Gita* in the office (where no work came and the striking employees only shouted outside my room) and the regular *japam,* which sustained me and gave me such remarkable strength to go through my life's most hellish experience. All this coming from the Guru and *guru-bhais!*

I have always been a very keen reader of the songs of the great saint-poets of Hindi literature. What they explain in those songs is the finest, most artistic and elevating spiritual teachings of the world.

In retrospect, now I realise, what Kabirdas, the poet, has said: the Guru destroys you from within and rebuilds you.

Sadhana has to be done all alone, never in a group.

"A-ratihi jana sansadi" in the *Gita* clearly means when *sadhana* is done alone then the *sadhak* progresses.

Group *sadhana* is appealing in the beginning but soul destroying in the end.

Batuk Bhai knew my condition. He could have done nothing. He told me often that he had taken some *guru-bhais* as his business partner and had indulged in tax evasion. He was betrayed by them. They got ruined themselves. Batuk Bhai overcame it when his son, who took over his firm and achieved fine financial success. But he had learnt the lesson too; the **rich** *guru-bhais* **were** what they were.

The *Gita* Saved Me

As a regular reader of the *Gita*, I found this greatest book of spiritual wisdom keeping me in the right spiritual frame, though life in the ashram was full of fires.

During this time, it was the instructions of my Guruji, and the Gita, which sustained me. What the Gita has taught me is summarized by me in my own way. But first a caution.

Etat-vigyaay madbhakto madbhavayopapadhyate Madabhkta
vimuktanaam hi shastra-garteshu muhyatam, Na gyanam na
mokshah syaatayesham janmashatairapi.
— *Adhyatma Ramayana, Baal Kanda, p.24)*

Those, who attempt to understand Me through the reading of many shastras (scriptures), get neither wisdom nor salvation even in hundreds of births because they fall into the pit of reading too much and do not take to the path of true devotion. The quotation given above from *Adhyatma Ramayana* literally means that only through the dawning of proper wisdom, when all dualities vanish, only then a devotee realizes that there is Cosmic Unity in the Creation of the Lord.

In the story of man's spiritual stages, the curtain of the Lord's Maya begins to lift when someone gets into the company of devotees and cultivates the habit of worshipping God himself. On the dawning of divine wisdom as a result of such worship, he now gets a right Guru, who shows him the Path. Then dualities vanish. *(Adhyatma Ramayana, p.52)*

Then there is no vast pantheon of gods as the ignorant British imperialists emphasized without understanding Indian scriptures. Narada states it thus addressing Lord Rama in the *Adhyatma Ramayana* (p.58):

"You are Vishnu and Janaki is Lakshmi: you are Shiva and Janaki
is Parvati: you are Brahma and Janaki is Saraswati: you are Sun
and Janaki is Prabha[1]: you are Moon and Janaki is Rohini: you
are Indra and Janaki is Shachi: you are Fire and Janaki is Svaha.[2]

References

1. Prahha is the illumination of the Sun.
2. Svaha is uttered during the recitation of mantras after lighting fire.

Gita's Sublimest Lessons

ᘓ৪৩

CHAPTER ONE

Gita and Rebirths

The theme of the *Gita* is the shining light of divinity. The preaching here is most optimistic-showing that Divine Illumination alone leads to liberation and freedom from the cycle of births. It is why the *Gita* is, and will always be, the greatest book on this earth.

The message of the *Gita* is clear: Salvation is the birth right of every being if he devotes himself to Him.

The theme of the *Gita* revolves round the problem of getting out of the cycle of births and rebirths. That hope exists for everyone becomes clear in the *Gita* unlike the fear of eternal damnation or hell fire preached by fear inducing fundamentalist religions. There is as much hope for those whom we call sinners and the downtrodden, as for others. The path of illumination is devotion to Him and surrendering the fruits of actions to Him. It never is stopping the doing of one's *karma* After reading the Gita, every wise man decides - start doing your *karma* properly but stop desiring.

A brief summary of what the *Gita* says about rebirths is given here.

ᘓ৪৩

CHAPTER TWO

To help Arjuna overcome his terrible mental confusion created by the agonizing feeling that in the battle of Kurukhshetra he would have to fight against his own cousins, uncles, gurus and respected elders, Lord Krishna started his preaching, the greatest ever done for man, by explaining three essential points first.

What is Life and what is Death?

1. It must be known what is death before knowing what is life.

   It must be known because the delusion caused by the grief of death must be overcome. Boyhood, youth and old age are the stages of life one has to pass through.

2. It is certain that those who are born will die and will be reborn. One should not grieve over these inevitable events.

3. An equanimous man renounces the fruits of his actions, frees himself from the shackles of birth and attains supreme bliss.

— *Shlokas 13, 27, 43, 47, 50, 51.*

ෆ৪০

CHAPTER FOUR
Lives before Lives

The Lord tells Arjuna that both He and Arjuna had passed through many lives which were known only to the Lord an forgotten by Arjuna.

The Lord is Unborn but manifests Himself through his *Yogamaya* (divine energy creating illusion) but keeps His own *Prakriti* (nature) under control. The purpose of this manifestation or incarnation is to protect the virtuous and destroy evil-doers. All this has to be done to establish *Dharma* (righteousness). It is for this that the Lord incarnates from age to age. God's incarnation and activities are divine. He who knows it gets liberated from the cycle of births.

In such a state, all attachments of the devotee vanish. Divine Knowledge is what he has now. He gets liberated.

— *Shlokas 5, 6, 7, 8, 23.*

ෆ৪০

CHAPTER SIX

Results of steadiness or vacillations in spiritual practice. Arjuna asks a very pertinent question: does not a person swinging like a pendulum between the worldly and the spiritual get himself torn within?

The Lord clarifies it step by step:

He who follows the spiritual path does not meet with an evil destiny.

If for. some reason he is not able to complete his spiritual *sadhana* and does not get final liberation yet, he attains to one of the higher worlds where he lives happily as a result of his meritorious deeds. Then he has to descend to the earth where he gets his birth in the house of pious and well-off persons (where he would get a favourable atmosphere for resuming his uncompleted *sadhana).*

Or such a person may take birth in the family of an enlightened Yogi though it is generally rare.

Having got such a birth and finding the atmosphere suitable for the pursuit of his *sadhana,* he now; impelled by the spiritual practices of his previous birth, becomes equanimous and overcomes the desire to achieve the fruits of his actions because the lessons learnt are really spiritual.

— *38, 40, 41, 42, 43, 44, 45*

ॐ

CHAPTER EIGHT
Thoughts at the time of death

The thoughts that are in the mind of the dying man decide the nature of his next birth. If he is contemplating on God, he gets liberation.

Whatever object one is thinking about at the time of death is what he attains after death. It is that predominant thought that determines his destiny of future life.

Therefore all the time one's *karma.* must be done and thoughts must be fixed on the Cosmic. I

He whose mind is so fixed gets liberation.

Therefore a yogic practitioner who uses breath control, concentrates on the spot between the eyebrows at the time of deat~ and devotes himself to God with unwavering mind, attains liberation.

Great persons who reach that high stage of liberation are not reborn in this world which after all is full of sorrow and is only transitory.

It must be remembered that even the Higher Worlds spoken of appear and disappear. But for he who concentrates on Him there is no rebirth.

The Path of a Yogi and time of his departure from this world are two important factors to be known. In uttarayana (when the Sun moves between Capricorn and Gemini, January to June) during day time and in the bright lunar half if the yogi leaves his body in a yogic state, he attains. On the contrary, when a Yogi leaves his body in a yogic state in the dakshinayana (when the Sun travels from Cancer to Capricorn) in the dark lunar fortnight, he takes a rebirth.

— *Shlokas 5, 6, 7, 8, 9, 10, 15, 16, 23, 24, 25.*

ॐ

CHAPTER NINE
Supremacy of Worshipping HIM

The difference between the worship of the Lord as a Form *(Sakar)* and as Formless *(Nirgunaor Nirakar)* should be understood to get freedom from the shackles of births. It is imperishable knowledge and must be practised. Those who have no faith in God have to go through the whirl of births.

The Wheel of the World revolves because the Lord, who is the Creator of the animate and the inanimate, causes it to revolve.

Those, who perform ritualistic rites with the definite motive of getting the results of their good actions, go to one of the Higher Worlds (the Iindra Loka) and enjoy celestial pleasures but have to return to the world of mortals when the stock of that spiritual merit gets exhausted.

Those, who worship the Lord, without any such motive, get God's full protection and attain liberation finally.

Where one will go after death, will depend on whom he worships. They that worship gods go to the world of gods: those who worship manes go to the world of manes those who worship spirits go to the world of spirits.

The downtrodden, women and sinners whosoever takes to the worship of the Supreme gets liberated. There is hope for everyone.

Those, who are already on the Right Path and have been doing the right worship sublimely attain that high state of liberation easily.

— *Shlokas 1, 2, 3, 10, 20, 21, 22, 25, 32, 33.*

ख़

CHAPTER TEN
When Worship Leads to Liberation

Those that worship the Lord with unflagging constancy gets liberation. The Lord gives to them the right intelligence to act wisely. God, dwelling in their hearts, illumines them from within and dispels darkness (creating bondage).

— *Shlokas 10, 11, 34.*

ख़

CHAPTER TWELVE
Importance of Constant Worship

Those, who worship Him, surrendering all the fruits of action to Him and have single minded devotion are given freedom from the cycle of births by the Lord quickly. Therefore fix the mind on the Lord, abide in Him.

— *Shlokas 7, 8.*

ख़

CHAPTER FOURTEEN
Prakriti and the World is Lord's Own Creation

Prakriti (the primordial matter), when imbued with consciousness by the Lord, creates the world which is enveloped by the three-layered *Maya* of the Lord, the *sattwa*, the *rajas* and the *tamas*. He, who transcends this three layered *Maya*, reaches that transcendental state which is liberation.

— *Shlokas 4, 20*

ශ්‍රව

CHAPTER FIFTEEN
What is Real Freedom?

Those, who have not freed themselves from the primordial matter, transmigrate from one body into another.

— *Shloka 8*

ශ්‍රව

CHAPTER SIXTEEN
Who are Punished by the Lord?

The evil doers, who are cruel and vile are born as demons. They suffer life after life because their objective is neither goodness nor sublimity associated with the spiritual path but lust, greed and anger. Lust, Greed and Anger are three pathways to hell.

— *Shlokas 19, 20, 21, 22.*

ශ්‍රව

CHAPTER EIGHTEEN
Devotion to Him is the Only Path to Liberation

That faculty of discrimination with which a person is able to

distinguish between deeds that create bondage or salvation is *sattwick*. The reason for all human delusions is the Lord Himself. He reposes in all hearts and makes beings dance to the tunes of his *Maya*. He, who devotes himself to Him and Him alone, gets liberated.

— *Shlokas 30, 61, 62.*

An analysis of what has been discussed in the *Gita* can be made thus —

1. There are those, who know that the human life must be devoted to seeking liberation.

    Their single minded devotion leads them to the path of salvation and gives them salvation.

2. There are those, who do all the worship with the sole aim of enhancing their enjoyments. But they lead good lives. This type of worship, with materialistic motivations, gives them long spells of celestial happiness but no freedom from the cycle of births.

3. There are those, who are not able to complete their *sadhana* in their present birth.

    They are given a happy and congenial surrounding to do it in their subsequent birth and attain liberation.

4. There are those whose lust, greed and anger are uncontrollable.

They take the three paths to hell.

Then there is method, a yogic method, of departing from the world. Fix the attention on the spot between your eyebrows and contemplate on the Lord when Death begins to walk into your life stealthily.

There is also a favourable time, uttarayana, to do it.

The royal road to liberation is - surrender to His Will, leaving the fruits of actions to Him. Your duty is to perform your *karma* most efficiently without keeping your eyes glued on its results. Surrender to Him sweetly.

...18...
Ecstacies Spring from Fires–III
(Batuk Bhai)

He was before his eyes the Luminous Person. In appearance he was
of the size of the thumb, but he appeared to be totally stainless.
—The Shrimada Bhagvatam

B atuk Bhai was from Gujarat, had met Guruji sometime in
1948 and had taken spiritual initiation. He had started
becoming very other worldly, very detached in 1968. I had watched
him closely till December 1969, when I got transferred to Rajkot, the
place from where Batuk Bhai hailed.

How the inner life evolves through constant spiritual practice is
the story of Batuk Bhai and many others whom I have watched for
thirty years now.

Life in Rajkot was peaceful. One day I got a letter from him that
he was coming to Rajkot to attend a marriage party but would not be
able to stay with me, to avoid misunderstanding with his relations. But
only after one day with them, he came running to my place, bag and
baggage.

He was a Jain and had never visited Dwaraka, the pilgrimage
associated with Lord Krishna. Would I take him? I decided that on a
Friday evening we would go to Dwaraka. I would come back and join
my office on Monday while he would stay there spending three nights,
a rule followed by *sadhakas* that they must spend three nights when
they first visit a pilgrimage.

I had watched Batuk Bhai very closely since 1968. "Sit down a
little more," he would often say. He would be sitting overrelaxed in
his office. He had created stillness and solitude around himself. He had
faced life and its turbulence and had decided from the age of forty five
that intense *sadhana* was not to be neglected. He did more, sitting

231

anywhere. I watched him, not him really; actually the rhythmic flow of his breath.

It was deep, mostly even. He would talk rarely. If he did, it was in monosyllables.

Then the breath seemed to stop. There would be a faraway look in his eyes. To talk to him would have been a crime, to disturb him a sin.

Then his eyes would close involuntarily. It could be for many minutes, twenty or even more.

Then when he opened his eyes, he did not like talking, or being talked to.

When it happened to me, I never allowed anyone to notice it. In 1966 when it happened in a bhajan of Swami Vikasanandji (known as Lambe Maharaj in Nagpur), I went into *samadhi*. Squatting on the floor, I lost my consciousness, my body becoming light, then very light. It was an experience of weightlessness. My spine, it seemed, was only a silken thread through which passed electric currents upward. The *Sushumna* was all that seemed to exist in my body.

I often told him, "We both are incurable patients."

When it happened to me intensely in the beginning, sex torments had troubled me. Guruji assured me that it would evaporate into thin air, but it was an unavoidable obstacle in the life of a *sadhaka*.

The sex torment ceases sooner than one expects, and then it is pure bliss. For Batuk Bhai, life had no attractions. It had to be spiritual life only now. I had no material ambitions yet Guruji told me and Batuk Bhai that we had to carry on with our work as we had the unliquidated load of past *karma* still on us.

I took him to Dwaraka as planned and he lost control of himself there. Very long and deep breathing occurred, and often he lay down on the floor or squatted.

The only great thing that had happened to him, he said often, was his spiritual initiation. His experiences were very powerful, blissful. How could the Guru be ever repaid for it?

I agreed with him but with a difference. To me the fires and the problems of the ashram were also like the responsibilities of house-holders. I told him that perhaps I could have handled two wives but managing one ashram with none interested in *sadhana* for which an ashram is founded, was to ignore chaos, which I could not do.

The one lesson that life in the ashram had taught me was never to accept anyone on face value as a *sadhaka, sadhu* or *sanyasi*, religious or spiritual. Your own experience and your own detached view, help you decide your choices and judge what we call the spiritual phenomena over a period of time.

Batuk Bhai had liked my house in Rajkot precisely for one reason. He had all the loneliness he wanted and no one to disturb him. We sat for hours without talking to each other, like two Buddhist Lamas, observing a vow of silence.

The Dwaraka experience of Batuk Bhai was revealed by me only to Sunilda and Guruji in a letter in 1970. I can reveal it now, twenty five years later (1995) and nearly five years after the death of Batuk Bhai.

In the first visit we made to the Dwarakadheesh temple in the morning, with the *Gita* in my hand, which I always recited there, I saw how much stamina Batuk Bhai had. He stood in the temple, holding the railings, with tears rolling down his cheeks in a continuous stream. The priest had closed the temple from inside for shringar (decoration) but had asked us to stay inside since the *Gita* was divine musical accompaniment for the decoration.

Back to the place where we stayed in Dwaraka, Batuk Bhai said, "How beautiful was Radha. So beautiful that Krishna seemed to pale into insignificance."

I then suppressed my reaction.

In the afternoon when we visited the temple again, he had the same experience and he called Radha beautiful, tears rolling down his cheeks.

It happened that night, for the third time, next morning the fourth time, and in the afternoon of the second day, for the fifth time, the same remark.

I was to leave for Rajkot on Sunday night and he on Tuesday morning after observing his three-night rule in a pilgrimage.

When we were making our sixth visit, the third on the second day, I quietly told Batuk Bhai that what had happened would have to be kept a secret according to the instructions of Guruji.

"What?" he had asked me, surprised.

"In the Dwarakadheesh temple, there is no idol of Radha. It is only Krishna. You have had darshan (realisation) of Goddess Radha five times by now."

In the temple he caught hold of my hands and told me, "Yes there is no Radha here. Only Krishna."

...19...
Ecstacies Spring from Fires–IV
(Mrs "S")

The incredible stories of my life should have been actually about the great Yogis I have met and whose spiritual powers and extraordinariness is what I am writing on. Having omitted many Yogis here, I do hope that someday when I am able to piece up some loose bits of information and better recollections, I may add them to this book or write another one. Such incidents are countless in my life.

More than even these Yogis, the great saintly women I have met are so many that if I were to record here what I remember so distinctly about the great spiritual housewives, the volume would be too large, and it would appear repetitive because their lives fall in a pattern too well-known. In these days of women's lib, those stories may not appeal to modern Indian women at all, not to speak of women of the west.

This story must begin from the very beginning of my quest as a regularly initiated spiritual disciple of my Guruji, Swami Paramananda Saraswati.

I was the tenant of a police officer, Shri Sudhir Datta, whose wife, Usha Datta may have been a mother of mine in some previous life. She was as if waiting for me to arrive in Shillong to defray some debt of filial affection of some unknown past life of mine.

She had an extraordinary sense of humour. One day she and her husband were arguing, after they had made some purchases from a market, as to whose choice was better. They asked me to arbitrate, which I refused to do saying, that taking the side of either of them would be not good for the future of the regular supply of food and tea I had from them.

Then they decided to settle it between themselves. Mrs. Usha Datta asked her husband to stand with her in front of a large size mirror, and asked him, "Now tell me whose is better?"

Mr. Datta was a very handsome person, with his sculpture-like face while she could not even have been called attractive.

Mrs. Datta's family introduced me to the family of the late Shri Amiyo Dasgupta, an administrative officer of the government of Assam. I had my initiation there in the month of April, 1962.

This gave me a chance from then on to see first hand the spiritual manifestations of some phenomenon in women and study them not as *sadhaka,* but as psychologists.

A daughter of Dasguptas known as Milee was known to go into trances often during *bhajans* and say something prophetic and even predict people's future, resembling I think, the psychics in the west. The crowd addressed her as "Maa" (mother) when she got into that states but I could never bring myself to that position. It annoyed many Guru-bhais and Guru-bahens. When a male asked me why I did not address her as Maa, my simple answer was that unless I had such feelings in me, I saw no reason why I should indulge in such hypocrisy.

Roundabout that time, my marriage was almost fixed and I was to have married a girl from south India. My eligibility as a bachelor in the Indian market was very inconveniently high and here in the crowd of devotees I was moving, I never suspected that some of the young women were interested in me.

In a trance one day, Maa said, "No, I will not allow my son to marry that girl, who does not have a long life."

My marriage could not take place. The girl I was to have married got married to someone else and died in a difficult pregnancy. This is her only correct and remarkable prophecy, otherwise most of what she said in trances, were mostly her own opinions and even her prejudices, as I came to know, later.

The Dasguptas were very warm-hearted people and served Guruji as I had seen no house-holder ever doing. They never monopolised Guruji, which is what I cannot say about other house-holders in whose houses Guruji stayed also, running away from the ashrams he had created. Guruji was never attached to the ashrams he created, yet why he created them at all remains till now a mystery to me.

Years later, when Maa had an unconventional marriage, *guru-bhais* and *guru-bahens* boycotted her, showing such ingratitude that hurt me deeply.

Slowly I saw the same hypocritical attitude towards sex in them, which a puritanical society uses more as a measure of social control rather than believing in it, as I have seen astrologers believe in their own personal greatness, without any valid astrological reasons. The minimum that astrologers should do is to examine their own horoscopes.

But there was one exception among them, a woman whom I will address as "S".

It is her story that I am narrating now.

Dasgupta had often taken me to the house of S and told me that in her house, he experienced spiritual vibrations and ecstacies, which he rarely experienced, even in the finest pilgrimages of the country.

The first time I went to her house, with her two small lovely daughters, and low-paid husband, I saw the familiar old picture of bliss amidst poverty, or shall I say a life in which only bare needs of life could be fulfilled. I, unable to speak in Bengali, named her two daughters, perhaps both under ten years then, "Rang Birangi" (of many colours).

"You know, these two daughters wearing such colourful clothes are hiding a story of utter poverty." Dasgupta told me on our way back and said that S collected colourful cut clothes from tailors for free and from these made these frocks for her daughters. And the daughters always appeared to be the best dressed girls, in any crowd.

For many years children have always been my best friends, companions - my oxygen bags, to borrow a favourite phrase from my late father.

My additional attraction to visit the house of S was her lovely children, who, now grown up, at least one of them happily married, must be in their forties in 1995.

One day one of the "Rang Birangis" slipped out of the house when we were there, returned after sometime and gave me kwai a betel leaf with raw supari (areca nut), which the tribals especially eat. How did she know that I was a rabid, incorrigible eater of betel leaves, and who asked her to get one for me, I asked S.

"I do not know. She must have done it herself. She had saved five paisa and must have spent it on this," S told me.

S lived in a wooden apartment with only two small rooms, Shillong being an earthquake-prone place. She had very ingeniously divided and sub-divided them into four rooms, using whatever verandah was available. She had converted her verandah into her kitchen, the first big room, if it could be called big, into her drawing room where we sat squatting; another big room into the family bed-room for all four family members, a smaller one for guests, and the smallest one into her room of worship.

We, Dasgupta and I, visited her house sometimes on weekends, mostly on Saturday evenings, avoiding Sundays when we had our regular *bhajans*. Every time I went to her house, I took enough sweetmeats from a shop which was owned by a very religious person and who prepared it with such care that they could be offered to god in worship. When once or twice I took some gifts for her children, S protested. I could see that by so doing, I was perhaps mocking at her poverty. I stopped that.

I noticed that she followed the instructions of Guruji absolutely to the letter, and in spirit.

She did her *pooja* twice a day.

Ate and prepared only sattwic food.

She kept the entire house so marvellously clean that it appeared as though in the entire city of Shillong no particle of dust had ever existed. Or if it did, it would not enter her house at all.

She never criticised anyone, ever.

Paraninda (malicious criticism of others) must be avoided for spiritual progress. This was an instruction of Guruji, which she followed, unlike anyone else.

I never saw a wrinkle of worry on her face.

A piece of her logic, when once I had taken some gifts for her children was, "Do not do that again. God will give to me and my children whatever is due to them."

"Get a balance and weigh in it the love I have for your children," I had then countered her argument.

"Convert that love of yours into blessings for these children. Gifts are only material expression of that love, and get reduced in II period of time."

"But I am on a transferable job. I may be transferred out of Shillong, before that love gets diminished," I persisted "You are too sharp for me. But remember my request. God will give it to them through his chosen instrumentalities, whatever these children are to get when. It must not become a regular habit. The expectations of my children will be a problem for me."

She had the soundest commonsense of a mature mother and that great aura of spirituality always around, which one could feel.

Sitting in my office, one day, on a Tuesday or Wednesday, I started experiencing a great pull in my heart to visit her house.

Dasgupta was not available. I walked, as we had to, five miles and reached the shop from where I bought prasad (sweets) for her *puja* every time I visited. This time, a strange urge in me was to take four times more than what I had ever taken before. And I did that. Just when I was leaving the shop, another *guru-bhai* met me and said that he had a strong pull in his heart, to take a lot of prasad to the house of S, and instead of going home straight from the office he had listened to the "call within". I asked him to buy another variety, since I too, going to the house of S, had bought enough. He told me that he had bought four times the normal quantity.

On our way we met another *guru-bhai,* who was going with two huge bags full of flowers and told us that he felt a strong urge to decorate the entire house of S with beautiful flowers.

Reaching her house, I called out to her. She said that the door was open and that I could sit down since she was busy cooking.

A few minutes later, she came, and we all explained to her how and why we had brought what we had and she shed tears of joy.

Later, finding me alone, she explained that her father-in-law had never visited her house after her marriage. It was his first ever visit, and in the last week of the month, she and her husband did not have even a penny to attend to him with decency.

'What did you do then?" I asked her.

"There," she had pointed her finger towards her *puja* room, and said, "I prayed there and asked the Lord to do what best He thought I should ... " and then she shed her tears again. "God chose you to save my prestige today."

She attended to her duties, as usual.

Were someone to tell me someday that S has realised God, I would be the first to believe it.

...20...
Ecstacies Spring from Fires–V
(The other Woman S.D.)

"Whether it is through one's own realisation or through the teaching of others, when one understands that the world is a storehouse of agonies only, one is impelled into self-control. With God in his heart, he renounces the world and becomes the paragon of man."

— *The Shrimada Bhagvat Jatam*

As a man who has watched persons go to saints with both devotion and their personal problems, to astrologers like me and other astrologers known to me, to doctors or psychiatrists, or even to persons claiming to have supernormal powers, the questions they ask, I find are the same.

All these problems relate to comforts, career and sex.

But by and large people are happy most of the time in their lives because inside them is *ananda* (bliss). Otherwise a beggar suffering from leprosy, as one can see outside some temples in India, or people suffering from AIDS in the USA would have committed suicide at the earliest. *Ananda* is the eternal spring of that bliss, which flows in every human from *Atman* (the soul), which is God or the *Paramatma inside* us all.

Yet seeing so many types of human beings from my childhood, including Yogis and those, who visit ashrams and places of pilgrimages, I can classify them into certain categories.

The Gross or the Physical

The majority of people live at the physical or gross level. Their demands, acquisitions, losses, lust, greed, anger, attachments, love and hatred, joys and sorrows, envy or admiration, pride and humility, all have physical expression. "If two males stay in the same room," said a woman to us, "in USA, we think they are homosexuals." Rustic folk in India, or semi-literate persons all over the world live mostly at the grossest physical level. "Beer, baseball and sex", said an American friend once.

The Subtle or the Intellectual

A tiny, *very* tiny, group in every society produces artists, writers, poets, singers, actors, scientists, and intellectuals in all fields of human activity. They live at the intellectual level. They develop the habit of transferring the gross and the dross to the subtle level. The ego they develop is always visible in their expressions and reactions. Their habit of intellectualising everything, and their dogma of scientism obstruct their understanding the brilliance of astrology and the finer and sublime spiritual laws.

The Subtlest or the Spiritual

The most evolved, finest human beings belong to the subtlest or the spiritual category. Sometimes their half-acceptance and arrogant opposition to spirituality come to them from vestiges of their habit of intellectualising what they think they have understood.

Understanding a Yogi

In understanding a Yogi, we, the educated, must create our own mental blocks, consciously or unconsciously, and inevitably prejudge a Yogi according to our own parameters. It is very useful when it helps us expose a pseudo-Yogi but quite disastrous in our understanding of a true Yogi.

Real and intense experiences still help us overcome such obstacles, if the spiritual quest is genuine.

My disbeliefs, or half-beliefs, even suspicions about some *gurubhais,* even *guru-bahens,* got transferred to my own Guru quite early, after my spiritual initiation. One day I put this problem to my Guruji and he said:

"You experience something, which you call spiritual. Do not accept it easily. Test it hundreds of times. If you are now convinced that it is a spiritual experience only, use it to annihilate your disbelief. It is a slow but sure process of steady progress in spiritual life. It is good to use *viveka* (sense of right discrimination).

This instruction has helped me all my life.

It is still an agonising process, unlike in the case of simple persons with unquestioning faith.

I have seen, Devaraha Hans Baba just wave his hand when poor women came to him with their ailments, and they got cured.

I have also seen fat, opulent and the filthy rich coming for many days, and getting no relief.

In this respect, I found women far superior to men, but at a stage when their development is very fine.

When only either of two conditions exists in their lives, either loss of body-consciousness, which is very difficult for women compared to men, or when they surrender to the will of the Lord, with all their burdens and problems intact, unsolved, they can be said to have reached this stage.

Therefore, I must tell you the story of SD, another woman. If someone, who was a walking enigma in the atmosphere of the ashram during her life time haunts you long after her death, without your knowing, layer by layer, the composition of that enigma, you may begin to feel, as I do. That enigma must remain as it was.

The biggest mystery in my attempt to understand how *sadhakas,* rather *sadhikas,* evolve spiritually, from within, will always be, that woman, "SD".

A brief background is necessary.

In my first posting, on transfer from Bombay to Calcutta in 1967, I was asked by Guruji, to stay in the ashram, which was as dirty as an ashram could be, with no paved cemented paths, water tanks never filled up. But there was great divinity in the ashram, bliss and pure bliss only.

I have seen ashrams, where the hygiene is top class, management very efficient, daily schedule planned very well, but all that without spirituality. The best ashrams in India may be those, which are managed by the western disciples of Indian gurus. In India or elsewhere most of them are like well organised spiritual firms, all efficiency and no spirituality.

My Guruji's ashram was a total reversal of this.

Slowly, I persuaded Guruji to have cemented paths instead of the wild shrubs through which our bridle paths were inconvenient to walk on, in the pitch darkness of the night, because there was no electricity, and snakes there all the time.

Then came my younger brother, K. Subhas Rao, also initiated by my Guruji, for a brief spell of four months to Calcutta. With his money he did some electrical fittings, after getting Guruji's permission, but chose wrong electrical wires.

I, together with Sushantoda and Achintoda, filled up the tanks during weekends when they came to stay in the ashram. I did this work the rest of the week.

After some time, an electrician in indigent circumstances, Tapan, became a disciple of Guruji and did magnificent work, for free, teaching me things like wirefitting. He loved the ashram, and wanted to see it well-illuminated. He charged nothing for all that work, suffering his poverty. I helped him with whatever money I had which he would not accept easily, till I thrust some currency notes into his pocket.

During this time my younger brother was attracted to a young girl, daughter of a very noble and prosperous *guru-bhai* of ours. A story was manufactured and there was hot gossip for some days. Someone protested. Guruji said, "These are natural attractions."

An excellent *guru-bhai,* Sunilda, experienced the nectar that oozes from the palate, and yet he, past fifty years, said that he suffered from sex-torments.

The characteristic answer of Guruji was: "It hardly matters. Sex is controlled gradually. Extinction of sex-reactions causes dry spells emotionally, if it happens early. It is a gradual process."

The staple conversation of most of the house-holders associated with the ashram was sex-gossip, still.

My second spell of posting from 1975 to 1978 witnessed some change. A young team of Bengali boys joined us and cleaned up the ashram regularly, filled up the water tanks. Their parents told them to emulate me, which they did.

The sweeping of that huge ashram was done everyday by a shrivelled up oldish looking woman. Who was she? Guruji had never acceded to my request to have some paid employees, a trust, and income-tax registration. There was some order in that chaos but the radiant spirituality was always there because of the extraordinary spirituality of Guruji.

Money offered at the ashram was stolen. There were thefts many times. Financial morality was absent. The spiritual half of me accepted the ashram so mismanaged. The managerial half rejected it.

Who was she, that oldish shrivelled up woman keeping the ashram so clean? Everyday when I sat down to do my *Gita* recitation, she sat somewhere down below and listened to it. Was she paid? I was told that she was only a recent disciple and did free service and took only the *prasad* of the ashram as her wages.

Tapan, the electrician, and SD, the haggard woman, were the only two persons interested in seeing the ashram in good condition.

For them, very rightly, it was a part of their *sadhana.*

She was always in tattered rags. She lived in some dilapidated house near the ashram. I picked up some bits of information. I watched her do her duty with devotion, always. Someone told me that once in the ashram she was bitten by a snake. "May not have been poisonous," I said. No, her body had become blue, but she only said that she would not die because Guruji would save her, and became unconscious. A Tantrik *guru-bhai* of ours, Nagendrada, then alive, came and performed one of the many miracles. Her body was restored back to her original colour, as though nothing had happened to her. I could believe all this because Nagendrada had once tied a thread round my stomach when I was having terrible pain and I was cured. Similarly he had helped a cow having difficulties in delivering her baby.

A young girl often came to the ashram accompanying SD. She was her daughter someone told me. Not her natural daughter but the daughter of the second wife of her husband, I learnt later. She, who could not bear children for her husband, had persuaded him, to marry a second time. When a daughter was born to her, SD mothered her with so much affection that the child rarely went to her biological mother, though living in the tattered hut, within the great peace and harmony of their house.

Then a senior and well-meaning *guru-Mai,* perhaps Sunilda, told me once, that SD had been a prostitute earlier.

One of the irritants in the behaviour of Guruji is still a bitter memory of mine. He had created in the Kamakhya Ashram at Gauhati, two fine blocks of apartments, one for young girls in their teens named the Kumari Wing, and another, for unmarried women, in their thirties, called the Devi Wing.

During the Pujas, which is better known as the festival of Dussehra in northern India, he gave saris to all of them.

My Guruji, who had started his spiritual life as a Tantrik, never allowed anyone to criticise women, however evil they might be.

The Tantrik belief, that women were God's highest creation, was hardly shared by us. I had reasons to be annoyed often because while the young boys did all the work in the ashram, and the young girls chased them, as the young girls do, with artistic coquetry, Guruji often scolded only the boys and called them scoundrels.

My private joke was that if women in the forefront of the lib movement in the USA came to know of my Guruji, they would have worshipped him more than anyone of us did or could.

The only touching moment I ever remember to have witnessed

during the annual sari-distribution functions, Guruji performed was when I once saw him give one sari to SD also, who as usual stood in a corner, at the back of his cottage.

"Come on, take it, SD Mai", said Guruji and gave her a sari too. Guruji did see in every woman Goddess mother.

We, the males, were either devilish or divine for him, pernaps. I remember SD for another reason. *Guru-bhais* who borrowed money from me on some excuse or the other, cheated me often. SD, who needed it most, never asked me for a penny.

During the Radhaashtami festival (fifteen days after Krishna Janmashtami), there was always a big celebration in the house of a *guru-bhai;* the only occasion when we were all invited from the ashram. Once SD requested me to take her because she knew that I spent a huge amount of money by taking many of them in a bus.

To make her comfortable, I hired a rather expensive taxi and took three other middle aged women, who would have found Calcutta's overcrowded buses very uncomfortable. No one manufactured a sex scandal against me this time. Some years earlier when I had given some saris and bought medicine for a young woman suffering from tuberculosis, I had become a victim of gossiping tongues.

On a holiday, sitting in the verandah outside my room, I noticed SD sweeping the ashram roads, as usual. Birds flocked round her and animals came and licked her. I decided to watch it closely. Those, who feed birds every day have such experiences. But SD never fed birds. She had no money to buy enough rice for her own family. Yet how and why all this?

Here I must say that the entire community of *guru-bhais* and *guru-bahens* never disliked SD. But it was a case of respect from a distance. SD worshipped truth. Once or twice when she said something, it came out correct, prophetically. The birds flocking round her and animals licking her was a rare sight. It was all as is described in the aphorisms of Patanjali Yoga, a state of high spiritual development.

I know nothing about her inner spiritual development. An enigma had to remain an enigma.

Acceptance of God's will and perfect peace and harmony within and without - she was the Shabari of the Ramayana.[1]

References

1. In the great Ramayana there is the story of a poor tribal woman, Shabari, who, when she heard that Lord Rama was to visit her area, wanted to give to Him sweet berries. To select sweet ones, she tasted each of them. Such food is not fit for offering to God. But Lord Rama accepted them all, ate them and gave her salvation; first by preaching to her, then blessing her.

...21...
Ecstacies Spring from Fires–VI
(A tale of two Divinities)

There is the assurance given by Lord Krishna that if for some reason a spiritual practitioner is not able to complete his sadhana in his present incarnation, he will still be given birth in such surroundings in his next birth that he would find it convenient to complete it.

In the story of Jada Bharat it has been shown how in the incarnation of a deer he had, learning from the mistakes of his previous life, taken precaution not to repeat them.

Two first hand experiences of mine were described by me in a published astrological article. That is being reproduced here.

I must relate two incidents, something inside me compelling me to do it, with just that much of astrology, as may help someone do a bit of research in such of those areas of human existence, from where may emerge, without our knowing, a spark of divine ecstacy, with a tinge of sadness.

Rahu was in Pisces then, and, Jupiter in Leo was preparing to transit into Virgo. My lagna being Libra and the Moon too being there, the Rahu-Jupiter axis had covered the 6/12 axis of my horoscope.

The year was 1968-69.

My late Guruji, Swami Paramananda Saraswati, had asked me to stay in his ashram, Sri Sri Bejoy Krishna Sadhan Ashram, 24 Parganas, during that first spell of my posting to Calcutta.

I have quietly done a research on the esoteric significance of the transit of planets by collecting the horoscopes of many *sadhakas* of India and abroad and have succeeded in pinpointing the likelihood of some non-worldly, spiritual events taking place which is what, we astrologers, would not do generally, as mostly it is for the worldly affairs that we make use of transits.

Here, instead of elaborating it, let me only explain briefly thus:

(a) Whichever house from the lagna of the *sadhaka,* Jupiter happens to transit into that house gets irradiated with divinity. Now the twelfth house being the fourth from the ninth (Guru) is the ashram of the Guru, Jupiter in the twelfth from my lagna took me into Guruji's ashram from where I went to my office everyday.

(b) Rahu is an extrovert and the sixth house represents *dharana* in Patanjali's *Asthanga-Yoga* scheme.

(c) The dasha I was running was of the fifth lord which is significant from the spiritual angle.

Before leaving for the office every morning, I recited the *Gita* before the ashram temple, hardly noticing the presence of a bitch, dark, lean-bodied in a half-slumbering posture. Ashramites addressed her as Kali and fed her sumptuously the *prasad* of the ashram.

How many days passed that way I cannot say. But it seemed to have become a constant feature, even before I noticed it, my loud *Gita* recitation and Kali's presence.

If I ever had any pretensions to being a singer, my best, often only audience, was Kali.

Now transit Rahu was in my sixth house which represents pets, aspected by transitting Jupiter from the twelfth house in my horoscope.

No more discussion about my horoscope. Let me revert to Kali. One day as I emerged out of the bathroom, Kali stood close to me, looking intently at me and wagging her tail. I knew nothing about pets, none in our family ever had one. But Kali could not be called a pet in the sense in which people keep pets. She had strayed into the ashram and attended all *bhajans* with more regularity than any human being, and was, in that sense, a better ashramite than any of us.

But why was she wagging her tail? Showing affection? I had never patted her.

"It must be 8-30 a.m.," said Gopalda, an ashramite. "How is that significant?" I had asked.

"Waiting for your *Gita* recitation," Gopalda had answered. I had of course read about Pavlov's experiment. But what was this I wondered.

It was surprising to learn that Kali's time-sense was better than mine or anyone else's. At 8-30 she waited for me everyday near the ashram temple and if I was anywhere else she would come running to me and wag her tail. Cloud or sunshine, I knew that the time was 8-30 a.m. I could have corrected my watch with her unerring sense of time.

It must have gone on like this for over one year, me the talentless singer and she my perpetual audience. Other ashramites had given me some bits about Kali.

She ate only the prasad of the ashram. She rarely barked. Then I noticed that during the Sunday evening *keertans* she sat ahead of us all, near Guruji till the *keertan* was over and she had her share of *prasad*.

Who was she in her previous life? The explanation Guruji had given to someone was more or less on the lines of the sixth chapter of the *Gita*. God, the Merciful, gives to his errant devotee a place, a surrounding, an atmosphere where his or her spiritual practice becomes possible even in the next birth, even if such birth is not in human form. In this case, it was in a canine body.

As both Rahu and Jupiter were preparing to transit I was transferred to Rajkot. Four years after, when I visited Calcutta and went to the ashram, I did not see Kali. Where was she? Dead, they said. Dogs do not have more than twelve years' life, someone told me. I checked up the *Brihat Parashara Hora* and found the upper limit of the longevity of dogs mentioned there as twelve years. Some dog lovers told me that it was correct.

How and when did Kali die? Gopalda told me that his foolishness had caused her a lot of agony. One day when he was throwing a bucketful of hot water out of the window of the kitchen, it fell on Kali who was reclining there. She had got burnt; her skin was peeled off; she suffered. But she never gave up her habit of eating pure Vaishnava food, and died a few days after.

A vague melancholy, a sense of void and an unforgettable memory!' Kali had become a luminous part of my life's many sacred memories.

Our family tradition of not keeping pets was broken by my eldest niece, Kasturi, the wife of an army officer Col. T. G. Shankar. Her dogs, a male and a female, gave birth periodically too many pups which she distributed to her friends. When she came to Delhi, her husband having been transferred, her dogs became a big attraction for the two small sons, Gautam and Gaurav, of my youngest brother, Subhas, whose family stayed with me.

These two nephews of mine talked about pets, a little too often which amused me, till one day the elder nephew asked me what would be my preference, a male or a female pup. An amusing situation it was. I was not being asked whether I would allow a pet in my house but was merely being asked to exercise a preference! If I had said that I would not allow pets in my house, it would have caused anguish to both of my nephews. Well, the choice should also be theirs.

Then arrived in our house a pup, which looked like a dimunitive rabbit, a whitish small creature, with a musically halting bark, violating all rules of everyone's privacy, demanding a lot of love but giving more back.

My sister in law, Vijaylakshmi, fed the pup milk every morning at about 6 a.m. and once or twice when she was late, he grabbed her sari within his jaws perhaps even once tearing off a bit once. I remembered Kali's unerring sense of timing and told them all that perhaps dogs could improve man's sense of 'punctuality.

Then they named him Tango. Too late for me to give the pup another name. And Tango grew up fast like a Vaishnava, eating only Vaishnava food, attending all pujas, every recitation of the *Vishnu Sahasranama* every morning, particularly my sister-in-law's, and ate *prasad.*

And Tango violated all laws. I had to get used to his pranks. One day a very important man was consulting me, astrologically. In came Tango running and jumped into my lap seeking protection from my younger nephew bent on teaching Tango a lesson in good manners. A paw of Tango was on a planet of the horoscope of that important visitor. In mute language Tango told me that my visitor would have to wait till I assured him that my little nephew would not beat him. The fate reading of the important had to wait.

When in a crisis Tango would run into my room and sit in my lap; otherwise he needed me less in the beginning. Then he developed the habit of waiting for me every evening when I returned from the office and would jump upto my waist. Later Tango developed the trick of taking up a posture on a chair or a cot and jump into my arms as we do with human babies.

Then one day I saw the cat that stealthily enters our kitchen from the backyard, enter the covered verandah without any' fear of Tango who was standing there. I had then asked my elder nephew if Tango would chase the cat away.

"No, they play together," my nephew told me.

I never saw them play together but it was clear that the cat was not afraid of Tango. But what I actually saw one day was when a mouse appeared on the scene, Tango merely chased it away instead of killing it, by putting his paw on it.

The food one eats, *sattwick, rajasic* or *tamasic,* gives one's astral body its spiritual texture. The ferocity of a carnivore and the mild domesticable temper of a herbivore, the spirituality of a *sattwick sadhaka* eating *sattwick* food and the boast of a *rajasic sadhaka,* we know all that. Tango generally ate only once a day, in the evening when we all had fed him bit by bit. Milk in the morning and solid food in the evening.

But Tango's behaviour posed before me a question which someone will have to answer: does a carnivore fed on herbivorous diet develop a herbivore's reactions? This is what had endeared Tango to me, a feeling of love welling up, which deepened in weeks.

How much we had spent to ensure that he did not get any attack of distemper or rabies I do not know. A very substantial sum, I believe. The doctor, who had injected Tango had a roaring practice.

On January 8, 1988 my younger nephew came to my room and shed tears. Tango was not well. Gemini lagna was rising.

In a horary horoscope, the seventh house so heavily afflicted showed the disease, whatever it might have been, as being incurable.

Ketu in the fourth house aspected by Saturn, also Jupiter, indicated that the medical treatment could reduce pain only. Mercury, the lagna lord in the eighth house was bad. Then Venus, the fifth lord in the eighth house, was bad.

From the pada lagna, (Leo) Mars in the fourth looked ominous. What could it mean?

I saw Tango. He was not lively. I put my hands on his head and was reminded of the day when he, early in the morning; had entered my room, and had licked me on the forehead. Startled, when I had woken up, he stood there as though asking me if I had disapproved of his demonstration of love. And he knew that I only loved him and had never even once frightened him.

Nothing abnormal except that he looked lack lustre, without the buoyancy with which he had scattered the sunshine of cheer all over the house, demanding love and giving it back in ample measure.

We ran from one veterinary doctor to another. Some, of them had asked us where we had the distemper injection from. Who was the doctor who had injected it. Then they said nothing about the doctor. Yes, that is how they prosper so fast, those rags to riches stories - do we not know the stuff in those stories?

On the night of January 10th, both the legs of Tango had become immobile but he never even expressed his agony through groans. Late in the night, he was in agony, and he started groaning which stopped in the morning. On the morning of the 11th, he was quiet and had heard the *Vishnu Sahastanama* sitting in the lap of my sister in law. Then he was taken to a hospital where the doctor did what he thought was his duty, he injected something lethal into Tango's body.

Venus had by then transitted into Aquarius and the Moon joined Ketu in Virgo. Tango, the flame of ecstacy in my life, was a lyric. Lyrics are always brief:

I remembered Kali then. Rahu and Jupiter had then covered the 6/12 axis of my horoscope. Now Rahu and Jupiter both in Pisces, about to transit out, had showed to me the divinity of a mute creature, my Tango, from the sixth house, the house of pets. And the Moon was aspecting my sixth house from Virgo.

...22...
The Seers

The Yogi is a seer who may or may not predict. When he does, as is rare, he sees the *predestined event* in a flash, and hints about it, if he so feels, without giving a time frame.

I have had thousands of such experiences because of which, I now understand why in the *Vishnu Purana*, India has been described as a *Karma-Bhoomi* (the land where spiritual deeds are done), unlike other countries which are *Bhoga Bhoomis*, (lands where sensual and sexual enjoyments are the philosophy of good living).

It is also for this reason, why India will always remain the greatest spiritual place in the world; where the acceptance of physical sciences and metaphysical sciences, the normal and the supernormal, becomes part of the Indian system.

It is also because of this reason that rarely an Indian will go to an astrologer to ask questions about his spiritual life, when the fact is, that for the psychological and spiritual understanding of human personality, Hindu astrology has always been an unparalleled branch of knowledge.

India is not what the foreign media shows in its low-taste coverages about this great country. It may also not be their fault. A vulgar eye can see only what it has been trained to see. The other reason, a good one, can be that they have had some bad experiences with pseudo-Yogis in India or in foreign countries.

I have been one of those few fortunate astrologers, who has examined many events through a horoscope and also through a Yogi's known clairvoyant prediction.

The earliest instance I had given of such comparative study was in my two part article, "Predicting through Clairvoyance and Astrology", discussing my astrological prediction to Dr. Nagendra Singh, former Judge of the International Court of Justice and the prophecies of seers.

The Yogi talks or hints. His foretelling is subtle, and is often difficult to interpret.

My Guruji

I had the great fortune of seeing many such instances of my own Guruji most, naturally, because as a disciple I had access to him, and also because when I looked after his ashram twice, occasions arose time and again to watch it. I have given in this book enough instances already. Let me give some more here.

Through Dreams

Many of us had experiences of dream messages conveyed by Guruji. Let me cite some of mine here.

On the Night of My Initiation (April 23, 1962)

In April, when he had decided to initiate me on the midnight between 23rd and 24th April of 1962, I was sleeping in the house of the late Shri Amiyo Das Gupta who told me that he would wake me up half an hour before the time fixed for my initiation.

I was wakeful and yet sleepy, that condition, which is known as *tandra*, when I saw Guruji coming to me and saying, "You will someday write a book on me and the Yogis you have met. It will be of immense help to *sadhakas.* ".

I woke up and wondered how could Guruji, who was in the other room, come and tell me this. I had read too much of Freud and the dream analysis of psychologists. I did not believe in my experience.

I lay down again in that condition and again in a spell of *tandra* I had the same experience but the person conveying it was Swami Vivekananda.

There was Freudian rejection again.

Thirty one years later, I was persuaded by friends who heard the stories of Yogis from me, to record them somewhere. I started writing series of articles, 'That Blissful Inspiration' for the *Astrological Magazine*, which may be the longest ever series run by the magazine in its sixty years' existence.

Friends prevailed upon me to bring the stories out in a book form. A lot of additional chapters and new information has been added here.

The seed for the writing of this book had sprouted on the night of 23rd April 1962 and it is being written, after starting it in 1993, in the shape of a book in 1995.

My Elder Brother

In a dream in 1963, my Guruji told me, "Your elder brother will run into difficulties in his job".

In 1979, my elder brother ran into serious difficulties and has migrated to USA.

Cosmic Vision (Repeatedly)

Many times a dream has occured.

"See how the world is going to get annihilated catastrophically", he would say, then I would hear great rumbling from beneath the earth. I would see the earth shaking and buildings collapse. One of the buildings I had seen collapse is in the Lodi Estate in Delhi. When I had seen it happen sometime in 1963, the building had not even been constructed.

After that, this dream repeated many times. I saw good parts of northern India collapse, get destroyed.

Nothing destructive of that nature has happened so far.

Transfers

I saw in a dream in May 1963, that I was walking inside a fortress where I was told there was an excellent museum of paintings. Suddenly, I found a crowd, which had collected there rushing in a direction. "Where were they going," I asked someone. "To have a *darshan* of Govindji," I was told. I too joined.

I found myself in front of a temple whose curtain was removed and I saw a magnificent idol of Lord Krishna.

Two months later, I was transferred to another place and I went inside a fort, where I was to see a picture gallery. I then saw a crowd moving in a different direction. I followed them. I saw a temple and a magnificent idol of Lord Krishna.

In a flash I recalled the dream I had in Shillong, in May 1963 and here I was in July, 1963, in the city of Jaipur, in western India.

In Jaipur, I had a dream that I was sitting in a very small Shiva temple, on the side of a tank of water, on the night of a Shiva Ratri, and doing *japam* whole night.

I was transferred to Nagpur where, when I aimlessly went to a Shiva temple, some months later, I found myself the Shiva temple, as I had seen-in my dream. I spent the whole night there.

In April 1985, Lord Jagannath came into my dream and told me to take some persons for a *parikrama* of Govardhan, the great pilgrimage about one hundred and twenty miles away from Delhi. Lord Jagannath also showed me a lady, who was having difficulty in walking.

A few days after, nearly fourteen of us went to Govardhan doing the *parikarma*, the wife of a friend of mine was finding it difficult to walk. She had, she told me, a surgical operation, recently.

Fifteen days or more after that, I got my transfer orders to Bhubaneshwar in Orissa from where I went almost twice a month to the temple of Jagannath in Puri, where there was a branch office, which I, as Accountant General was required to visit frequently.

Guruji had asked us all to maintain a diary in which we should record our dreams. Many did it but I did not. I still remember many divine dreams which I will not reveal, perhaps, ever.

ೞೞ

Shri Aurobindo

Shri Aurobindo, the great Yogi, came into a dream of mine once and showed a woman in a skirt and warning me to be careful with her.

A few months later in a new office, I was required, for the first time, to deal with some top secret material. I soon found a woman chasing me, wanting to cultivate friendship with me.

I recognized her as the same face which Shri Aurobindo had shown to me. I kept her at a distance, after I saw, that this, woman was, in a spy ring.

Meher Baba

If some devotees of Meher Baba had recorded this instance, I would have appreciated their honesty. These devotees had it spread that Meher Baba was an *Avatar* and, had kept a vow of silence, which, when he would break, would be the end of the world.

I had a dream in which Meher Baba came and said, "I am going to leave the world without breaking my vow of silence."

It was in Nagpur, sometime in 1965, when I had this dream.

I asked some of the devotees of Meher Baba in Nagpur, to find out from the Baba who was then alive, the meaning of the dream. They wrote to someone in Poona and got a rather rude answer.

In 1967, I told this dream to my *guru-bhai*, Sunilda, in Calcutta.

Sometime, perhaps in 1969, Sunilda told me that my dream had come out true. Meher Baba had taken *samadhi*, without breaking his vow of silence.

In most of such dreams, Guruji was either personally present or his voice was heard from the background.

Actual Foretelling: Person to Person

I will give some instances of actual person to person telling instances.

(1) I praised someone in 1975, who was thousands of miles away achieving material success.

"No, don't praise him," Guruji said curtly.

Soon, he took to heavy drinking and ruined himself.

(2) Guruji looked at the shape of the arms of a woman, who was quite an ordinary person, in 1975, and said, "her *anga lakshana,* physiognomy shows prosperity." She has two houses, two cars and a good job with a good bank balance, with a very happy married life.

(3) In 1975, India's Prime Minister, Indira Gandhi, was grooming her second son, Sanjay Gandhi as the future prime minister of the country. Guruji was getting down from the hills of Kamakhya in Gauhati, when in a procession, Sanjay Gandhi was going towards the city.

"He does not have *rajya lakshana* (signs of royalty)," Guruji said. We, many *guru-bhais,* knew about the statement. Sanjay Gandhi died in an aeroplane accident in 1980, without even becoming a cabinet minister.

(4) In May 1963, I was to have returned from Calcutta, where I stayed in the ashram, to Shillong where I was posted. My leave was to expire on May 21st. I had the choice to buy either the air ticket for the 12th of May, and join office early or leave on the 20th and join my office.

Guruji asked me to buy the ticket for the 17th, which I did, unhappily.

At the Gauhati airport, we were told that there had been no flights between Calcutta and Gauhati for five days.

In Shillong, I came to know that again there were no flights between Calcutta and Gauhati for the next three days, also.

(5) In 1968, Guruji told Nirmalda, "Rao will go to Delhi and from there fulfil an international mission."

In 1978 I got my first posting to Delhi, twenty one years after joining the government service without my trying for it.

I delivered my first speech on astrology in December, 1981.

In 1987, the largest ever astrology school in the Bharatiya Vidya Bhawan, all according to the planning I had done, by training and grooming some astrologers.

In 1993, I went to the U.S.A. as the chief guest of the

second Annual Vedic Astrologers' Conference.

(6) In 1977, my mother was critically ill in Lucknow while I was in Calcutta. My younger prother, K. Vikram Rao, told me that doctors asked him to inform all relatives, which Indian doctors do when they feel that the end is inevitable.

I told Guruji about my mother.

"Not Now," he said. He gave no other time frame. My mother died seven years later, in December 1984.

(7) "Do not move out of the ashram till I come out of the *kuti,*" Guruji had told a *guru-bhai.*

But without telling Guruji he left.

Guruji came out of the *kuti* and not finding him there, asked some people to rush and see him.

If these people had not reached him, he would have been brutally murdered.

(8) A young man trying to get a job asked Guruji, if he would! "Not for three years," said Guruji.

I definitely know that for the next two years he did not get any job.

(9) A friend, who survived an air accident in 1968, came to Guruji and told him of his terrifying experience.

Looking at his face, Guruji said, "Your forehead shows a long life."

In 1995 as I am writing this book, he is alive, hale and hearty.

(10) Shri Bimal Chandra Ghosh, a famous poet of Bengal, had many dangerous heart attacks. Though a communist, his wife succeeded in bringing him to Guruji.

Guruji nearly admonished him, saying "You will live for some more years without any heart attacks. Remove fears from your mind." He died eight years later.

(11) Shri Toroni Chaudhary, younger brother of Tarini Chaudhary, was diagnosed as having a serious ailment of kidney by famous doctors of Calcutta.

"Doctors are wrong," was Guruji's comment.

Later, Toroni Chaudhary was cured with ordinary medicines for some minor ailment.

I have recorded here perhaps only five percent of what I could have.

From this it will be clear why I believe in predestination.

In the Mahabharata, the great rishi Narada tells Yudhishthira, the eldest of the Pandava brothers, "You will be chosen as the instrument, the offence will be of Duryodhana, killings will be done by Arjuna and Bhima, and there will be destruction of Kshatriyas."

This prophecy was given before the great battle of Kurukshetra. Guruji used to say, "Unflinching belief in the *Shastras* is a sign of a very good spiritual development;"

References

1. Issues of Jan and Feb. 1984 of the *Astrological Magazine*.

...23...
Astrology when it is
an Illumination

Compared to Yogis, I have found astrologers most unimpressive, in fact a menace to human society. In no age, in no country, except the communist governments, which have collapsed, could astrology be banned.

The best that the world governments can do is to recognize astrology as a serious subject of academic pursuit and, as a licensed profession.

Serious penalties, including twenty year's imprisonment, confiscation of property and the like should be imposed on professional astrologers, who cause more anguish than joy to human society.

There must be strict licensing of the profession. Since the menace of astrology cannot be eliminated, it must be contained.

There is no serious research in astrology, no sound teaching methods existed until I evolved some, which however, will have to be refined more and more as time goes by, by generations of academic minded astrologers. It is a hard battle, which has to be fought because in the days of the printing press and mass media, the abusable knowledge called astrology will spread more and more. I have seen the menace of astrology spreading; in India, in the gimmickry that passes for political predictions by quacks, and in USA I found persons, who needed counselling themselves to help them overcome their own bouts of insanity, taking upon themselves the roles of counsellors through astrology.

Nothing can be done to stop it as I know, having fathered the academic group among astrologers in India and, in the process, starting and running the largest school of astrology in the world. The world will never really have great astrologers, but there will be, in any human society, psychics, fortune tellers and practitioners of occult and astrological sciences, with very imperfect knowledge, high claims, loud boast, low morals but high profile, who will be editors of astrological journals, and even writers of books. I have met great Yogis, who have been of great divine inspiration, but have met no astrologer, who could be called even a tiny fragment of a Yogi. They are mercenaries pure and simple or dangerous mountebanks.

Yet astrology, which I studied, to test its effectiveness and usefulness, reveals so much about human life and destiny. It is and will always remain the best subject that man can study to help man. I have been impressed by many astrologers, but none can be ranked by me as truly and technically great in the rishi tradition of the country. I have been involved in the academic movement to revive astrology more than anyone else in India. In so doing, I had to interact with astrologers, in thousands.

Let me give my impressions about them, since I will be held guilty of not giving my assessment, by those very students who have learnt the subject and will have a right to question my sincerity in getting astrology established as a serious academic discipline.

I can give my assessment about some of them only though I have met over five thousand astrologers in nearly four decades, studied their methods, understood them, assessed them, and finally got thoroughly dissatisfied with their imperfect knowledge. Naturally I came to the conclusion that in a lifetime an astrologer can acquire good command only in a certain branch of this magnificent science, and that I cannot be better than those whom I criticize.

Yogi Shri Shivananda Murthy of Andhra Pradesh

Very impressive, very spectacular and most artistically satisfying is the presence of many of those I have met, who were house holders doing *sadhana,* serving in a job and also doing astrology. As they progressed in their *sadhana,* they reduced their astrological activities. Then, after discharging their burdens as householders, they reached a stage of spiritual development when they separated from their families.

Yogi Shri Shivananda Murthy of Andhra Pradesh, who comes to Delhi once or twice a year, is the best example of such a paragon of a person I have met in recent years.

I first met him in the house of Shri J. Choka Rao, a Member of Parliament, sometime in 1989 or after. His humility made me feel ashamed of myself. He was doing astrology, *sadhana,* being a follower of the famous Ramana Maharshi, and was a police officer of Andhra Pradesh.

The picture of equipoise that a Yogi is, one who has faced life's problems, done office duties, and has yet continued his *sadhana* and has now become a seer in the fullest and the happiest sense of that term, is Yogi Shivananda Murthy.

Often when people come and ask me which living Yogi they should meet, I tell them, if they are English-knowing Indians or foreigners, to meet him, discuss their spiritual problems with him and get clear spiritual guidance.

The first time I met him, he said that when he saw my articles in the *Astrological Magazine,* he read them, otherwise astrology is what he had given up. The run of the mill articles written on astrology by others revealed the limitations of other writers. Mine, on the other hand, showed boldness, an insight into the real content and meaning of some astrological principles. I felt that I should divert his attention from this subject and talk of other spiritual life.

I have rarely met, in recent years, a better conversationalist in English, with such clear idea of man's spiritual goals of life as he. Coming from the background of a house holder he impressed me and my friends, more because like us all he has faced the fires of life and then evolved into what he is.

In such a state of development as he is in, does he need astrology which is a confused and chaotic picture of destiny patterns for most of the astrologers? He is a seer, who can see that without astrology, without a horoscope, which he might have needed earlier when he was doing *sadhana.*

Like all great men of India, in the true spiritual tradition of the country, he encourages astrology because it is the science of illumination, and if the astrologer is a mercenary, self-propagandist as some editors of astrological journals are, he feels that they do more damage to astrology.

Then came in 1993, an invitation for me to visit the USA, as the chief guest of the Second International Symposium of Vedic Astrologers, at San Rafael, California. I was telling him about it.

"You must go. The Americans have not seen an astrologer of your type. What you have to offer is what no other astrologer that has ever visited the USA could ever offer. Others must have been either fortune-tellers or self-propogandists.

"You will see how Americans will respond to you. They will. call you many times in the future. It is good, very good. You must accept the invitation and go to USA."

Later, I had an occasion to tell him that David Frawley summed up the impact of my tour in his report, part of which appeared in the *Astrological Magazine,* in a sentence, "Vedic astrology in USA before Rao and after Rao."

Semetime in 1994, I met him again, this time with someone, who was having difficulties professionally. He looked at him and said, "Your trouble will be over soon. Your will have one more promotion." Part of what he has said is already fulfilled.

I have seen how astrologers evolve into seers. I have referred to my astrology gurus, my mother and Yogi Bhaskaranandaji.

I must make it clear that I have given to Yogi Shivanand Murthy a very high place.

I must here refer to my late mother to show how an astrologer evolves into a seer.

Let me discuss my assessment under certain heads: their outlook, their techniques, range of predictions, special interests, limitations and their last years.

My Mother

The highest in my rank is my own mother, **Shrimati K. Sarasvani Devi**, for whom astrology was a spiritual pursuit, which it has been for me also, with the difference that it has also become for me, an academic discipline.

Outlook – She was deeply spiritual and not a ritualistic Hindu Brahmin woman at all. She believed in the infallibility of the subject, and had the most fantastic memory among astrologers, I have known or seen. She remembered hundreds of horoscopes and did mental calculations, with great speed. After she became stone-deaf, her concentration on a horoscope had Yogic splendour about it. She successfully turned her handicap into her greatest asset, but it prevented wider communication with people at large.

Techniques – She studied both Vedic and western astrology. She was totally open minded and was prepared to accept, any good astrological research, from any part of the world. If she had wanted, she could have done deep researches in the use of the extra-Saturnine planets and helped us. Being a house wife, she had her own limitations with eight children, and a husband, my father, K. Rama Rao, with his patriotic fervour in the days of the British rule, landing in jail and taking all risks a patriot had to take.

The birth horoscope, the navamsha, the divisional charts, sometimes ashtakvarga in which she had unusual success and some of which she taught me, prashna (horary), in which she was the greatest I have seen so far, and the limitlessly brilliant use of transits, which inspired my statistical researches in the use of Saturn and Jupiter (the double transit phenomena, as I called it), was her strength.

Her approach to the use of, and experiment with, techniques was purely utilitarian, in the sense that if she found it not working, she never hesitated to discard it.

Range of Predictions – Her range of predictions was the widest I have seen, though I feel that following other techniques, I have surpassed her. She gave predictions to people telling them what would happen twenty or even thirty years, later. The predictions came out mostly correct.

Interests – She confined herself mostly to marriage and children horary only. It disappointed me terribly and she discouraged me from going into this area, warning that I would find no time for any research, which she knew I could do.

But these limited interests gave to her spiritual outlook that needed depth, which astrology has to give to those, who do it as part of their *sadhana,* and not as a career or for mercenary or other worldly motives.

Limitations – She had all the limitations of a Hindu house wife and rarely got interested in other areas of human life.

Last Years – In her last years, she did not need a horoscope. She had developed supernormal powers. She had told me in 1972, that her own mother would be born as the daughter of my younger brother, K. Vikrarn Rao. When Vikrarm's daughter was born in September 1972, I started watching my mother seriously.

My younger brother, Vikram had invited very important men for the birthday party of his son on March 22, 1979. During the preparations, when suddenly the then prime minister of India had announced in Parliament that the great leader, Jaya Prakash Narayana was dead.

My mother told Vikram, immediateiy after the Parliament adjourned, that the news was totally wrong.

Some important persons thought that my mother had gone mad. Later, the Prime Minister announced that he had got wrong information and apologised. I know more than one hundred such predictions of my mother, given without a horoscope. It must have come about so because astrology was a purely spiritual pursuit and she never made any money out it, ever.

How it happened is described later.

Once in 1981, I, Dr. R K. Caroli, cardiologist and Dr. K.S. Singh, an I.A.S. had gone to Vrindavan and did not return home till ten in the night, which was unusual.

My mother was sleeping and my younger brother and his wife

and a friend, G .K. Shukla, were sitting and talking. It must have been late in the night when mother got up from her bed, suddenly, and told my younger brother, that I had got involved into a vehicular accident with friends.

That was true but we were saved.

Yogi Bhaskaranandaji

Outlook – His outlook was purely divine. He was a rishi and the greatest worshipper of truth, I had ever seen in my life. When I met him, he was like a spiritual bud ready to blossom out. That happened soon after and, he gave up-astrology.

Techniques – His techniques were limited to the birth horoscope, the navamsha and the vimshamsha.

Range – He never predicted or if he did, very rarely. When he discussed a horoscope, it was the most brilliant in-depth, most satisfyingly four-dimensional analysis describing the physical, the mental, the intellectual and spiritual levels of human personality.

When he discussed a horoscope in that manner, an intelligent man could infer what all he was predicting, without predicting, an art I never developed because I never had his moral and spiritual stature.

Interests – He was the best read astrologer I could hope to see. He had an academically brilliant career, had studied Hindu and western philosophies thoroughly, knew politics and mundane astrology.

Limitations – Like my mother he had limitations; the limitations of a blossoming Yogi, who had to avoid human company. He could have glided into any branch of astrology very efficiently. His limitation was born of his dislike of people treating astrology as a piece of fortune-telling.

Last Years – He had developed many supernormal powers. He did not need any horoscope. If he blessed you, your trouble was over.

I have seen only three cases in which one has become a seer or evolved into a seer, the greatest of them, Yogi Shivanand Murthy, is still with us.

The other two, my mother and Yogi Bhaskarananda, are no more.

I have heard about a ninety year old astrologer of Varanasi, who is now not doing astrology and has become a seer.

The Contrast

There are two contrasts, now. The first between astrologers and and astrologers. Those, who pursue it as part of their spiritual practice, never become famous and known, and they give up astrology, when the divine purpose, which it has to fulfil is served, whether or not they had high academic standard in any research in it or not. Then, there are the professionals, for whom the purpose of astrology is no better than buying daily bread to sustain their lives, to do which they have to follow all that becomes necessary to succeed, whatever may be the means adopted to succeed.

The contrast between Yogis and astrologers strikes the eye at once, the Yogi with his *ajna chakra* open, sees it all, while the astrologer struggles his way through, first with unrectified birth time, which he does not know how to rectify; then he struggles with a doubtful ayanamsha as Raman has all his life. Finally, if he has overcome these handicaps, if at all, he has no support of a sound research to help him predict properly.

Technical deficiency, intellectual handicaps in the absence of debated and accepted researches which, say doctors use so well in their treatment, and lack of ethics, the last, the worst of the' three handicaps, virtually cripple astrologers.

Yet, if astrology survives, it is because a good astrologer with honest intentions is a good guide in the encircling confusions and chaos of his client. This good astrologer is only making use of the knowledge made available through ages by seers, who were great Yogis.

If good Yogis are rare, they are great still. A good astrologer is rarer because of the three handicaps referred to. Yet astrologers are in millions, because there are billions in any society wanting to seek light in the darkness of their lives. But the astrologer finding such easy gullible people, has no scruples and exploits him to the full, in his own way and through his own methods. Astrology then is not that light which illumines, but the menacing fraud with its fatalism, or its psychological bluff, poured down the throat of its hapless victim. And it works.

But astrology is a divine science, which needs something of Yogic insight to understand it even, and not merely method and some formulae. It is for this reason that this is one of the six limbs of the Vedas and is described as *Vedanga*.

The only hope is for the academic group to come out with its own replicable techniques. Astrologers will not have a standardised approach, which is the prime requirement of our age.

The present astrological scene is bleak. For a decade or two, there will be substandard astrology till the academic begins to replace, gradually, the mercenaries and charlatans. It will need efforts of some decades. Till then, astrology will be of limited utility to mankind but, that too when sound and honest astrologers take it up with a good conscience and save it from becoming a piece of fortune telling, bluster and money demanding threats, or skating through the workable labyrinthine bluff of psychological readings.

The astrologer preserves all the gifts King Parikshit gave to the Ruler of this Era of Kali, known as Kaliyuga.

Seek the blessings of a good Yogi, pray to God and do not go to astrologers whose training is imperfect, and tools of readings so imprecise and high profile too bloated, for their tiny mortal frame.

Summing Up

1. Astrologers are ordinary human beings. The good ones among them are well read and quite successful in the art of prediction. But they cannot see the ultimate like Yogis, infallibly.
2. There are many good astrologers in India, who predict well but cannot discuss the subject with the disciplined mind of academicians. I have met hundreds and I respect them. I give them credit for part successes only. They work in narrow orbits with reasonable success.
3. Those I have listed here are or were all-rounders. I have gone running to astrologers when I heard about their reputation and have seen their predictions and analysed the horoscopes they had read. Even if, those predictions were successful, they were so clear that anyone could have given such predictions.
4. Many of the successful predictions I have given could have been given by others also.
5. Yet there is no great astrologer anywhere in the world.
6. World's best astrologers are Indians or, those non-Indians who do Hindu astrology.
7. Yogis do not give predictions. But they help their disciples.
8. Astrologers will therefore have some useful role in the society always.
9. Those, who depend too much on astrological predictions are the mentally sick persons or timid human beings.
10. Those, who do not seek guidance from astrologers may sometime or the other misplan their lives.
11. Astrology is a human necessity yet it can make you fatalistically stupid.
12. Astrology is that spark divine, which illumines your path but with the ever present danger of blurring your vision of life

...24...
Memory Glows

Thus when through sweet devotion to God, worldly desires melt away and the heart is filled with bliss, does one experience Cosmic Truths.
Realizing that Great Being, the knots in the heart of the devotee get untied, doubts vanish and the bondage of Karma loosens.

— The Srimada Bhagavatam

In **1962 and later years** — In July 1962, after a three month-tour of Assam, I went to the hill of the goddess mother, Kamakhya, at Gauhati, where our Vaishnava ashram was to be founded. Guruji would be there I knew.

Who else? It was not necessary to know.

I had gone with *Guru-bhais* from Shillong and found in the ashram rich persons from Calcutta.

There an eight-feet-long and six-feet wide pit, about six-feet deep, was dug up to store flowing water from a very thin, rope-like current down from the hill.

The ashram was very beautiful with three backs of tortoises-like mountainous blocks and above them, quite high, was the flat land where cooking was being done for over three hundred of us.

All of us were bathing there, washing our clothes. We carried a hundred buckets of water to the top high flat land for cooking, drinking and cleaning it, all twice a day.

I made a mental calculation on the very first day and, thought that by the next morning there would be no water for us.

We stayed in the ashram for three days.

The water level never went down, even by one inch. In subsequent years, till 1977, when we went there, more storage tanks had been built up, larger in size. But we always had water scarcity.

Why only in 1962 did we not have any water difficulty?

Someone said that he had seen Guruji praying and saying that devotees, coming for the first time should have no difficulty.

1975 and Before

It was my second posting to Calcutta and I was again in the ashram. A change there, had created nostalgia and pathos.

Earlier, Guruji used to sit in his cottage, where in the verandah, there was a tree. In 1968, one night I, Sudhanshuda and two others were sitting and talking with Guruji. It was a starry and windless night. A branch of the tree above was suddenly being shaken by some one whom we could not see.

"*Ke tumi, jao,*" said Guruji loudly meaning, "Who are you, go away."

It stopped but, happened again. Guruji shouted loudly this time and it stopped completely.

In 1975, that tree was not there except its trunk.

Who lived on the tree and came and sat sometimes, remained a mystery.

1968 and 1978

Yes, I remember once in 1968, when the sun was setting, we three — I and two sons of Kanuda were walking between Garia and Kamalgazi. Crossing half the way, when it had grown dimmer, I saw a woman, whose face I could not see, in dazzling white sari, crossing our path, expecting us to stop and give her the way, I guessed. I had stopped but, Kanuda's son continued walking and went about fifty yards ahead of me.

Soon, when I joined them, they had asked me why had I stopped.

I had accused them of bad manners, not giving way to the woman in white sari, walking right across.

If that was true, where could she have gone, they had asked me. They had then shown to me that on left side where she would have gone, there were only fields with barbed wires.

They were right.

What was it then?

The Goddess of a temple sometimes walks and appears. It was well-known in that area, they had said.

They had never seen her.

In 1978, I had returned from the office, entered the ashram. It was what they call in Calcutta, load-shedding, no electricity.

In dim moonlight, I was walking towards my room.

Guruji was in Assam those days. In the absence of Guruji, no woman was allowed to come to the ashram. But in front of me, I had seen a woman in dazzling white sari, walking very majestically, with a gait that had enraptured me.

I had asked in Bengali, very courteously, "Who are you, mother".

No reply.

I must have repeated it twice or thrice.

No reply.

Then she had walked right into the room adjoining mine, which I knew was locked in the morning.

Had anyone come to stay ?

I had asked them in the ashram.

No, none, was the answer.

Two inmates brought a lantern and checked.

The room was locked.

But I had seen her enter the room.

The same Goddess!

I do not know.

I only know that, that night I was in absolute bliss.

Flash Back to 1964

My mind went back to 1964. My Nagpur days.

My reputation as a bridge player had preceded me. They had asked me to play for the team in the national championship and, I had refused. Then, they had asked me why could I not coach them up.

They had touched a sensitive chord of my heart.

Knowledge, which is sharable must be shared, I had said always.

It is why I give my case-studies in astrology.

I was the coach of their bridge team for the nationals.

I used to return late in the night, walking through semi- darkness, towards the huge bungalow allotted to me, in which I had lived.

One night, in front of the house allotted to the Commissioner of the National Savings, I heard a wailing sound. It then increased in volume. Then I felt, as though someone was walking towards me.

For a moment I was nervous.

Should I do my *guru-mantra* or the *gayatri mantra?*

I decided that I should not.

The next moment, I felt distinctly that some weightless and invisible entity had sat on my right shoulder and its wailing, so voluminous, was not disturbing me any more.

It continued, till I had reached the bungalow, just before mine.

It then stopped. Perhaps that entity had entered that bungalow, in which had lived Mr. Bombawala, then a Deputy Inspector General of Police.

269

Next day, I first thought that I would take another route for my mid-night walk. But then I argued with myself, why not test it again. Do not accept any supernormal phenomena till you have tested it hundred times, Guruji had said. By hundred, he had meant many times, till I was convinced.

It continued for a month, and then stopped.

Everyday, that entity had entered the bungalow near mine.

Swami Vikasanandji or Lambe Maharaj

That reminds me of Swami Vikasanandji, who was the Guru of M.N. Barve, who used to work under me and was a great classical music singer, whom his jealous rivals had prevented from rising to the national level. His daughters, Madhavi and Nilambari, had sung so many good bhajans for me.

I had met Vikasanandji in 1963. His Thursday and Saturday all night *bhajans* were, the best two weekdays of my life then.

There was rumour that I was getting transferred out of Nagpur.

One evening Swamiji had asked me if it was true.

I took more liberties with him always. I had said, "You with your supernormal powers should tell me."

"Not till the Goddess of Chattisgarh gives the permission."

That was the place where he had done his *sadhana* for years, the area in Madhya Pradesh associated with black magic.

When will that be, I had asked.

"I will let you know."

The rumour of my transfer had not died down. I had continued in Nagpur for another twenty months.

Then one day, Vikasanandji had said, that we would go to Chattisgarh.

We went in cars. There I started cleaning a lantern and, in trying to fix the nail of a window, I hurt a finger and there was profuse bleeding. None could stop it. His doctor disciples had done their best but there was no stopping. It went on and on and Swamiji looking at it, smiling had gone on with his *bhajans*.

Next morning he told me, the Goddess mother has taken her due.

It was all so mysterious. I did not understand it all.

"Is it linked to my transfer as you had said nearly twenty months ago?" I had asked.

"Yes," he had said smilingly.

On Monday, when I reached the office my transfer orders were waiting for me.

That Great Bhajan

A farewell bhajan for me in the house of the police officer, my neighour, had been arranged, the same bungalow, where I had felt that wailing invisible entity had entered.

I had talked of ghosts. Swamiji had said that there was one in the outhouses, of the police officer's bungalow.

I had then narrated my experience with that wailing entity.

That entity had lived there, Swamiji had said. He said that the *bhajan* of that night would relieve that wailing entity of its agony.

It is that night's experience that I have described, my experience of total weightlessness and that experience of *samadhi*.

Swamiji's disciples had grown jealous of me.

Too late.

I was under orders of transfer.

Thank God.

Back to Calcutta, 1968 and 1978.

Let me get back to the lingering memories of the ashram.

Why had Guruji stopped living in his original cottage and had shifted to the new construction called the library room? I had asked and they had told me, as I expected, a gory story of someone polluting that.

Scandals and scandals and scandals, the mental food of the majority of men and women in the world.

I had felt very bad.

In 1968, I was the last ashram inmate to see Guruji before he closed his cottage. I would stand there check his back door to make sure whether it was bolted properly or not.

One night, I saw a cobra crawling, without fear along the wall of the cottage, towards Guruji. I thought I should do something. Guruji had waved his hand, reading my thoughts, as though, telling me to do nothing.

The cobra had continued undisturbed, passed near Guruji's feet and completed the circumambulation of the cottage, and then left.

It happened every night. Till the cobra had completed the circumambulation Guruji would not close his cottage.

I was instructed not to talk about it.

In 1978, Guruji had left living in that cottage. Was the cobra coming and doing the circumambulation ?

I tried to watch it once or twice. There was no cobra.

That mystery must remain a mystery.

Yes, I am a strange creature. I believe in the achievements of physical sciences and technology and, also in the supernormal.

Astrology provides the link between the two.

My jyotish Guru, Yogi Bhaskaranandji was right.

If you do not know how to view life holistically, you are a fool. And we have more fools, among the educated.

...25...
Why Astrology at All?

Long before anyone knew me and knew that I was an astrologer, I thought I should give it up. Finally, astrology has to become fortune-telling. The questions they ask in India have to be about their material demands of life only because of India's socio-economic life. The spiritual guidance they want is what they get from their family, from gurus, from Yogis. They do not need an astrologer to do it.

Mundane predictions are mostly negative. Read the predictions given by anyone known in this field and you have forecasts of destructions, devastations, deaths which are easy to give and will never go wrong, because that is what newspapers and newscasters the world over report. To give such predictions one need not know much astrology. It is guess and private information used to make it look like astrology when a little jargon of astrology is used.

Astrology, even if done with the best of intentions, can never give that bliss, which sadhana, done in solitude, must give.

But Guruji would not merely not allow me to give up astrology, but give me a lot of astrological work which I did. I have given enough instances in various writings of mine.

Then the astrologer is hardly spiritual. Jealous, petty publicity seeking, ever bitter with his lack of achievements, ever ready to criticise the other astrologer. My disenchantment with astrology has only grown over a period of time. But then came Moorkhanandji and astrology continued.

They talked of my international mission. It has started with astrology. But again the spell of disenchantment creeps in.

"Do Kaal Chakra dasha," Guruji said one day and quoted some couplets from Khana the astrological genius, who was a poetess, and had given some method of doing it easily. Neither could he explain it nor could I make head or tail of it. But I continued with it and got results, which are unbelievably good.

Then one day, he asked me to do his Kaal Chakra dasha. I was surprised. I did it. Then came the surprise.

"Calculate my span of life," he said and I tried to avoid. I could not. He repeated it often and I had to do it.

The sixty fifth year and I got confused. Could I be correct?

"Astrology is for the body. This body too must come to its terminus. Astrology shows it," he had said.

Then, I met a young Maharashtrian brahmin, who looked at one's forehead and predicted. He had very poor vocabulary in Hindi and he talked rather bluntly, very curtly and sometimes his predictions were deeply hurtful. He had told a businessman in my presence, "Why are you planning so much? You do not have much life left not for more than fifteen days."

That man was healthy but he died within the span indicated.

He came to meet me in the ashram, naturally went to my Guruji, who encouraged astrologers. Some ladies were sitting there.

He looked at the forehead of Guruji and said, *"You will be betrayed by a disciple of yours. If you survive the sixty-fifth year, if at that time you overcome your desire to give up your body, then and then only grander things will happen."*

The woman there resented this prediction. Guruji quietened them.

Guruji gave him a lot of money.

Others forgot all about it. They thought that it was like the normal treatment of courtesy of Guruji who was allowing him to say, to say it all.

But the prediction haunted me.

Jealousy is man's commonest instinct, I feel sometimes. It is the product of ego. Ego is the worst enemy of a spiritual aspirant.

There is no ashram without intrigues, there are no astrologers, who do not envy other astrologer's better predictions and life readings, there is no Yogi, who after building an ashram, can make it a haven of bliss which ashrams should become.

In 1967-69 period, it was the rich group of *guru-bhais* that had dominated and I had to quarrel with them. Now, there was a younger group, who manipulated everything with concealed skill and not blatant arrogance. They had done all this in the period between 1969 and 1975, before I was posted to Calcutta for the second time.

May be, because of all this, Guruji avoided the ashram more this time.

I have referred earlier to my own discussion of his horoscope with him. *"Jupiter in the eighth house but aspected by Saturn was good for yoga sadhana but it had a sinister implication for him."*

It was the younger group of manipulators now. I had no intention of quarreling with them. I would be transferred soon and after that I would free from all this pettiness.

I got my transfer orders. I told Guruji, "If I meet you at all in future, it will have to be sometime outside the ashram," I said.

"You have suffered in the ashram. You will now see how your spiritual life progresses. Whatever happens to anyone is the Will of God. The peace you search is within you."

In June 1980, when he left us, it did not surprise me. I could collect only some information. One of those manipulators had given him poison through a young woman.

.... Guruji took it, digested it, fell sick, recovered and for the next six months lived only on two leaves of tulsi and water.

Thereafter, our *guru-bhai* Dhirendra Da, read out the Srimada Bhagvatam for him.

He went into total seclusion.

Then, he went to his sprawling ashram at Silchar and gave up his body.

Saturn's aspect on the fifth lord in the eighth house and the prediction of the young Maharashtrian brahmin, who was a worshipper of Lord Dattatreya, showed how correct can be these occult sciences, which every great Yogi I have met has en-couraged, describing it as a sacred *vidya*, particularly astrology or *jyotisha*.

Where is that sacredness associated with astrology?

I am now, I feel, reaching that stage of giving it up.

My life and world was better without astrology. Unfortunately, too many of my predictions given to very important persons privately clicked too fast. In its wake, came fame. Fame brought in jealousy and jealousy, even from those who in their very advanced age, should have shown some ethics.

Astrology was meant to teach wisdom to its practitioner. It was meant to be a bridge between the *para* (divine knowledge) and the *apara* (worldly knowledge).

The last meeting...

"Wait," Guruji said and went inside his cottage with an apple in his hand, came out and said, "This is my parting gift to you."

"Please explain," I said.

"It is charged," and then after a pause said, "He who will eat it will get spiritual bliss."

I kept it and in Lucknow, when I met my mother, asked her to eat it without giving a bit of it to anyone else.

  It was after that, that my mother gave up astrology completely and her supernormal powers increased. She could predict without a horoscope, till the end of her life, in her last six years, with unfailing accuracy. It was not astrology, but as we do, as she had taught me.

...26...
Poetical Guidance

I had picked up enough Bengali in 1968, to be able to read the vast literature Bengal has on saints, most of which I found raising one's Guru to the level of an *Avatar*, or Incarnation of God. Some great devotional poems of Thakur Ram Prasad, and some great songs sung in classical form, of the great Muslim poet, Kazi Nazrul Islam, held me in thrall for months.

During that period, a famous literary critic of Bengal, Narayana Chaudhary wrote a review of my Guruji's poems, comparing them with the Upanishads in their sublimity and divine wisdom, but most defective in prosody; defective in many ways, if the rules of grammar were applied rigidly. They were yet great pieces of literature worth reading, as, they took us into the rare realm of divinely inspired compositions.

Between me and Narayan Chaudhary, had existed a very sweet bond of friendship. He was an uncompromising critic of whatever he thought was the result of excessively narrow views of the great classical traditions of India. He was also a famous music critic of his time. Once when he, the external examiner of the Rabindra Bharati University, wrote that the Rabindra Sangeet, an obsessive love of Bengalis, was ruinous as it prevented the growth of fondness for genuine classical music, he lost a lucrative source of income.

Similarly, in spite of his fondness for my Guruji, he criticised the way his ashram was run, and agreed with me that an unmanageable ashram was a slur on society.

He liked my forthright opinion that a disciple need not have the same political opinion as his Guru. My Guruji, who had started his spiritual life as a Tantrik, never allowed anyone to criticise women, may be because, in Tantrik literature, woman has been treated as the highest point of God's creation. Up to this point, one need not have any difference with him. Indira Gandhi, then India's Prime Minister, was not liked by me as I thought that she was the devil who had ruined all good democratic traditions. Yet, Guruji never criticised her, nor would anyone, except me, ever criticise her in his presence. Narayan Chaudhary said that he liked my forthrightness and liked my line of demarcation, between my Guru's real spiritual greatness and his chaotic political preferences.

Narayana Chaudhary's admiration of my Guruji impelled me to read my Guruji's poems over and over again. I translated them into English without telling any one, keeping rhymes, wherever, in the original, rhymes existed. Wherever there was free verse, I put them into English in that prosodic form, to come nearest to the point of verisimilitude in English.

I felt that I had retained the spirit of those poems. One day, I showed them to Narayana Chaudhary and he thought that my translations were very good. In the meantime, a *guru-bhai* of mine had also translated them into English. He being a Bengali, must have done better, I thought. But one day Guruji who had heard of my attempt to do the English translation, said himself, "Rao has understood the spiritual message of my poems and his translations are the best." But I lay low, as life in an ashram has more politics than sweet reactions. Some of my *guru-bhais* liked them and as late as 1989, wanted me to give whatever poems I had translated, for publication. I did not allow them to do that. Here are some of the many such attempts.

ଔଚ

In the Temple of Light,
Secluded, He dwells,
Away from world's din,
Within.

ଔଚ

Pleasures dance in attendance,
At the threshhold of the opulent door,
That door is barred to God.
Reposes, in devotee's bosom,
Meekness in beggarly grace,
Gracious, ready in silent adoration.

ଔଚ

Agony is a desert stretch,
Very long, it may stretch.
Yet in Naam Kalpataru's shade,*

Peace spreads, many a glade.

ⓒ⧓ᴐ

Arrogate to myself when God's power supreme,
Proud, inflated, vision is rendered blind.
Ghoulish is the world of sorrows, wilderness all,
Gloom's intense, Cruel World Wheels grind.

ⓒ⧓ᴐ

A favourite piece of mine, made many of my *guru-bhais* uncomfortable. *What is religion?*
I quoted a poem of Guruji.

ⓒ⧓ᴐ

Truth is the soul of religion,
It's content, compassion soft,
Transcendental knowledge,
It's dizzy height, aloft.
Cleanliness, good conduct,
Art bodily ornaments,
Innocence, a ray serene,
Of heart's firmament,
In love, its fruit is found,
Ripened, round.

ⓒ⧓ᴐ

I found among all religious groups, Bengalis to be the most dress conscious, even when they came to attend sacred functions in the ashram. Women dressing tastefully for such occasions, seemed rarer in Bengal, where they came in white saris, with red or blue borders. But men came in the finest garments, with the ends of their costly dhotis tucked inside the pocket of their kurta.

Perhaps, they and similar other persons, inspired the following poem.

Bodily cares, their lives occupy,
Funeral pyres, impious food,
How much of life's vistas,
They ever know, or would.

ⓒ⧓ᴐ

Many of us often had our divine experiences and told Guruji in the early years of *sadhana*. Guruji forbade our discussing such experiences. Spiritual experiences are not meant to be broadcast. The greater their secrecy, the greater is their potency to take a *sadhak* to a higher stage. Yet he gave hints about such deve-lopments and experiences.

ೞಬ

Celestial light when adored Gods fill,
In devotees' lives, joys fill.
All worship becomes still.
Pulsates in body-bounds,
Rippling, and resounds,
Primordial Mystic sounds.

Here the reference is to the mystic light seen in meditation and the twelve types of mystic sounds, from Anahat Chakra.

ೞಬ

Wealth of bliss,
I get in sorrows' glow
Under Mayas' veil,
World's illusions flow.

The entire world is engaged in a race to earn more money and yet it talks of spiritual demands of life. There is a contradiction.

ೞಬ

Who is God? See an Upanishadic echo
How is the Creator?
Like a mouse,
With a hill in His womb,
Reposes in all,
Removed, from all.

ೞಬ

Even if heaven,
Was a dream-figment,
It's sweet still,
Disbelief, darkness spreads,
As if it were,
Death's perpetual chill.

൮ഇഇ

Sweet surrender to God, the ecstacy of that divine love as the great woman saint, Mirabai experienced, is the *ultimate in the life of a devotee.*

൮ഇഇ

The nectar shower of Love,
Stills carnal tingles.
Dead then, now resurrected,
Man lives a life a new.
Shrinks mortal frame,
Of fleshly urges,
LOVE, all-encompassing,
Surges.
A love-tryst of two hearts,
A testament,
Sparkles, star-like,
In firmament.
A saga timeless,
In bliss boundless.

൮ഇഇ

Therefore,
On life's lute,
Play love's lyric.
Undying and rippling
Melodies solemn,
Will Gods awaken,
And will resound,
In Inner Temples' dome,
Mystic sound,
of ringing OM.

൮ഇഇ

Not Love's sweet blossoms alone,
A thorn or two to prick me too,
Soul's immortal undertones'
Are inscribed,
In blood's red tones.

281

ೞ

Books impart not learning,
Only speech,
They teach,
Parading riches,
Other's riches.
Kindles when,
The lamp Within,
A peep makes known,
The Great Unknown.

ೞ

Blessed is he,
That many, on him,
Loving, lavish love,
He that on many,
Loving, lavishes love,
Deserves respect,
Due to Gods above.

ೞ

Men are flesh, flesh bare,
Kindred souls are rare.

ೞ

Serving without veneration,
Brings inner damnation,
Nectar-sweet service, captures,
To heart's content, raptures.

ೞ

Riches increase pride,
And dwarf the mind,
And may cause,
Many hurts.

ೞ

Be thou blemishless,
Supreme-oriented,
Grace, so augumented,
In life's bowl pour,

Lord's grace, sure'
Mercifully,
Brimful.

ՇՑ

Out of over two hundred such pieces I had done, which Shri Narayan Chaudhary had approved, only some pieces are available. Others lost during my transfers or mislaid, has been a loss mainly because my Guruji's preachings, were always poetical and graceful, pieces on which meditation opened out a spiritual vista.

My own well-read *guru-bhais* and *bahens* did not seem to realise their beauty and value till Shri Narayan Chaudhary found in them Upanishadic wisdom.

I remember noticing my Guruji, who sat on his *aasan*, inside his cottage, in short to long spells, thrice a day, getting down to compose poems, soon after. Most of them he composed late in the night. He went to bed very late in the night, got up very early in the morning and kept himself busy throughout.

It was in the evenings mostly that groups of devotees came to him, most of them with their worldly problems, and unmarried young men and women, with their sexual problems, or attractions as well.

Ashrams are generally good meeting places for young men and women to exchange glances, through which they convey, good deal of their feelings. From purely platonic to highly physical, such attractions often became the staple of the scandals, discussed in hush-hush silence. A hypocritical and puritanical society, where sex inspite of being looked upon as a divine decision for the human race to continue, a strong and primary instinct, is discussed, secretly while in the west, the role of India's scandal-mongerers has been taken up by newspapers and tabloids. Scandal-mongering is and has been, man's chief conversational pre-occupation, all through the ages.

I know that often, though Guruji never allowed anyone to criticise women, it was they that came, with their problems, their repressions, and created odd situation.

After they left, he composed his poems in which his own feelings about such feminine reactions seemed to be different from his open admonition to us to never criticise women.

ೞ

Marriage is a bondage.
Changes it still,
With love's infusion,
Into freedom,
From mundane illusion.

ೞ

Frail and fickle when woman's heart,
Her love, like water, stays not.
Where she sees pleasure's slopes,
There she glides, renewed her hopes.

ೞ

Renunciation glows,
True Path shows.
Pleasure is a charm,
Darkened mind's harm.

ೞ

Sparkles not when divinity,
Defiled is life's sanctity,
Passions, deformed, howl,
Sinister shadows prowl.
Whirligig of Time,
Turns dust into gold,
Satsanga* shapes,
The divine mould.

ೞ

Dwells man,
In five elements,
Dictate devils,
Their chosen dance.

ೞ

To be disposessed of,
"My" and "mine",
Is discerning,
The pure and the fine.

ᘉᘏ

Anger is, as if fire burning,
Deadly its countenance,
Devours like dry twigs, leaves,
All fruits of penance

ᘉᘏ

Hatreds emphasize,
The dissimilar,
Ill-tuned hearts,
The notes familiar

ᘉᘏ

Lust, with its infinite pains,
Sighs secret, its secret sobs,
Mind glued to myriad colours,
Desires, death, Maya-throbs.

ᘉᘏ

Often, I had put a ticklish question to many religious preachers why when there was so much sinning in the world, there was no Incarnation of the Lord. Linked to it have been two other more ticklish questions. Lord Krishna had given his *Virat Roopa Darshan* to Kauravas, who should have been, after seeing Lord's Great Form, reformed. Similarly Arjuna had the *Vishwa Roopa Darshan* (Lord's Cosmic Form), yet why was he disinclined to fight the great battle of Kurukshetra?

I guess some answers to questions like these were in some of the poems of Guruji.

ᘉᘏ

Knowing the Lord,
Is knowledge's end,
Life's demands,
Vanish and end.

ᘉᘏ

From the darkness,
Of the womb,
Man emerges.
And the Holy Great
When darkness,

285

Age submerges.
But the Avatar,
When Evil,
World submerges.

ೞ

It was Narayana Chaudhary's assessment of my Guruji's poems that prompted me to see them closely. Then came the inspiration to translate them into English.

During the period I was doing it, I got into sublime meditative moods, which were my greatest spiritual gain. I never sent them anywhere for publication. It is only now, finding some of them after twenty eight years in my records, that I thought that I should include them in this book.

...27...
Bliss and Confusion

There was great bliss inside me after Guruji left us. The true Yogi has to take upon himself some part of the *prarabdha* of his disciples. Every time after giving initiation, Guruji's face used to get darkened. We had seen him suffering. It should stop, I decided, and it stopped. I asked people not to flock round him for spiritual initiation. There were quarrels and I was blamed. I had invited it. Guruji defended me without annoying others. Why should he initiate those who never took to spiritual life seriously?

That suffering would be over now.

How would his ashrams run now?. They formed a trust, as I had argued with Guruji. They have paid servants also and have built up very good temples also. It is what Guruji never allowed me to do. Now they want me to be its head.

Why do they want to inflict on me the same old suffering?

The Guru lives not in those temples but in the *mantra* he has given.

Later, when some *guru-bhais* came to Delhi and said that they had not expected Guruji to leave them, I asked them, could they not see that when in the last six months he was taking only water and two tulsi leaves, as they had seen him do, he was preparing to leave.

Anandmoyee Ma, the great woman saint, had not eaten anything in the last month of her worldly existence.

That is what Ranga Avadhoot had done.

That is what Devaraha Baba had done.

They know that the End is coming or they invite it.

Reg No. 40050/2001

Telephone : 011-22721624
Telefax   : 011-22721625

the Society for Vedic Researches and Practices

(Registered under the Societies Registration Act XXI(1860) of Govt. of NCT of Delhi)

F/291, Saraswati Kunj
25, I.P. Extension
Delhi - 110092

Members of the
Governing Body

K.N. Rao
Consultant and Teacher

K. Subhas Rao
Journalist

Ms Swati Chawla
Consultant

R.C. Dadwal
Consultant and Teacher

A.K. Jain
Practising Lawyer

M.S. Mehta
Consultant and Teacher

Deepak Bisaria
Consultant and Teacher

The Society was founded a few years ago by Shri K.N. Rao and the likeminded scholars of the subject to evolve more and more avenues to disseminate this ancient science as far as possible and as much as possible. And so far the Society has been successful in this exercise. They have sponsored a few research projects and got the findings published in the forms of monographs. The Society has also undertaken the publications of the translations of some of the earlier works of various scholars in Hindi.

The **preamble** of the Society lays special emphasis on

undertaking original research in the science of Vedic astrology, and Indian/Hindu philosophy,

organising discussions and seminars on various researches and the subsequent publication of the findings,

helping the projects financially for conducting the research and its publication,

promoting scientific exchange of knowledge between various groups engaged in similar researches in India and abroad,

and

raising funds through various sources mainly from donations and contributions from time to time upon such terms and conditions as deemed necessary.

IMP: All donations to the Society are exempted u/s 80 G of the Income Tax Act 1961

E-mail: ● knrastro@hotmail.com ● kn_rao@yahoo.com
● subhasraokraju@rediffmail.com

ß5